# QUEST
# FOR THE
# PAST

# QUEST
# FOR THE
# PAST

9459

## GREAT DISCOVERIES IN ARCHAEOLOGY

## BRIAN M. FAGAN

ADDISON-WESLEY PUBLISHING COMPANY
Reading, Massachusetts • Menlo Park, California
London • Amsterdam • Don Mills, Ontario • Sydney

**Library of Congress Cataloging in Publication Data**
Fagan, Brian M
  Quest for the past.

  Includes index.
  1. Excavations (Archaeology)   2. Archaeology—His-
tory.   I. Title.
CC165.F3        930'.1        77-14664
ISBN 0-201-03112-4
ISBN 0-201-03111-6 pbk.

Copyright © 1978 by Addison-Wesley Publishing Company, Inc. Philippines copyright 1978 by Addison-Wesley
Publishing Company, Inc.

ABCDEFGHIJ-DO-798

# FOR JOHN STAPLES

" A man who has once looked with the archaeological eye will never see quite normally. He will be wounded by what other men call trifles. It is possible to refine the sense of time until an old show in the bunch grass or a pile of nineteenth century beer bottles in an abandoned mining town tolls in one's head like a hall clock. This is the price one pays for learning to read time from surfaces other than an illuminated dial. It is the melancholy secret of the artifact, the humanly touched thing."

Loren Eiseley, *The Night Country*

# AUTHOR'S NOTE

All measurements in this book are given in miles, feet, and inches. We have made no attempt to present metrical equivalents. Place names are spelled in accordance with the usage in the *Times Atlas of the World,* with the exception of ancient Egyptian and Mesopotamian spellings, which follow common archaeological use. In the case of ancient Egypt, I have followed the spellings used by William C. Hayes, *The Scepter of Egypt* (New York: Metropolitan Museum of Art, 1959).

The locations of sites and cities mentioned in the text are indicated on maps found in Chapters 2-10. A chronological table in Chapter 1 gives the rough time periods of the sites described.

# ACKNOWLEDGMENTS

It was John Staples who first had the idea for this short book over five years ago. That it has finally appeared is because of his constant encouragement through several drafts. The best way of thanking him is to dedicate the book to him. Warren Stone, Ann Dilworth, and Martha Drum, as well as the production staff at Addison-Wesley, helped me immensely. I am grateful to the various colleagues and friends who read through the text in draft. In particular, I want to record my deep gratitude to Professor and Mrs. Richard Daugherty for their warm hospitality on a visit to the Ozette site. Professor Daugherty gave up several days of valuable time to show me Ozette and his remarkable discoveries. Mr. and Mrs. Jerry Grosso were kind hosts in Neah Bay, where I was able to examine the many artifacts they preserved in the Project Laboratory. Marge Mahoney of Santa Barbara kindly typed the manuscript.

# CONTENTS

# CHAPTER

# 1

# THE QUEST FOR THE PAST

ARCHAEOLOGISTS ARE COMMONLY THOUGHT TO BE EC-
centric old gentlemen who wear rumpled khaki shorts and
sun helmets and spend their lives unearthing crumbling ruins
in the shadow of mighty pyramids. They live in a world of lost
civilizations and buried treasure, deep mysteries and unex-
plained phenomena. The archaeologist of novel and television
seems to be continually off on a "dig," searching for missing
links and unwrapping innumerable Ancient Egyptian mummies. Sometimes, too, the angry mummies chase the unfortunate archaeologist, intoning dreadful curses that lead to his
premature death. Many of us, at one time or another, have
dreamed of pursuing such a romantic—if, in fact, mythical—
career.

This is a book about actual archaeological discoveries,
about remarkable archaeologists whose explorations have
dramatically expanded our understanding of human history. It
is a book about the excitement of archaeological discovery,
about a scientific world that many consider to be one of the
most engrossing frontiers of science. Its heroes are ar-

1

chaeologists of extraordinary ability who have made fascinating discoveries, often after years of patient effort. Each was a pioneer who pursued a dream, a conviction that spectacular archaeological finds awaited his spade.

The face of archaeology has changed considerably in recent years. Archaeologists of the 1840s, and even as late as the 1930s, could hope to uncover hitherto unknown civilizations: the Assyrians and Sumerians of Mesopotamia surfaced in the mid-nineteenth century, the Maya of Mexico in the 1840s, the Mycenaeans of Greece in the 1870s, the Shang civilization of China in the late 1920s. All of these discoveries captured the public imagination, for they were made under conditions of great difficulty, conditions that often required near-heroic efforts. The early archaeologists had few resources and no advanced excavation techniques. By constant improvisation, by drawing on their own wealth, and by acute political maneuvering, they frequently achieved miracles. They learned digging the hard way, made brilliant finds, and, regrettably, sometimes irreparably damaged vital clues to the past.

Some of our archaeologists belong to this heroic era; others, to our own generation, where there are simply no lost civilizations left to find. But today's archaeologists still make remarkable discoveries, often as a result of applying such advanced tools as the computer to archaeological data. Modern archaeology is big business; thousands of people all over the world are currently involved in digging up the past. Practically every nation now employs a few archaeologists—as museum curators, university professors, or conservators of national culture. All of these archaeologists use excavation techniques that have evolved over generations of archaeological discovery. The newer techniques enable them to tackle problems that would have boggled the mind even a few years ago.

One of Mexico's earliest cities, Teotihuacán, is a case in point. Early archaeologists could only gasp at the size of Teotihuacán, sample a portion of a pyramid or a few houses, then turn away in despair. They simply did not have the technology needed to carry their explorations further. It has taken a team of modern archaeologists over a decade to map the entire twelve-and-a-half square miles of Mexico's largest prehistoric city. Their task would have been impossible without a mosaic of air photographs and highly sophisticated computer programs that enabled them to store inventories of archaeological finds and millions of other items of information on computer tape. When the time came to put the data together, the archaeologists could recall and classify thousands of data items in a few seconds. The result: a whole new picture of Teotihuacán.

How do archaeologists dig up the past? What makes archaeological excavation different from ditch digging or the treasure-hunting activities of our mythical, sun-helmeted archaeologist? To get some idea of just how far the field of archaeology has progressed, let's look back over its colorful history.

Archaeology has a long and disreputable line of descent: its ancestors were, quite literally, grave robbers and adventurers. A century and a half ago, even serious archaeological excavation was little more than licensed treasure hunting. Everyone, whether archaeologist or treasure hunter, had the same objective—to recover as many valuable objects as possible in the shortest time. Serious archaeologists would not hesitate to use gunpowder to blast their way into a burial chamber or a pyramid; everything was cast aside in a frantic search for the valuable and spectacular. As a result, most excavations resembled untidy vegetable gardens.

Mummy hunters in Egypt literally waded through piles of discarded coffins to reach their prey. The famous Italian collector Giovanni Belzoni, who worked in Egypt from 1817 to 1820, would crawl hundreds of yards into the rocky hillsides behind Thebes in search of mummies and papyri. Exhausted, he would perch in the darkness for a few minutes on a convenient mummy. Sometimes his perch would collapse in a cloud of smelly dust. "I sank altogether among the broken mum-

| | MESOPOTAMIA | EGYPT | AEGEAN | CHINA | AMERICAS |
|---|---|---|---|---|---|
| A.D. 1950 | | | | | |
| | | | | | OZETTE |
| A.D. 1000 | | | | | TULA |
| | | | | TEOTIHUACÁN | |
| A.D. 1 | | | | HAN | |
| | | | | | |
| 1000 B.C. | | | | CHOU | |
| | | TUT-ANKH-AMUN | TIRYNS / MYCENAE | SHANG | |
| | KING HAMMURABI | | TROY | | |
| | KING SARGON | | THERA | | |
| 2000 B.C. | ASSYRIANS | | KNOSSOS | | |
| | | PYRAMIDS OF GIZEH | | | |
| 3000 B.C. | SUMERIANS | | | | |

OLDUVAI GORGE      BED I SITES      1.75 MILLION YEARS

Chronological table showing the approximate time periods of the major sites mentioned in this book.

mies, with a crash of bones, rags, and wooden cases,'' he remembered. It was a good quarter of an hour before Belzoni could extricate himself.

Belzoni and his contemporaries were quite open about their efforts to ''rob the Egyptians of their papyri.'' No one thought this either eccentric or wrong. Rather, Belzoni's audiences would be agog as he related his eerie experiences in the dark burial chambers, where, in the flickering lamplight,, the

EXPLANATION OF THE CHRONOLOGICAL TABLE

This table* covers the main sites, civilizations, and dynasties described in this book which date to after 3000 B.C. It shows, for
example, that the Sumerians were in power in Mesopotamia at the
time the ancient Egyptians were building their greatest pyramids,
and that Knossos was steadily evolving into the powerful center of a
far-flung empire while the Assyrians were achieving domination in
northern Mesopotamia. Tut-ankh-Amun was buried soon after the
eruption of Thera and the devastation of Minoan civilization by one
of the greatest natural catastrophes to affect humankind. The
Mycenaeans rose to power while Troy was still important—like
Knossos, an ancient and long-occupied center—and fell from power
while the Shang people in distant Asia were making the finest
bronzes in the world. And Liu Sheng and Tou Wan were laid to rest
just as Teotihuacán was reaching the zenith of its power and influence. Meanwhile, in the Pacific Northwest, the Makah Indians were
already living at Ozette, a settlement they continued to occupy until
modern times. Written records, and hence historical times, began in
about 3000 B.C. in Egypt and Mesopotamia, in the second millennium B.C. in the Aegean, and around 1600 B.C. in China. Western
civilization first encountered the American Indians in the fifteenth
century A.D. Olduvai Gorge, of course, dates to a much earlier period
than this table shows.

---

* Dates given in the table are approximations. For more detailed and accurate information, please consult the sources listed at the end of the book.

---

mummies seemed almost to converse with one another and
the naked Arab workmen, coated in layers of dust, resembled
mummies themselves. The audiences would gasp as Belzoni
produced pieces of desiccated ancient Egyptians, remarking
casually that "mummies are rather unpleasant to swallow."

  In general, the nineteenth century was a time of frantic
search for ancient sculptures and fine artifacts, whether from
Egypt, Greece, Mesopotamia, or the Americas. Everyone

wanted items for their collections and no one had any scruples about the means used to dig up their pet acquisitions. All too often we read in their early reports that such and such a find "crumbled to dust" on discovery or that exposure to the open air caused the finds to "dissolve before our very eyes."

One cannot entirely blame Belzoni and his successors. Basically, they were ignorant. No one had ever tried to dig a large archaeological site at all systematically. Even today, the technology of conservation is in relative infancy and modern archaeologists are still at a loss how to preserve many delicate finds satisfactorily. Considering the state of the art, it's a miracle that so much is preserved from early excavations. But the archaeological price of filling the British Museum, the Louvre, and other great museums was simply enormous: witness Austen Henry Layard's excavations in Mesopotamia at ancient Nineveh and Nimrud from 1845 to 1851.

Layard started digging Nimrud with precious little money and absolutely no archaeological experience. He simply tunneled into the huge mounds reputed to be the remains of these ancient cities and went on digging until he hit a fine sculpture or a stone-walled palace room. At Nimrud he was lucky enough to find two palaces. But, as he dug through mud-brick walls and houses, he failed to recognize invaluable inscribed tablets of unbaked clay. To his unskilled eyes, the bricks and tablets were indistinguishable from the brown soil of the mound. Later excavators recovered thousands of these tablets from areas of Nimrud that Layard left untouched. They had developed the skills and techniques to find them.

The deep tunnels that Layard dug along walls or lines of sculptured slabs at least sheltered him from the merciless sun and sweeping winds of the open plains. He would shovel out the contents of each room with dispatch, then sit down to record the intricate details of prancing horsemen and fighting warriors that flickered in the somber shadows. When his trenches were open to the elements, clouds of blinding dust stirred by savage gale-force winds would bombard the workmen. Layard himself would take refuge behind a giant sculpture until the sandstorm subsided. Under the circumstances, it is remarkable that he succeeded in excavating at all.

Austen Henry Layard shifted thousands of tons of soil, discovered nearly two miles of bas-reliefs, and cleared seventy rooms in the Palace of Sennacherib at Kuyunjik alone. Although he did keep some records, he more or less shoveled his way into the past. He tore Nimrud and Nineveh apart and, in the process, wiped out priceless archaeological information—data on daily life and ancient diet, details of houses and storerooms, and, above all, the complex sequence of layers that made up the occupation mounds.

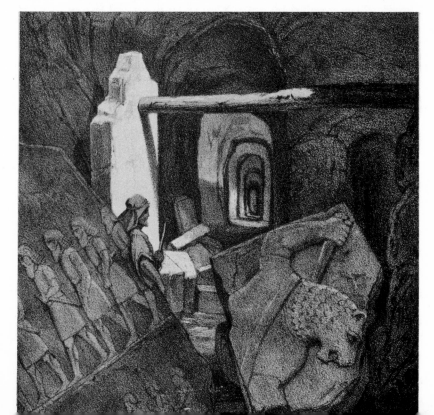

Layard's excavations in a tunnel at Kuyunjik.

Every Mesopotamian city mound was formed over centuries of occupation through complex processes of rebuilding houses, dumping garbage, and the natural actions of rain and wind. Many years before Layard came to Nineveh, geologists studying railway cuttings and canal excavations in Europe and America had observed the layered strata of the earth and established the classic principle of superposition. Very simply stated, this means that the lower levels of a succession of geological horizons were laid down earlier than the higher levels. The law of superposition had obvious applications to great city mounds like Nimrud or Nineveh, for every site started as a small settlement on a low ridge. The first occupation levels were soon covered by later settlements built in the same place. A thousand years later, the same city could look down from the top of a high mound of age-old occupation debris. The archaeologist wishing to understand the history of the city would have to dissect this mound layer by layer.

Layard himself was well aware that his mounds had gone through many changes. He knew that many kings had ruled his cities. But his excavation methods were simply too crude to permit him to dig the mounds period by period. One cannot blame Layard. If anything, he was more conscientious than his contemporaries, for he at least wrote popular accounts of his findings.

Many of the excavations of Layard's time were little more than picnic parties. Wealthy country gentlemen would open Indian burial mounds or Bronze Age earthworks for the sheer fun of it. When the English antiquarian Thomas Wright attended the opening of an ancient burial mound in 1844, he found a large party of interested gentry assembled for the sport. While the workmen opened eight burial mounds, the ladies and gentlemen "continued to spend [their] time, at intervals between digging and picnicking, in games of various descriptions . . . and in other amusements. The weather was fortunately exquisitely fine." When a sudden shower threatened to drench the party, they took refuge in the trench

Burial mound excavation—
1840s style.

under a shield of umbrellas. The burial mounds contained "skeletons, more or less entire, with the remains of weapons in iron, bosses of shields, urns, beads, armlets, and occasionally more vessels." All of these finds vanished into the landowner's private collection, which the party inspected after partaking of a "sumptuous repast." This burial-mound dig was in no way exceptional; rather, it was typical of thousands.

The techniques of excavation were still in their infancy when Heinrich Schliemann began work on the great Hissarlik mound, site of ancient Troy. Schliemann, a millionaire, attacked archaeological problems with the same single-minded intensity he applied to business ventures. His wealth gave him the means to work on a truly grand scale, with resident experts and hundreds of workmen. He arrived on the site in 1871 with the vague notion that the mound contained many different settlements. So he set out to dig to bedrock, on a scale that almost beggars description. In 1872, for example, he borrowed a railroad engineer and employed three overseers to direct over a hundred men. They sliced into Hissarlik with a cutting over 230 feet wide that eventually penetrated over 40 feet into the huge mound. The city walls found in the uppermost strata were ruthlessly cleared away as Schliemann dug his way down through the centuries, toward his Homeric city.

Eventually, Schliemann identified the remains of seven cities, one above the other. His excavations exhibited a notable lack of finesse. In his books, he refers to the clearance of entire ancient streets, to the removal of "older walls which I am also having broken through," and to thousands upon thousands of potsherds, ornaments, and other small finds that were shoveled out as thousands of tons of soil were dug out of Hissarlik. At one point, he boasted that he had removed 325,000 cubic yards of soil from ancient Troy.

Schliemann's motto was speed, more speed, and yet still more. When he dug, he cleared an entire landscape. Every day he described his findings in a comprehensive diary, which he eventually published. Unlike many of his contemporaries, Schliemann kept his finds and recorded all of them, not just the spectacular pieces. And, although he has been castigated

The Hissarlik excavations in progress, using techniques employed in digging the Suez Canal.

as little more than a treasure hunter, he in fact undertook the first large-scale dissection of a city mound where, unlike the situation at Nineveh or Nimrud, there were no sculptures to guide the way to ancient structures. As his digging experience increased, Schliemann began to rely more heavily on expert diggers, who were able to refine his methods drastically.

While Schliemann was working at Troy, German archaeologists had begun a quiet revolution in excavation methods that was to affect both the Troy excavations and many other digs as well. The Austrian archaeologist Alexander Conze dug at the site of Samothrace in Greece between 1873 and 1875. He dug with the help of architects and a photographer, who recorded the progress of the excavations.

The Samothrace report was a beautiful production, the first to be illustrated with photographs. Conze's example was not lost on the German Archaeological Institute, which started work at Olympia in 1875. For six winters, Ernst Curtius directed a brilliant campaign of excavations on the site of the original Olympic Games. The Kaiser himself paid for part of the dig. Every find was carefully preserved and housed in a special museum built at the site. No artifacts were exported. Curtius and Wilhelm Dörpfeld worked out every detail of the stratigraphy at Olympia with the aid of new and very precise record-keeping methods. The Olympia excavations set new standards that the ever-energetic Dörpfeld took with him to Troy. In his later years at Hissarlik, Schliemann became what one authority has called "a constitutional monarch among expert ministers." Dörpfeld refined Schliemann's seven cities into the complex history of a mound that, he said, flourished from about 3000–700 B.C., the Homeric city dating from 1500–1000 B.C.

Curtius and Dörpfeld were concerned with the trivial as well as the spectacular. Their excavations were far more meticulous than those of their predecessors, although still crude by modern standards. A retired British general named Augustus Pitt-Rivers revolutionized the art of excavation even further. The general, a formidable personality, spent much of his military career working on the development of army rifles. His experimental research involved him in the history of firearms and the study of different types of primitive artifacts from all over the world. Pitt-Rivers was deeply interested in the evolution of human technology. He became an avid collector of artifacts of all types—masks, shields, weapons, even canoes. His collections became so large that he donated them to Oxford University, where they are to this day.

In 1880, Pitt-Rivers inherited an enormous estate in southern England, an estate littered with ancient burial sites and earthworks. The general decided to devote the rest of his life to investigation of the sites on his property. He did so with ruthless efficiency, diverting enormous sums from his fortune into leisured excavations that lasted twenty years, until his death in 1901. Pitt-Rivers had a mania for records and detail. "Every detail should be recorded in the manner most conducive to facility of reference," he wrote. "I have endeavored to record the results of these excavations in such a way that the whole of the evidence may be available for those who are concerned to go into it." He had realized a cardinal point: all archaeological excavation is permanent destruction and all objects found in a site have a vital context in time and space that is just as important a piece of information as the find itself.

The learned general was far ahead of his time. He trained archaeological assistants, had "before" and "after" models of his sites constructed, built a special museum to display his finds, and even marked his filled-in trenches with special medallions that said, in effect, "Pitt-Rivers was here." His ideas were revolutionary. Consider some of his basic principles of digging: "No excavation ought to ever be permitted except under the immediate eye of a responsible and trustworthy superintendant." "Superfluous precision may be regarded as a fault on the right side." "Tedious as it may appear to some to dwell on the discovery of odds and ends that have, no doubt, been thrown away by the owners as rubbish . . . yet it is by the study of such trivial details that archaeology is mainly dependent for determining the date of earthworks."

Hundreds of man-hours went into each of Pitt-Rivers' sumptuous reports. Each was published privately, complete with detailed plans, accurate measurements of every artifact, and precise information on every aspect of the site from pottery to hut foundations, stratigraphy to animal bones. It was to be years before anyone would equal or surpass Pitt-Rivers' painstaking work. He deplored the destruction of earthworks by plowing, laid out picnic grounds for people visiting his museum, and urged his fellow landowners to follow his example. Not a particularly endearing gentleman, the general, but his legacy to archaeology is unquestioned. An interesting glimpse into the man comes from a photograph of the excavations which is tersely captioned: "The figure standing *at attention* in the foreground gives the scale." Evidently Pitt-Rivers was a military man, as well as an archaeologist, to the very end.

Few people followed Pitt-Rivers' example. One could still become an excavator without any training at all, although well-known archaeologists like Wilhelm Dörpfeld and the immortal Egyptologist Flinders Petrie were busy training students to follow in their footsteps. Petrie begged his colleagues to be quit of "the brandy-and-soda young man . . . of the adventurous speculator. Without the ideal of solid continuous work, certain, accurate, and permanent, archaeology is as futile as any other pursuit." He went on to urge informal attire: "To attempt serious work in pretty suits, shiny leggings or starched collars, would be like mountaineering in evening dress." "It is sickening to see the rate at which everything is being destroyed," he once remarked, "and the little regard paid to preservation."

Some of the better digging that stemmed from Pitt-Rivers' work took place on Roman sites in Britain. Still, to modern eyes, the efforts appear to have been terribly amateurish and the excavators incredibly ill-equipped. Young Leonard Woolley, for example, later to become famous for his skilled excavations of royal graves at Ur-of-the-Chaldees in Mesopotamia, found himself in charge of a major Roman excavation without any experience at all or the least idea of how to survey a site or make plans.

The early part of this century also seems to have been a difficult period for female archaeologists. When a little-known archaeologist named J. P. Droop wrote a small manual on excavation in 1915, he spent a lot of time worrying about male/female roles. "I have never seen a trained lady excavator at work," he admitted. "Of a mixed dig, however, I have seen something, and it is an experiment that I would be reluctant to try again." His reasons were twofold. "In the first place, there are the proprieties." Excavators should respect the etiquette and mores of the countries they are working in. Droop's other reasons were more personal. It seems that, in his experience, the "charm" of ladies vanishes during an excavation, for the dig lays on its mixed participants "a bond of closer daily intercourse than is conceivable." Droop found this irritating. "The ordinary male at least cannot stand it," he added. He cited the strain of "self-restraint in moments of stress, moments that will occur on the best regulated dig, when you want to say just what you think without translation, which before ladies, whatever their feelings about it, cannot be done." Droop was never to know of the key roles played by twentieth-century women in major archaeological excavations the world over.

The lax standards of Pitt-Rivers' contemporaries and successors were assaulted by archaeologists of the 1920s and 1930s. "There is no right way of digging but there are many wrong ones," wrote one of Pitt-Rivers' most avid disciples—Mortimer Wheeler. Wheeler, who was ten years old when Pitt-Rivers died, came to archaeology through the good offices of Arthur Evans, discoverer of the ancient palace of King Minos on Crete. Wheeler spent his lifetime digging large sites with meticulous precision and training new generations of archaeologists in methods that owed their inspiration to the Victorian general.

Wheeler worked first on Roman forts, notably the famous Iron Age fortress at Maiden Castle in southern Britain. From archaeological evidence, he was able to reconstruct a blow-by-blow account of the Roman storming of that fort. After a distinguished military career in World War II, Wheeler was asked to head up the Archaeological Survey of India. With characteristic and flamboyant energy, he took up the task of organizing archaeology out of chaos. He found Roman imported pottery in southern India and dug deeply into the ancient city mounds of Harappa and Mohenjo-daro in the Indus

Valley. There he sketched a fascinating picture of a long-extinct Indian civilization that had traded with Mesopotamia and developed its own distinctive, and still undeciphered, script. Mortimer Wheeler's excavations were, quite simply, meticulous, and the results remarkable. Most modern excavations build on the basic principles that he and Pitt-Rivers, as well as a handful of other pioneers, set out.

"The archaeologist is not digging up things, he is digging up people," Wheeler would begin. Good excavation takes imagination, an ability to understand what one is digging up. According to Wheeler, people who do not have this kind of imagination should collect bus tickets instead of digging. He believed the key to excavation was accurate observation and recording of occupation levels and architectural features, of the layout of burials and minute artifacts. The relationship between different objects in the ground can tell one much about the behavior of their makers, he taught his students. Wheeler's excavations were models of tidiness, with straight walls and carefully swept trenches to make the tasks of observation and discovery more precise. The observation of superimposed layers and the features and artifacts in them would give one an accurate chronology to work with, an essential framework for studying the numerous pot fragments and other finds from the dig. He pointed out how buildings should be dissected with great care, so that the foundations could be related to the underlying, dated strata and the contents isolated from those in other parts of the site. The burials Wheeler found were exposed bone by bone and carefully photographed in position before removal.

All of Wheeler's excavations were carefully designed not only to find artifacts but to answer specific questions about chronology or other matters. These questions were formulated in advance or as the dig was in progress. The staff of the excavation was organized into a hierarchy of specialists, led by the director himself, whose task was to "cultivate a scrupulous accuracy and completeness in the observation and record of his factual evidence." Wheeler's ideal director had "the combined virtues of the scholar and the man of action," an ability to achieve accuracy "not for accuracy's sake, but as a basis for using his imagination to interpret his finds." "Archaeology," wrote Wheeler, "is primarily a fact-finding discipline." But, he would always add, we have to dig sites as a means to an end, the end being the understanding of humanity's complex and changing relationship with its environment.

Schliemann dug up the past of Troy. He and many other early archaeologists taught us that archaeological sites contain many treasures. Curtius, Dörpfeld, Pitt-Rivers, and Wheeler developed techniques for recording the contents of each site in meticulous detail. And Wheeler himself threw down the gauntlet to his successors—he challenged them to apply these recording methods to such complex problems as "estimating the density and social structure of populations." His words were prophetic, for that is what leading archaeologists are now trying to achieve.

Mortimer Wheeler died in 1976 after witnessing a revolution in digging methods all over the world, a revolution whose impact is still being felt. His students and their students, as well as those of other pioneering archaeologists, have refined his methods even further. Some idea of the complexity of a modern excavation can be gained by a brief look at the investigation of an ancient camp site at Olduvai Gorge in Tanzania. The site dates to more than 1.75 million years ago.

"Archaeology," wrote British archaeologist Stuart Piggott some years ago, "is the science of rubbish." And rubbish is precisely what Louis and Mary Leakey had to dissect when they excavated the ancient campsites in the lowest levels of Olduvai Gorge. All that remained of the campsites were small scatters of discarded animal bones, stone tools, and waste chips, lying in irregular concentrations on the very land surfaces ancient people once trod. Often the scatter of artifacts and bones was only a few inches thick and was sealed under dozens of feet of sterile sand and lake clay. How old were these campsites? What activities took place there and how large were the settlements? Could any information on prehistoric diet and food-getting methods be obtained from the floors? These and many other questions came to mind as the Leakeys began clearing these small but complicated sites. They had no doubt as to the importance of their excavations: these were probably among the earliest human settlements in the world. To avoid damaging any human fossils and to prevent disturbance of the artifacts from their original positions, only the most delicate methods could be used.

Each floor lay within a major geological horizon of Olduvai Gorge, one that the Leakeys knew dated to the earliest millennia of the human experience. But dating samples had to be obtained, that is, lumps of lava that could be dated by laboratory tests for their radioactive content. These samples had to come from the living floors themselves, from lava fragments that had actually been carried to the site by those who had lived there. The Leakeys had no choice: they knew they must excavate each entire living floor, plot all the objects on them, and obtain dating samples from among the finds in the camp.

One living floor yielded the famous skull of *Zinjanthropus* in 1959, a discovery we describe in Chapter 2. Mary Leakey originally found a portion of the fossil outcropping from the lower lake beds of the Gorge. A small excavation was immediately undertaken at the site of this discovery to aid both in the removal of the precious skull and in establishing the exact level from which the fossil came. The immediate surroundings of the skull were sifted carefully in case additional fragments had already fallen down the slope on which it was found. The trial excavation yielded broken animal bones, some rodent fragments, and a few stone tools that lay in place near the skull. There seemed a strong possibility that the skull was directly associated with the tools—indeed, its owner might have made them.

It was seven months before Mary Leakey could return to the site, for the skull had been found at the very end of the 1959 season. When the time came for larger-scale excavations, she did not attack the living floor at once. Her task was to establish the precise position of the campsite in the Olduvai geological strata. To determine this, she dug a six-foot trial trench in steps through the entire forty feet of the geological bed the skull had come from, right down to bedrock. She found that the living floor was halfway up the bed.

Once the stratigraphical position of the fossil skull was established, Mary Leakey set out to determine the extent of the living floor itself. The workmen removed the sterile overburden of lake bed from the area around the trial trench. This unproductive soil was removed with picks and shovels in rough levels. When they reached a whitish-yellow volcanic-ash zone that Mary Leakey knew directly overlay the precious living floor, they stepped aside. The trench was now divided into four-foot-wide strips that were worked one by one with great care. Skilled workers carefully pared away the volcanic ash to within a few inches of the underlying living floor. Sometimes bones and other finds protruded through into the ash. So dry was the soil that the excavators had to dampen it before removal to guard against damaging valuable fossils underneath.

The living floor proved to be about a foot thick. With great care, Mary Leakey worked each strip of the trench from one side of the floor to the other. Whenever possible, every find was cleared from the surrounding soil with dental probes and small paintbrushes. Every find of any size, whether a stone tool or an animal bone, was marked with black or white ink and plotted on the floor plan before being lifted. A complete photographic record of the floor was maintained as well. Once the larger finds had been removed, the floor soil was wet- or dry-sifted through one-sixteenth-inch screens so that even the tiniest stone chips and bone fragments were recovered for laboratory analysis. As a result of this painstaking excavation,

Photograph by Robert F. Sisson, © National Geographic Society

the position of every significant find on the floor was known to within an inch or less. What a contrast to Belzoni's burial chambers or Layard's palaces!

The man-hours expended on the *Zinjanthropus* floor were well worth the expense. The amount of detail about early human life-styles that came from the *Zinjanthropus* floor was truly astonishing, all of it the result of meticulous excavation. In addition to the dating samples gathered—which proved the site to be 1.75 million years old—the Leakeys obtained data on the dimensions and layout of one of the earliest campsites

The Leakeys at work on a 1.75-million-year-old living floor at Olduvai Gorge.

in the world. Mary Leakey found and took apart a concentration of stone tools and flakes and over a thousand broken bone fragments covering an area 21 by 15 feet near the spot where *Zinjanthropus* was found. This central zone was separated from another concentration of bones by a less densely covered area that she felt might have been the site of a crude shelter. We know that the inhabitants used crude stone choppers and many flakes in the preparation of food and the butchering of small animals. They smashed up the limb bones of antelope and zebra and broke open the skulls to remove the brain. But large scavengers like hyenas visited the site as well and chewed up some of the freshly broken bones—presumably after the inhabitants left. None of this information could have been obtained without rigorous excavation techniques. The Leakeys literally drained the living floor of information.

Each excavation has its own distinctive problems of preservation and recording, but burial sites are among the most challenging of all archaeological problems. Howard Carter spent ten years clearing and preserving the finds from Tut-ankh-Amun's tomb in Egypt. In this case, the diggers were more concerned with removal and preservation of funerary furniture than with actual excavation. Still, before removal to the laboratory, the position and context of each piece of grave furniture were carefully recorded.

Cemeteries and even individual burials can provide vital information on the social status of the people buried there. Their costumes, grave furniture, and the circumstances of their burial often reveal a great deal about the individual and the society. Burial excavation involves recording the arrangement of the grave goods and the position of the skeleton even before the find is removed from the ground. Once the presence of a grave is suspected, the first stage is to outline the burial pit and its filling and to identify any surface features that may have marked the ancient grave. Then the pit filling is carefully removed with dental probe and light brush, until the bones and grave furniture appear and the general orienta-

Excavating the dead: a human skeleton from Wheeler's excavations at Maiden Castle, England. The position of the bones and the shape of the burial pit can clearly be seen.

The head of Tollund Man,
Denmark.

tion of the skeleton is established. Many hours later, the complete burial and the pots, ornaments, or other grave furniture are picked clean of clinging soil, so that the grave, its furniture, and the skeleton are all clearly exposed for the eye of the camera. Only when every detail of the burial is described in notebook and recorded on film will the grave be removed. Especially important burials may be lifted in one piece, using a casket of plaster of paris and steel rods. Less important skeletons are disarticulated and removed piece by piece.

Archaeological literature abounds with stories of remarkable feats of recovery in which extremely delicate or highly fragmentary artifacts have been rescued from oblivion. Waterlogged conditions on a site create colossal excavation problems, but often result in spectacular finds. The Danes have recovered two-thousand-year-old corpses from damp bogs, sacrificial victims with clothing, hair, and skin still intact. Richard Daugherty had to use pressure hoses at Ozette in the Pacific Northwest to uncover long-buried cedarwood houses and their highly perishable contents. Dutch archaeologists were able to trace the outlines of corpses in the sandy subsoil under burial mounds, even though the actual flesh and bones had long since vanished. Discolored stains left in the soil from the process of decomposition were exposed by careful scraping of the subsoil.

The Dutch achievement pales considerably beside Leonard Woolley's recovery of the long-vanished wooden harp of Queen Shub-ad of Ur-of-the-Chaldees. Woolley's first clue to the whereabouts of the harp was a gold cap of the upright, found loose in the soil of the royal cemetery. Next, some isolated gold nails came to light. Exploring further, the excavators found a small hole angling steeply down into the ground. A flashlight revealed more gold nails deep in the hole. Woolley inserted a small stick into the shaft and filled the interstices with liquid plaster. As the soil was cleared away, the stem of a harp, preserved in plaster, emerged from its burial place. By using paraffin wax and fine muslin, Woolley was able to recover the mosaic inlay of the sounding box and the gold and lapis lazuli calf's head that had decorated the front of the instrument. Subsequently Woolley could reconstruct a very accurate version of the entire original instrument, simply because he was able to record all the instrument's salient details from the impression they had made in the ground before they decomposed. And he was able to recover fragments of the harp that a less skilled or less experienced excavator would have completely missed.

Modern archaeology has undergone a revolution not only in digging methods but in dating methods as well. Early archaeologists had to rely on guesswork to date their finds, unless they could relate their sites to historical civilizations. Many ingenious methods were devised to date the past until physicist Willard Libby invented radiocarbon (C-14) dating in the late 1940s. Libby's invention took the archaeological world by storm. It provided a reliable means of dating organic materials, such as charcoal or wood, found in archaeological sites ranging in age from 50,000 to 500 years old. For the first time, archaeologists had a common method of dating sites as far separated as Afghanistan and Patagonia, a means of developing a worldwide chronology for human prehistory.

The principle of C-14 dating is based on the fact that normal, nonradioactive carbon has an atomic weight of 12. The nucleus of the carbon atom has twelve protons and twelve neutrons. The radioactive isotope of carbon (carbon-14) has two additional neutrons in the nucleus. Carbon-14 is produced in the upper atmosphere by the constant bombardment of nitrogen atoms by cosmic rays. There is a constant ratio of carbon-14 and normal carbon in the atmosphere, a ratio that is found in all living things, whether plant or animal. However, when an organism dies, the C-14 is no longer replenished from the atmospheric reservoir. It is unstable and, in time, will radiate its additional neutrons and revert to carbon-12. The C-14 decay starts at death and proceeds at a measured rate. Libby calculated this decay rate and determined the ratio of C-14 to C-12 in charcoal, wood, and other organic substances from objects of known age, like funerary boats from Egypt. He related these readings in years to the actual historical dates for the objects and found they checked out. He then extended the method to prehistoric objects and sites.

Now, over a quarter of a century later, thousands of radiocarbon dates provide us with a global chronology for more recently prehistoric millennia. Although comparisons with dates from tree-ring chronologies developed on ancient logs and beams found in the deserts of the American Southwest have revealed some inaccuracies in radiocarbon dates, methods of correcting these are being developed. The radiocarbon revolution has truly opened up a new dimension for probing the past, a dimension we see explored at Ozette, Teotihuacán, and other sites described later in this book.

Most archaeologists, at one time or another, feel they are in touch with the people they are studying. This sense seems to have been highly developed in Louis Leakey, Heinrich Schliemann, and Howard Carter. Carter experienced an almost eerie bond with Tut-ankh-Amun. He summed it up well when he wrote: "I stood in the presence of a king who reigned three thousand years ago." One suspects Carter was not speaking strictly figuratively: he felt he *really had.*

Sometimes, as I have stood gazing over a long-deserted prehistoric settlement, silent on a cool evening as the sun casts long shadows over earthworks and eroding occupation deposits, I have experienced a sudden collapse of time. The site comes to life: thatched huts rise from the ground, scented wood smoke ascends in the evening still, dogs bark and children laugh in play. Outside their huts, old men sit and gossip quietly for a brief evening hour. Then, just as quickly, the image recedes and the village once again becomes a deserted archive of archaeological information, a silent complex of mud-hut foundations, dusty pot fragments, and broken food bones. For a moment, the ancient inhabitants of that village sprang to life, shedding their cloaks of anonymity to reach out across the millennia. Heady emotions, perhaps, but, for a moment, one understands why archaeology is so much more than just a set of techniques and tools for digging up the past.

# CHAPTER

# 2

# LOUIS LEAKEY'S VALLEY OF BONES

OLDUVAI GORGE IN EAST AFRICA WAS A QUIET AND WARM place on July 17, 1959. The Gorge's steep slopes shimmered in the African heat as Mary Leakey crouched over the dry sands of its lowest geological beds. For weeks, she and her husband Louis had been looking for traces of ancient campsites. Now, while Louis lay sick in their base camp on the lip of the Gorge, Mary continued the unending search for ancient human fossils. This particular day she was working at a place where the Leakeys had found traces of bones and stone tools months before.

Mary worked slowly and painstakingly in the hot sun. The only sounds to be heard were the scraping of trowels and dental picks and the labored panting of the family's two dalmations, Sally and Victoria. Suddenly, Mary spotted some bone fragments eroding out of the sloping wall of the lowest levels of the Gorge. Electrified, she carefully scraped away the clinging soil from two large teeth. They were unquestionably those of a humanlike fossil, the first to be found in Olduvai Gorge. Mary jumped in the Land Rover and tore up to camp.

"I've got him! I've got him," she cried as she burst into the tent. His illness forgotten, Louis leaped into his clothes and, together, husband and wife rattled down the track to the site. With great care, they examined the teeth and prised away more soil. There could be no doubt: Mary Leakey had uncovered a fossil skull of tremendous antiquity. A search that had begun twenty-eight years before was finally crowned with success that hot July day.

The destinies of Louis Seymour Bazett Leakey and his wife Mary were inextricably intertwined with a "valley full of bones . . . they were very many in the valley, and lo, they were very dry." The valley is Olduvai Gorge in northern Tanzania, East Africa, and the bones are those of some of the earliest humans ever found. Together, the Leakey family has added more to the story of early humanity than have any other archaeologists. Some of their discoveries resulted from sheer luck, most from dogged hard work, and a few from a sense of vision that only truly great archaeologists possess. Like the prophet Elijah, the Leakeys displayed an uncanny prophetic sense that enable them to conjure bones from the ground and rewrite human prehistory.

The whole of Louis Leakey's long life was linked in some way with East Africa. His father, a pioneer missionary, settled in Kikuyu country near the young town of Nairobi in 1902. Louis was born a year later, the first white baby many Kikuyu had seen. As an infant, Louis learned both Kikuyu and English and was partially initiated into the tribe. For the rest of his life, he called himself a white Kikuyu. The Kikuyu lore that Leakey learned as a child was to prove invaluable later in his life.

Although his father saw to it that Louis had a solid schooling, young Louis's main preoccupations were hunting and trapping small animals. From his Kikuyu mentors, he learned the importance of keen observation and patience, two qualities essential for an archaeologist. "My Kikuyu training taught me this," he wrote in the *National Geographic* many

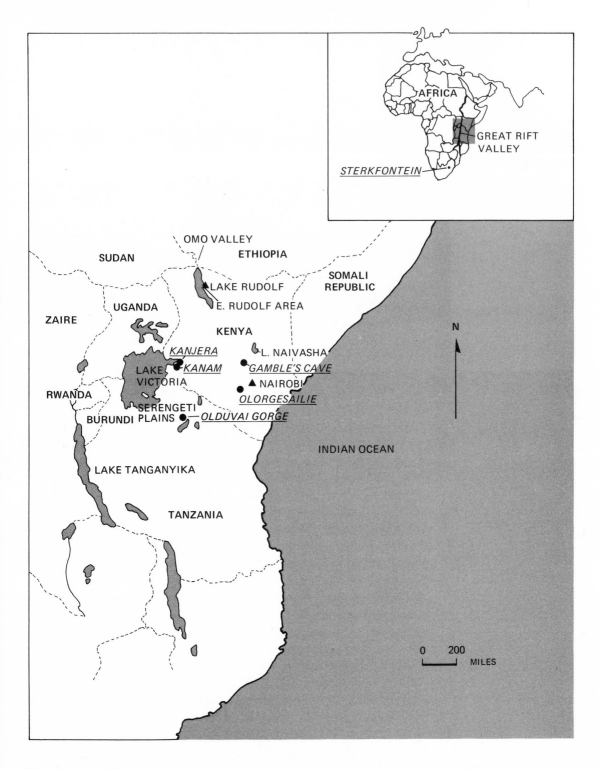

Locations and sites mentioned
in Chapter 2.

years later. "If you have reason to believe that something should be in a given spot but you don't find it, you must not conclude that it isn't there. Rather, you must conclude that your powers of observation are faulty."

At the age of thirteen, Louis met Arthur Loveridge, curator of the new museum in Nairobi, who encouraged him to study wildlife instead of hunting it. When a loving aunt in England sent Leakey a book about prehistoric stone axes, it was Loveridge who encouraged him to look for similar tools in Kenya. Within a few weeks, Leakey had found several boxes full of stone tools that looked just like the European examples illustrated in his book. Thus was kindled a lifelong interest in archaeology and natural history, pursuits that required all the patience and powers of observation that the Kikuyu had taught Leakey to cultivate.

By the time Louis applied to Cambridge University, he had already decided he would become a great scientist. Since anthropology, his chosen subject, was only studied at an advanced level, two modern languages were required of degree candidates. One was easy for Leakey to choose—French. His father had insisted that he study it from an early age. Characteristically, Leakey chose Kikuyu as his second modern language. The university authorities were at a loss. Indeed, Kikuyu filled the modern language requirement, for it was a language spoken by large numbers of people. Furthermore, Leakey's own father had translated the Bible into Kikuyu. It was thus a written tongue. In addition, one competent examiner in Kikuyu resided in England at the time, duly registered with London University—Louis Seymour Bazett Leakey himself! Displaying a touch of genius, Leakey had taken the precaution of registering himself as an examiner a few months before. And his certificate of competence was signed not only by a missionary, but with the thumbprint of a Kikuyu Senior Chief as well.

Leakey started his Cambridge career by teaching his examiner in Kikuyu the language—for the standard university fee.

He threw himself into all manner of pursuits and was ejected from the tennis courts for playing tennis in shorts, dress considered to be grossly indecent. He took up conjuring and sawed women in half, and acquired an interest in handwriting that was to stand him in good stead when he became involved with police work in later years. His brand of Rugby football was so violent that, when he was kicked in the head, the doctor advised a year out of school.

Instead of moping in England, Louis got himself a job as an assistant on a British Museum dinosaur-hunting expedition to Tanzania. After a hectic year, during which he learned how to lift fossils with plaster of paris, Louis returned to Cambridge in January of 1925. He was literally bankrupt and supported himself by giving lectures on dinosaur hunting at private schools. For the first time, Leakey learned how to thrill an audience with his tales of exciting discoveries and far-off lands. It was another skill that was to prove invaluable.

Louis went on to study archaeology and anthropology and came under the influence of the great ethnographer A. C. Haddon, a formidable personality with an encyclopaedic knowledge of the world's primitive tribes. He encouraged Louis to study early technology and, when Louis graduated with first-class honors, helped him find money to return to East Africa with his own archaeological expedition.

With Haddon's assistance, Leakey found himself with enough money to support himself and a companion for several months and enough time to find out something about the archaeology of Kenya. There was little to go on. Although a geologist named E. J. Wayland had recovered tons of prehistoric artifacts during geological expeditions in Uganda, Kenya remained a complete archaeological blank. Leakey had corresponded with Wayland for months and was certain he would find similar sites in the Great Rift Valley near Nairobi. In his letters, Wayland had described a sequence of dramatic climatic changes—alternating periods of heavy rainfall and drier conditions—that had persisted in Uganda throughout prehistoric times. Had such climatic changes occurred in Kenya as well? How long had Stone Age people lived in East Africa? These questions were to occupy Leakey's mind throughout his career.

The 1926 expedition had been in the field only a short while when Mr. Gamble, a local resident, showed Leakey two rock shelters that looked promising. So expedition members took up residence in one of Gamble's disused pigsties and proceeded to dig into the deep deposits under the cliff. By the time funds ran out, Leakey had found abundant signs of prehistoric people in Gamble's cave and thought he had evidence of ancient climatic change in the Rift Valley, too. Wayland came, saw, and approved. Louis immediately began to make plans for a second expedition. He obtained a small income for himself and managed to recruit a party of five people to accompany him. He also married Frida Avern, whom he had met in Kenya the year before. Her first home was the Gamble pigsty, which also served as base laboratory for the new excavations.

Gamble's Cave proved to be a prehistoric gold mine, one that took over seven months to excavate. Leakey dug through twenty-eight feet of occupation deposit and was soon finding over seven hundred stone tools a day, each of which had to be catalogued and examined in the evenings. The finds provided a chronicle of prehistoric peoples that went back, Leakey claimed, over 20,000 years. He found traces of ostrich-eggshell beads, large numbers of small tools delicately fashioned from black volcanic glass, and numerous animal bones from slaughtered game. So complicated were the geological events of the Rift Valley that Louis appealed to the Governor of Kenya for assistance. He was granted a thousand pounds, sufficient for Leakey to cable A. C. Haddon in Cambridge: "Find me a geologist." And Haddon did. Soon Leakey had the evidence for ancient periods of high rainfall that he had been looking for since 1926.

By this time, Leakey's reputation as an archaeologist was well established; he was regarded as an up-and-coming young man in his field. Anyone planning a scientific expedition to Kenya automatically consulted Leakey. The Kenya government used his expertise, too: he served on the Kikuyu Land Commission in 1929 and, while a member, looked into the grievances that erupted ultimately into the Mau Mau rebellion of the 1940s.

One particular archaeological discovery continued to fascinate Leakey during this time, a report of a human skeleton found in 1913 at a remote gorge in northern Tanganyika named *ol duvai* (Masai: "place of the wild sisal"). The Olduvai Gorge was discovered quite by chance: one day in 1911, German entomologist Wilhelm Kattwinkel literally stumbled across it while hunting butterflies. He is rumored to have tripped over the edge and bounced over three hundred feet to the bottom. As he made his way up the side of the Gorge, he picked up some fossil bones outcropping from erosion gullies. The experts on fossils who examined the bones back in Germany were very excited. Kattwinkel had inadvertently picked up fragments of a three-toed horse and other unknown extinct animals. So the geologists asked Dr. Hans Reck, at that time a member of the Geological Survey of German East Africa, to look for more.

The interior of East Africa was so unfamiliar to Europeans at that time that Reck had considerable difficulty finding Olduvai. He knew it was somewhere on the Serengeti Plains, a vast grassland that teemed with herds of antelope and other game, just as it had for thousands of years. So, outfitted with a hundred porters, he trekked to the Serengeti and, after considerable difficulties, managed to find the Gorge. For three months, Reck searched Olduvai from one end to the other. He recovered hundreds of fossils and spent a great deal of time trying to untangle the geology of the Gorge. At least four distinct sandy beds could be seen in the walls, all dating from several hundred thousand years ago. Millennia before, a large freshwater lake had extended over the Serengeti Plains. Herds of extinct mammals had once drunk from its waters, some of them dying nearby. The lake then rose and covered their rotting carcasses with sand. Much later, a series of earthquakes cut through the deposits of the dry basin, exposing the long-forgotten lake, along with the bones of the animals that had died on its shores.

Just as Reck was about to leave Olduvai, he made his most dramatic discovery. He nearly stepped on a human skeleton eroding out of a grave deep in the lake beds. Reck was astonished. If the grave actually belonged to this deep level, it must date to hundreds of thousands of years ago. The skeleton lay in a crouched position and was obviously of a modern anatomical type. But why was it lying in such early beds when, presumably, more primitive people were in existence at that time? Was this an early human fossil *in situ*? Reck himself went home and claimed it was, touting "Olduvai Man" as a truly ancient find. Most scientists disagreed with him. The German Kaiser himself was so interested in the finds that he sponsored a new expedition, a venture that was aborted by the First World War. So Olduvai Man remained a mystery until Leakey came along.

Leakey first heard of Reck in Munich in 1925. The two men—the one ambitious, fast talking, and excitable, the other tall, fair, and more easy going—struck up a friendship at once. When Leakey finally saw the Olduvai human remains, he was struck by the close resemblances between Reck's find and the skeletons he had discovered at Gamble's Cave. He was convinced that the burial was much more recent than Reck claimed. Without further ado, he invited Reck to accompany him to Olduvai in 1931—and this, long before he had obtained the money to go! With his usual luck, however, Leakey soon raised some 2,500 pounds from various sources and obtained the support of the British Museum, which was interested in fossil mammals from the Gorge. The Museum sent A. T. Hopwood, a fossil expert, along with the party.

Until very recently, getting to Olduvai was a mild adventure; in 1931, it was a major undertaking. Leakey hired an ex-Indian officer as a guide to blaze a motor track to the Gorge. Captain Hewlett was also an expert shot, which, as it turned out, was extremely fortunate—he shot two lions while protecting members of the party. Leakey himself had to kill a wounded rhinoceros that charged him. In late September 1931, Leakey, Reck, Hopwood, and Hewlett set out with eighteen Africans on a four-day trek along Hewlett's pioneer trail. The three trucks and one automobile bounced along the rough track at a snail's pace, a journey that Leakey always recalled with pleasure. When they reached Olduvai, the pools of water that Reck and his men had drunk were dry. Alternate supplies were eventually found twelve miles away.

An early Leakey expedition ready for departure.

Incredible as it may seem, Reck had never found a single stone implement in all his weeks at Olduvai. He had seen hundreds of them in museums, all European specimens made from fine-grained flint and very easy to identify. There were no flint deposits in East Africa. Prehistoric peoples used coarser materials like lava and quartzite, and occasionally obsidian if they could find it. Expecting flint, Reck had found nothing. Leakey, however, although interested in fossil mammals, was certain even when he first heard of Olduvai that prehistoric tools would be found there. The German was unconvinced.

"I bet you ten pounds that I find a handaxe within twenty-four hours," countered the brash Leakey.

Quietly the geologist agreed. The bet was a sizable chunk of Leakey's valuable research funds. But only a few short hours after starting down the walls of the Gorge, Leakey gave a cry of triumph. He pointed to a stone handaxe protruding from one of the upper beds of the Gorge. Ten pounds duly changed hands.

Leakey was wild with excitement. For six weeks he and his colleagues combed the sides of what turned out to be a vast treasure house of prehistoric sites, as well as of Pleistocene animals. There were over eighteen miles of main and side gorges to traverse, many of them steep cliffs and sharp rocks. The Gorge was dry and very hot, with a resident population of rhinoceroses who resented human interference. All supplies had to be brought in along incredibly rough tracks at great expense. Yet Leakey was in his element with an archaeological challenge that he realized would take him back earlier into human history than anyone had ever been before. With the extraordinary vision that characterized so much of Leakey's work, he felt certain that one day he would find the bones of early humans in this arid place. He also knew it would take years to locate them.

The first step was to work out the geology of Olduvai Gorge. Even today many features of its complicated strata remain a mystery. Leakey and Reck were able to identify five large geological beds, most of them consisting of fine sands and clays that had been laid down in the shallow water of a long-dried-up lake. It was at the edge of this lake that the many animals whose bones lay in the Gorge had drunk. When the two men looked more closely at the strata, they found that the lowest two beds, which they labeled I and II respectively, were closely similar—indeed, passed into each other with few signs of a break. The lowest lake deposits lay directly on a thick layer of vocalnic ash, the result of a large eruption millions of years before. A striking, red bed overlay the lowermost two beds. Its red earth could be seen for miles, in marked contrast to the whiter levels above and below it. Originally Reck argued that this bed was laid down at a time when there was no lake at Olduvai, but it is now thought to have been deposited

Olduvai Gorge.

under much the same conditions as the earlier beds. Bed IV lay directly above the red horizons of Bed III and seemed very similar to the lower levels of the Gorge. Fish and crocodile bones came from Bed IV, as did fragments of hundreds of large mammals. But, at the close of Bed IV, major earth movements cut a deep gorge through the long-established lake, in some places right down to the volcanic bedrock under Bed I. The edges of the Gorge were subsequently covered with wind-blown sands, a thin Bed V that is comparatively very recent.

The four older geological beds were found throughout the length of the Gorge. Reck was able to trace them not only in the main gorge itself but also in a side gorge that extended southwestward from the middle of Olduvai. The lowermost beds were particularly well exposed in the mouth of this side gorge—indeed, it has proved to be one of the richest areas of Olduvai. The floor of the main gorge was affected by several geological faults. A stream ran through Olduvai on the rare occasions when there was any lengthy rainfall. It took Reck weeks to work out the geology, for the four major beds were twisted and convoluted by earth movement and erosion, and often covered with dense scrub vegetation. Then, too, there was always the danger of meeting a stray rhinoceros among the thorn brush. Reck achieved miracles under very difficult conditions. He concluded that the Olduvai lake existed during a prolonged period of relatively dry conditions, during which there were several periods of increased rainfall. The many animals found in the lake deposits told him that the lake had existed during the earlier millennia of the Pleistocene epoch or "age of humanity," the most recent of geological periods. Olduvai lake was several hundred thousand years old. But Reck had no means of knowing actually how old the various beds were. At the time, no one had developed a way of dating sites as early as Olduvai. It was to be a quarter of a century before the earliest beds could be dated at all accurately. And when they were, the readings caused a sensation.

As Leakey and Reck fanned out over the Gorge they found that its many gullies were crammed with fossils and stone tools. Each locality received a name after its discoverer—for example, RK for Reck's Karongo, *karongo* being the Swahili word for gully. They worked over an area within five miles of the camp and found stone tools in all of the four Olduvai beds. Most of the stone implements found in Beds II to IV were axe forms, with sharpened edges that became progressively better trimmed and straighter as time went on. But the lowermost bed contained much cruder tools, coarse choppers formed by chipping off a few flakes from a lava lump to make a very simple jagged cutting edge. These remarkable tools were obviously flaked by a human hand and, in their simplicity, seemed to be the earliest and crudest in the world. The first examples were found in a gully Leakey named Frida Leakey Karongo (FLK), in honor of his wife who was in faraway Nairobi. Twenty-eight years later, his second wife Mary was to find a fossil skull only yards away.

While these exciting discoveries were coming to light, Leakey spent some time puzzling over Reck's ancient skeleton, which seemed such a chronological anomaly. On the face of it, the skeleton seemed to be contemporary with Bed IV, for its find spot was sealed by the dense and very hard deposits of a later Bed V, which would have been hard for anyone to dig through. It was some years before they guessed the truth, that the skeleton had been deposited on the surface of Bed IV before Bed V was deposited, but much later than Bed IV itself was formed.

The expedition sent over a hundred boxes of stone implements and fossils back to Nairobi. Leakey realized that he was probably sitting on the richest early archaeological site in the world, one that was worth not only extensive excavation but years of careful research. His normal inclination would have been to excavate at once. But on this occasion he held off, determined to get to know the Gorge intimately before putting a spade in the ground. An obvious first stage was to examine the thousands of implements and fossils collected during the 1931 expedition. But it was not until after the Second World War that Leakey could start large-scale work at Olduvai.

By the time Louis returned to Olduvai, his first marriage had ended in divorce. Some time before he had met Mary Nicol, a young woman with a passionate interest in prehistory. Together, they worked at Olduvai and other sites in 1935 and were married the following year. Mary Leakey's introduction to Olduvai was a rough one. Heavy rains turned the streams in the Gorge into raging torrents, the roads were awash with mud, and it took them three-and-a-half days to travel sixteen miles. Once they arrived, their work was complicated by prides of lions and by angry rhinoceroses. But the expedition was a profitable one. In examining the side gorge, they found no less than twenty promising sites in an area that was later found to have been a long–dried-up shore of an ancient lake, where small bands of hunter-gatherers had camped.

Although Olduvai was still a very promising locality, Leakey faced trouble on other fronts. In 1932, he had led a small party to investigate the fossil-bearing beds on the east shores of Lake Victoria near the Gulf of Kavirondo. The ancient lake beds yielded fossils of similar age to those found at Olduvai and, most exciting of all, some fragmentary human remains from two sites at Kanam and Kanjera. Unfortunately, Leakey was in a hurry to return to Olduvai and failed to double-check where precisely the fossils had been found. Unwisely, he went ahead and published the new fossils, claiming them as ancestors of modern humanity. His scientific colleagues were a bit dubious and an investigation of the circumstances of Leakey's find was launched. When a geologist named Percy Boswell visited Leakey's sites, Leakey was unable to locate the precise spots where the fossils came from. Boswell returned to England and wrote a scathing account of the incident that nearly ruined Leakey's career. For the rest of his life, Leakey was almost fanatically careful about double-checking his finds in the field.

Leakey had suffered a professional setback, but, fortunately, was offered an unusual opportunity by the Rhodes Foundation, an organization deeply interested in African affairs. In exchange for two years' salary, he was to record the customs of the Kikuyu tribe. Time was of the essence, for many of the older tribe members—those most knowledgeable in tribal customs—were nearing the end of their lives. This proposal was the result of an appeal by a group of anthropologists who knew of Leakey's extraordinary reputation among the Kikuyu. Louis accepted this new job with some reluctance, as it would mean abandoning prehistory for a while, but, once the decision was made, he tackled the assignment with extraordinary energy and characteristic shrewdness. Despite his unique qualifications as a white member of an age-set and a fluent Kikuyu speaker, the project was beset with difficulty. Louis started by consulting the Senior Chief of all the Kikuyu. Chief Koinange put Leakey's proposal to the elders and, to allay their obvious suspicions, appointed a nine-man advisory committee who sifted through all the research materials. The resulting study—recorded in a three-volume monograph that ran to some 700,000 words—must rank as one of the more remarkable achievements of Leakey's career. The first volume deals with Kikuyu history and tradition, as well as with their way of life, the second with the life of a Kikuyu from the cradle to death, and the final volume with social organization, religion, and ceremonial life. The Rhodes Foundation was amazed, but was unable to pay for publication of the study. Leakey, deeply hurt by their response, flatly refused to cut the length of what he considered to be a definitive study. The monograph has languished in the files ever since.

The Second World War broke out just as Leakey finished his Kikuyu research. He spent the war years in government service, working in intelligence. During his spare time, he worked at the National Museum in Nairobi. A little archaeology

Photograph by Melville Bell Grosvenor, © National Geographic Society

Louis Leakey.

could be managed during leaves, but it was impossible to get down to Olduvai. Meanwhile, one remarkable site came to light in the Great Rift Valley forty miles from Nairobi. Years before, a geologist had reported some stone axes from a white clay deposit at the foot of a moutain called Olorgesailie, but failed to record exactly where. The Leakeys combed the area on weekends, and their diligence paid off. One day, both Louis and Mary excitedly called out at the same moment: each had made a find. Mary's was particularly spectacular—an unbelievable concentration of stone axes lying on a gentle slope. It transpired that Olorgesailie had been a lakeside camp, used year after year by small groups of hunter-gatherers who preyed on the big game that came down to the water's edge to drink.

As the Leakeys dug into the fine lake deposits, they came across the tools of the hunters lying exactly where they had been dropped. Artifact by artifact, bone by bone, they uncovered the ancient campsites, recording and photographing each object in place. Olorgesailie is now an open-air museum. Radiocarbon dating indicates that the site is more than 400,000 years old.

When the war ended, Leakey was appointed permanent curator of the museum in Nairobi, a post he was to hold for many years. During that time, he built up the museum into a research institution of international reputation, renowned not only for archaeology and palaeontology, but for natural history as well. All the diverse interests Leakey had acquired among the Kikuyu came together in the job of curator. He lobbied long and hard for new galleries and facilities and, with these improvements, the number of museum visitors increased a thousandfold. The Leakeys also found time to lead hunting expeditions to geological beds near Lake Victoria. Here, they made another important discovery—an early ape fossil, which they named *Proconsul.*

Louis also moonlighted for the Kenya police as a forensic expert, an interest he had developed while a student. One case involved a young man accused of murdering his wife with a shotgun. Leakey was able to prove, in the best Sherlock Holmes fashion, that the shooting had been an accident. He took plaster casts of a dent in the woodwork of a piano near the body. The casts fitted the gun butt perfectly, for it had flown from the accused's hands and hit the piano. The young man was eventually acquitted. Louis also played an important role in the government's handling of the Mau Mau emergency, a nationalist uprising that resulted in the death of hundreds of innocent Africans and Europeans. He acted as an interpreter at the trial of Jomo Kenyatta. It is greatly to both men's credit that neither bore a grudge against the other after independence was achieved.

But always at the back of Leakey's mind was the call of the great Valley of Bones. Olduvai Gorge was still unexcavated. A preliminary report on the early expeditions finally appeared after long delays in 1951. Louis described a slowly evolving

Plan of Olduvai Gorge. (Adapted from L. S. B. Leakey, *Olduvai Gorge,* vol. 1, Cambridge University Press, 1965, p. 95.)

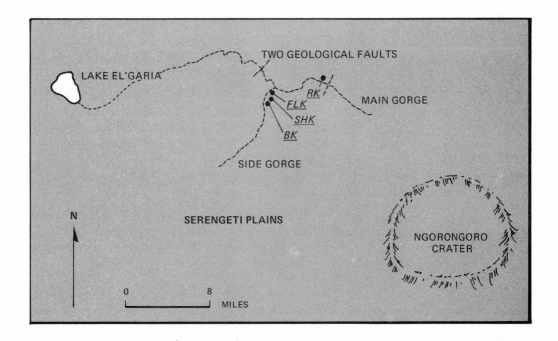

history of stone-tool technology, from the simple choppers of the very earliest beds up to the finely shaped stone axes of the latest campsites in the Gorge. Obviously, Olduvai had been the scene of a long history of human cultural evolution, one that could be fully charted only through long-term, large-scale excavations. The year the book appeared was the year the Leakeys returned to Olduvai to dig. They were to remain there, on and off, for the rest of Louis's life.

Louis and Mary pitched camp near two sites in Bed II labeled BK and SHK. For seven seasons, between 1951 and 1958, they worked on these remarkable localities. They found an incredible profusion of over 11,000 stone choppers and other early tools. Both sites were veritable charnel houses of Pleistocene mammals, many of them of enormous size. One such creature was a form of buffalo named *Pelorovis*, an awe-inspiring animal with horns over six feet across. Louis speculated that a band of hunters had one day driven a whole herd of *Pelorovis* into a swamp, where the creatures became bogged down and were unable to escape. Some of the smaller animals were dragged to the shore and cut up. At least one complete skeleton was found upright in the deep clay, standing where it had perished hundreds of thousands of years before.

The entire area was littered with stone tools and waste flakes where the people had cut up their quarry at leisure. BK and SHK were major sources of information on fossil animals, including not only dozens of pigs and other large mammals, but also small rodents, birds, and even frogs. And, unlike many fossil finds, the Olduvai specimens were very often from more or less complete skeletons of animals that had died in the shallows of the ancient lake. But there were no signs of human fossils, except for two large teeth found at BK in 1955. Leakey was not worried. I remember hearing him lecture on *Pelorovis* and these two teeth at Cambridge University in 1956. "One day soon we will find more complete human remains," Leakey predicted. How right he was!

The 1959 season crowned nearly a decade of strenuous effort. Exactly a century after the publication of Darwin's *Origin of Species*, Mary Leakey unearthed a large and robust hominid skull on floor FLK in Bed I. The find caused a tremendous sensation. Louis immediately recognized that the new skull was very similar to a series of early hominids found in South Africa, fossils known as *Australopithecines. Australopithecus*, the "southern ape," had been claimed as an ancestor of modern humanity by anatomist Raymond Dart back in 1924, but scientific opinion had laughed him out of court. Although subsequent finds had made people take Dart's claim more seriously, here was additional evidence that *Australopithecus* was close to the human line. But the Olduvai find was of a very robust individual, one with huge teeth and a massive skull. Leakey named it *Zinjanthropus boisei* (African Man of Boise—the name of a Leakey benefactor). Within the Leakey family, the skull was affectionately known as "Dear Boy." The public preferred the catchy "Nutcracker Man," coined because of the skull's huge teeth.

Within a few months, the Leakeys were international celebrities, feted at lectures and public receptions. Olduvai was flooded with visitors. The National Geographic Society and other foundations gave large sums of money that enabled Louis and Mary to put in 92,000 work hours at Olduvai in 1960, more than twice the total number of hours spent there since 1931.

Most of these 92,000 hours were put in by Mary, who spent a whole year at Olduvai. Louis was tied to the museum much of the time. Operating from a camp far more elaborate than they had ever had before, Mary set the workmen to stripping the sterile soil from above the *Zinjanthropus* living floor. Meanwhile, she sat down to plot the position of every artifact and bone found over an area of five to seven square yards. She found thousands of tiny bone fragments, literally smashed to ribbons for their meat and marrow by the campsite's inhabi-

The jaw of *Zinjanthropus boisei* when first discovered.

tants. A strip of ground almost bare of finds lay outside this concentration of debris. Outside was a zone where more complete bones and larger tools were found. Since the bare patch lay to windward of the central concentration of occupation debris, Mary theorized that the people had built a simple wind barrier of branches to protect themselves from the prevailing winds. Unfortunately, the jaw of *Zinjanthropus* was nowhere to be found.

In November of 1960, son Jonathan found some more fragments of hominid only three hundred yards from FLK—a jaw and two skull fragments. Although the find came from a slightly lower level than *Zinjanthropus*, the bones were much lighter than those of the earlier discovery and seemed more "human" than Nutcracker Man. When Mary excavated the site, she eventually recovered traces of no less than four individuals, two adults and a juvenile of the less robust form, and some fragments of another creature that resembled *Zinjanthropus*.

Then, only a month later, Louis himself came across a small gully no one had ever examined. There he found a small pile of bones that had eroded out of Bed II. The pile included a thick skull cap with massive brow ridges, obviously from a being less ancient than *Zinjanthropus*. Although the new find was not associated with any living site, Leakey soon realized that it was the remains of a later hunter-gatherer who had made some of the many stone axes found at Olduvai.

In 1961, the excavations were shifted to other localities in Bed I. Mary started digging at a site named FLK N, near the *Zinjanthropus* floor. She came across five campsites stratified one above another. At one of them, the hunters had butchered an elephant where it had fallen. Mary found no less than fourteen thousand rodent bones as well—also lizards and frogs. Fish and bird bones were abundant, the latter from all kinds of wading species that fed by the shores of the ancient lake. Presumably the hunters caught them when the birds roosted after dark.

Mary was surprised to find a strange concentration of rocks on the oldest Olduvai floor of all. When she uncovered and plotted them, she found they lay in a circle about twelve feet across. There could only be one explanation: the rocks evidently had served as the foundation for a crude shelter of branches and thorns that protected the inhabitants from the sweeping winds that bombard the Serengeti Plains. This is still the earliest known human dwelling in the world.

It was now time for specialist work at Olduvai. Louis himself was overwhelmed with all kinds of commitments—fundraising lectures, other excavations, and museum work. Mary shouldered most of the excavation and laboratory analysis. Professional geologists and fossil experts were called in to unravel the myriad details of Olduvai's geology and animal life, a job that could be tackled only by specialists. Louis Leakey's greatness lay in his ability to look at the broader picture, to fire other people with his enthusiasm for archaeology and anthropology. He had a natural flair for publicity and made the most of it to gain support for his excavations. Above all, he encouraged younger scientists to engage in bold re-search, investigations that took the study of human origins in new directions.

How old was Olduvai? No one really knew. The first indica-tion came from two University of California scientists, Jack Evernden and Garniss Curtis, who applied a new radioactive

Field worker clearing and re-cording the world's earliest structure—a semicircle of stones at Olduvai Gorge.

Photograph by Baron Hugo van Lawick, © National Geographic Society method named potassium argon dating to the Gorge. This technique was highly effective at dating very old lava beds but had rarely been applied to recent strata. The Olduvai campsites, however, were ideal for experimental dating, for the early hominids had used lava for tools and other purposes. After prolonged study of many samples, Evernden and Curtis came up with an average date of 1.75 ± 0.25 million years for the base of Bed I and the early Olduvai campsites. The dates caused a sensation, for everyone had guessed that *Zinjanthropus* was about 600,000 years old. At one fell swoop, the scientists had doubled the length of time that humans had lived on earth.

Increased resources and worldwide fame meant that the Leakeys were never short of helpers. They were now able not only to excavate but to search for new Olduvai campsites as well. More hominid fossils came to light, among them a fragmentary skull from the lower levels of Bed II, somewhat later than *Zinjanthropus*. The skull resembled those of the lighter individuals found in 1961. Leakey spent many hours puzzling over the relationship between this new find and *Zinjanthropus*.

By the time the Olduvai excavations ended in 1964, the Leakeys had found some twenty hominid fragments, pieces of an extraordinary anthropological puzzle. What could be made of them? When *Zinjanthropus* was first found with stone tools, Louis claimed that the skull was that of the earliest human toolmaker. But when the lighter and less primitive finds came to light in Bed I, Leakey had to eat his words. Were these the people who made the tools found with *Zinjanthropus*? Did they kill their robust relative at Olduvai? Who was the first toolmaker? The question was still wide open. Leakey characteristically took the bull by the horns. When the anatomists told him that the foot bones of the lighter individuals looked astonishingly human and came from a relatively short primate who walked upright like humans,

| DATE (in years) | | |
|---|---|---|
| | BED IV | |
| Not less than 700,000 | BED III | |
| Not less than 1.0 million | BED II | *Homo erectus* ("George") |
| Possible break in sequence | | *Homo habilis* finds |
| | BED I | — "*Zinjanthropus*"<br>— Early gracile hominid<br>— Stone structure |
| 1.75 million | | |
| 1.8 million | | |
| c. 2.2 million | | Volcanic lava |

Schematic diagram of the geological beds and fossils mentioned in the text.

Leakey was convinced he had found his early human ancestor at last.

Meanwhile, anatomist Philip Tobias of the University of the Witwaterstrand in Johannesburg had started to examine the skull of *Zinjanthropus*. Leakey and Tobias pored over the Bed I fossils and compared *Zinjanthropus* with lighter individuals. Eventually they decided that they did, indeed, have a new genus of human that was contemporary with *Zinjanthropus*. This being had walked upright; stood about four feet, six inches tall; and had a brain somewhat larger than the *Australopithecines*. It was also capable of manipulating its hands to make stone tools and was thus the first toolmaker. Leakey and Tobias named this human ancestor *Homo habilis*.

I remember meeting Tobias as he passed through Livingstone in Zambia on his way back from Nairobi.

"We have a new man from Olduvai," he told me excitedly, "a Handy Man."

"A Handy Man?" I asked. "Why?"

He then explained how they had hit on the term "habilis," a word that implies dexterity of mind and hand. Fittingly, it had been Raymond Dart, the discoverer of *Australopithecus,* who had coined the label.

The announcement of *Homo habilis* generated yet another heated Leakey controversy, one that rages to this day. Leakey was a confirmed splitter of fossils into new categories. His opponents felt that *Homo habilis* was an *Australopithecus* and that Leakey's argument was based on very slender information. Even Tobias and John Napier, who had studied the feet of *Homo habilis,* were somewhat uncertain about the classification. It was the sheer power of Leakey's personality that eventually carried the day.

By now, son Richard had begun to take an interest in archaeology. After leaving school, Richard had started a successful safari business that had taken him into remote parts of Kenya. Then, in 1967, he joined an international party of scientists who were to look for early humans in the remote Omo Valley of southern Ethiopia. It was Louis who had persuaded the Emperor of Ethiopia to authorize the expedition. American, French, and Kenyan anthropologists were involved in a team effort that brought back thousands of mammal fossils and numerous examples of *Australopithecus.* To Richard's disappointment, the Kenya sector of Omo was rather sparse in fossils. But during the expedition he traveled by helicopter over the eastern shores of remote Lake Rudolf in northern Kenya. Looking down from his lofty perch, he spotted some promising-looking deposits where fossils might be found. The helicopter pilot was persuaded to land for a short look and, sure enough, the locality looked very exciting.

Using the powerful Leakey techniques of persuasion, young Richard managed to convince the National Geographic Society in Washington, D.C., to pay for a season's look at the area. They gave him the money on condition that he would never return for more funds if he found nothing. The East Rudolf area where he chose to work turned out to be a fossil treasure house. There were over two thousand square miles of fossil-bearing beds that, within six weeks, had yielded dozens of

Gracile *Australopithecus africanus* from Sterkfontein, South Africa, compared with *Australopithecus boisei* from Olduvai Gorge. The latter, far more robustly built, has a reconstructed jaw.

mammals and several hominid fragments. A few years later, Richard found an almost complete skull, "1470," which he considered to be from a creature more human than *Australopithecus* had ever been and related, at least in a general way, to Louis's *Homo habilis.* The East Rudolf sites were older than Olduvai, dating from one and a half to four million years old. Another Leakey generation had added a new chapter to the history of humankind.

Louis Leakey's interest turned in other directions in his later life. The study of fossil mammals and early human evolution was becoming an increasingly professional field, one where Leakey's impatient and flamboyant gestures were sometimes counterproductive. He was never good at detail, preferring to leave the minute affairs of excavation to Mary and others. He was particularly fascinated with primate behavior. Surely, he argued, studying living apes in the wild should tell us something about the behavior of early humans who were, in many respects, like apes. He felt women were best for this type of sensitive research and encouraged, among others, Jane Goodall and Dian Fossey to undertake what became classic studies of the chimpanzee and the gorilla. Goodall's research showed that chimpanzees were perfectly capable of using small sticks to gather insects. Their behavior was astonishingly human in many respects. The transition from ape to human might have been less of a jump than some people believed. A new field of research was born from this work.

During the last four or five years of his life, Leakey suffered greatly from health problems, including a stiff hip and a bad heart. By this time he had become the idol of millions. Despite considerable suffering, he insisted on keeping up a hectic lecture schedule in the United States. At college after college, university after university, he lectured on the latest fossil discoveries, on primate behavior, and on his African research. Invariably his lecture halls were filled to capacity; hundreds were turned away. Leakey never slowed his pace. In October

Photograph by Baron Hugo van Lawick, © National Geographic Society

Chimpanzee using a stick as a tool to fish for insects.

1972, while on his way to another lecture tour, he collapsed with a heart attack in London. The world mourned a great anthropologist and public figure. Even his old adversary Jomo Kenyatta sent a wreath to his funeral.

Louis Leakey must rank as one of the most remarkable archaeologists of all time, a man who, with his family, added whole new dimensions to the study of human origins. When Leakey started digging in the 1920s, no one knew much about prehistoric Africa and the oldest humans were thought to be not much more than a million years old. Leakey's fossil discoveries in the Valley of Bones doubled the time span of human history. He was one of the last of the Renaissance men in archaeology; today, a new generation of specialist scientists have taken over at Olduvai and elsewhere. Without Leakey, few of us would be conscious of the immense chapters of human prehistory that stretch back into a past almost too distant to imagine. He made the public at large aware of its ancestry, an ancestry which, the Victorians had discovered, was among the apes. The Victorians had not liked this; Leakey helped us love it. Today, his family carries on his work and keeps his vision alive.

# 3

# THE MAKAH FIND THEIR HISTORY

SOUTH OF VANCOUVER ISLAND, THE RUGGED PACIFIC coast of North America sweeps southwards in a series of wide bays fully exposed to the winter force of the ocean. Rolling swells batter the coast and carry driftwood from far-off lands to its deserted beaches. The mighty fury of hurricane-force southwesterly gales brings high tides and floods to the forested shore. Few spots on this wild coast offer shelter for canoes or small vessels. Yet, for thousands of years, Makah Indians settled on this exposed coast, living off the incredible bounty of the ocean and forest. They selected their village sites with great care, settling where offshore islands and kelp beds offered shelter from the perennial swells and where seals and other sea life flourished in profusion. One such Makah settlement nestled in a sheltered bay behind a small island named Ozette, protected by Ozette from southwesterly gales and from the northwest by two further islands, massive kelp beds, a sandspit, and offshore rocks.

Five hundred years ago, a visitor to Ozette would have found a cluster of weathered cedarwood houses ranged along the sheltered beach, their natural wood tones merging with the greens and browns of the forested slope behind. Viewed from afar, the village would blend almost imperceptibly with the landscape of ocean and forest. Indeed, the naive observer would believe it had nestled there since time immemorial. To get a clearer picture of the Makah way of life, let's pay a visit to the settlement as it might have appeared on a fine summer day five hundred years ago.

As we approach, we can see children playing among the houses and adults working on the fine cedarwood canoes drawn up on the beach. Each plank house is alive with domestic activity, humming with conversation and laughter on this pleasant day. As we near our host's house, we can see a bleached whale skull and a line of vertebrae lined up in front of the dwelling. Our host is a whale hunter, respected for his skills with the harpoon. The weathered planks of the house show signs of constant repair and replacement. Some of them are fresh, obviously recently brought to Ozette from the forest; others have been in place for generations, held in position by regularly spaced uprights. In one place, the side of a long-abandoned canoe has been pressed into service as a house plank. The worn gunwale of the canoe overlaps the plank below it. Two men are clambering around on the planked roof, picking their way through the large boulders that hold the overlapping planks in position on windy days. They lift a roof plank and place it on one side as a cloud of woodsmoke billows upward into their faces. Laughing voices come from inside the house as the occupants begin passing up salmon to the sunlit roof. The men lay the fish out in the sunshine to dry, all the while keeping up a steady flow of banter with the women below.

The house opens onto the beach and the entrance is open on this warm afternoon. A wooden partition keeps the wind out of the interior, placed so as to act as an effective windbreak. The interior seems very dark to us after the bright sunlight. A few shafts of sun filter through the roof, making their way

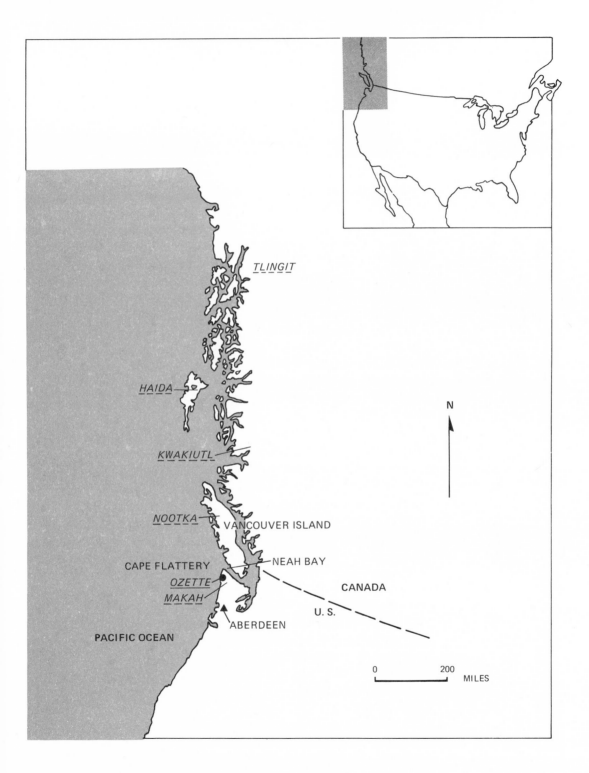

TLINGIT

HAIDA

KWAKIUTL

N

NOOTKA — VANCOUVER ISLAND

CAPE FLATTERY — NEAH BAY

OZETTE

MAKAH

CANADA

U. S.

ABERDEEN

PACIFIC OCEAN

0          200
MILES

Locations and tribes
mentioned in Chapter 3.

between the tools, bundles, and skins hanging from the massive rafters. The house is divided into family areas with low partitions, each lined with cedarwood sleeping benches, some decorated with seashells. A young boy, his bow and arrow by his side, sleeps on one of the benches, oblivious to the noise around him. An old women sits with her back against a nearby bench, gazing into the fire, a partially completed basket forgotten on her knees. Under the sleeping bench is a row of cedarwood boxes. A girl squats near an open box, going through the skin-working tools stored inside. The rafters seem to reach down into the house, festooned as they are with bundles of dried cattails, dozens of dried salmon, and loads of seaweed. A row of large sealskins bulging with oil hangs nearby, blackened with hearth smoke from the cooking fires below. Two large whale-harpoon shafts hang on the walls behind the sleeping bench. A fine canoe paddle lies on top of a sleeping bench near a woven blanket. The smell of dead fish, wood smoke, and seal oil pervades the atmosphere. Everything seems slightly oily to the touch. The wooden oil-storage bowls by the fire glisten with seal oil and everyone's hands and bodies seem to exude oil.

Three women are watching over a pair of fresh salmon spread out on sticks and roasting in front of the fire. A wooden carved seal club lies close by, black with smoke and oil. A young fisherman squats near the hearth, intent on mending a well-used fishing net. His old father sits on his right, binding a wooden barb to the curved halibut fishhook in his hand. At intervals he admonishes the small boy by his side who is poking around in a large storage basket and fiddling with a shell harpoon head wrapped in a fine storage sheath. A murmur of voices, of soft laughter and occasional caustic comments to the men on the roof, keeps the family around the fire in touch with the rest of the house.

Softly the old man greets us and bids us welcome. The talk turns to seals and salmon, and then to whales, as he shows the young boy how he fashioned the harpoon head that lies in the basket. He tells us about the ultimate quarry—the whale. Proudly, he boasts how the Makah are one of the few tribes bold enough to hunt the whale for its rich bounty of meat and oil. He speaks with authority, for he is a whale hunter, a person of high rank in Makah society, closely connected to important spirits.

Whale hunting is surrounded with elaborate rituals and taboos; the whale hunters themselves are important members of the community who inherited their roles from earlier generations. As we listen raptly, the old man tells stories of whale hunts of old and recounts the tale behind the bleached whale resting in front of the house. When the Makah spotted a pod of whales, he remembers, the whaling parties would set out in eight-man dugout canoes. The whale hunters wore nothing but a coating of oil and red ochre to protect them from sun and rain and, sometimes, woven hats to keep the rain from their faces. They frequently painted their faces with ritual designs. For several days before the hunt all crew members abstained from sexual relations. Magic charms and spirit tokens, perhaps even the skull of a skilled whale-hunting ancestor, went along on the hunt in a wooden box. As the canoe paddled out to the unsuspecting pod, the whale hunter would invite the whales to come and be caught, referring to them as "noble ladies," never as "whales."

Once a blowing whale came into sight, the canoe would paddle up behind it as it cruised along. With silent strokes, the captain would direct the craft to a position above and slightly to the left of the unsuspecting whale. The hunter stood in the bow with raised harpoon. The whale would blow and start to submerge directly under the hovering canoe. At that precise moment, the harpooner would drive his heavy weapon into the whale. The sharp, mussel-shell tip penetrated deeply into the wounded animal as it plunged away from the canoe. For hours the paddlers would follow their wounded quarry, pursuing the bobbing sealskin floats that revealed the position of the whale. As their quarry tired, the whale hunters would

approach carefully and try to kill the whale with a deep lance stroke aimed behind the great flipper.

Our host also remembers how the whole village would follow the progress of the hunt blow by blow. The captain's wife played out the whale's role, lying quietly at home, willing the whale to do the same. Once the strike was made, she would chant incantations, inviting the whale to visit the village. And, when the rejoicing villagers beached the carcass, the captain's wife would greet the visitor and bring the whale a drink of fresh water. Then the entire community would help cut up the carcass with blubber knives. The meat and blubber were distributed by rank and the entire community enjoyed a feast. Everyone was continually on the lookout for stranded whales, too, for strandings, of course, saved the hunters a great deal of trouble. Every whaling village had its own whale shrine, where the hunters and canoe captains performed the powerful rituals that ensured the continued arrival of whales off the coast.

We listen spellbound as the old man continues his stories of long-forgotten whale hunts, of great ceremonies, of canoes lost at sea, of raging storms and strange happenings. It seems as if the Makah have been living and hunting at Ozette since time began, living off the incredible bounty of the ocean. On this gentle summer day, we feel that nothing could interrupt the even tenor of life in this remote bay.

But we are wrong. Only a few years later, life at Ozette came to a temporary full stop. Several houses vanished suddenly under a dense blanket of slippery mud. The mud slide arrived abruptly and without warning in the early morning; few people were astir. The planked dwellings vanished completely in a few moments, their loose roofs sliding onto the beach on a conveyer belt of oozing mud. A few muffled cries could be heard, then silence. Much of Ozette disappeared totally and instantly. Although the Makah continued to live at Ozette until as late as 1910, they cherished only a few folk memories of sudden mud slides and terrible tragedy. In effect, their past was buried under a canopy of mud, sealed from the destructive atmosphere so effectively that it survived almost intact until the 1960s.

The Makah continued to hunt whales until the early twentieth century. Like other Northwest Coast Indian groups, they suffered at the hands of white settlers and traders in the nineteenth century until only a fraction of their original population still survived. Ozette itself was abandoned when the Indians moved closer to the public school in Neah Bay in the 1920s. Over a quarter of a century was to elapse before a young archaeologist named Richard Daugherty was lucky enough to find one of the most remarkable archaeological sites in North America.

Richard Daugherty is a native of Aberdeen, Washington, a small coastal town sixty miles south of Cape Flattery. In his youth, he spent many days wandering along the remote beaches north of Aberdeen. He studied anthropology in college and was appointed to the faculty of Washington State University in Pullman, a post he has held ever since. Daugherty developed a strong interest in the archaeology of the Washington coast and started recording sites along his favorite stretch of the Pacific. His research forays were sporadic, for he was deeply involved in salvage archaeology in eastern Washington and Idaho. Still, by the fall of 1947, Daugherty had already recorded fifty coastal sites, most of them thick concentrations of charcoal, fish bones, and shells. The richest sites lay at the mouths of salmon rivers. Daugherty found time to walk out to a protected beach named Ozette, a hike through dense forest on a muddy trail. Twenty or thirty years before, a Makah community had lived at Ozette, but the inhabitants had gradually moved away. Except for occasional fishermen, Ozette was now silent and deserted. Some of the abandoned houses were still visible, the only remains of a substantial village that was now rotting away into the soil. The ruined structures lay on a low terrace that overlooked a sheltered landing and a sandy beach. The terrace was black with ash, charcoal, and shells. Daugherty knew that hundreds of people had lived at Ozette for centuries. But how long ago? he wondered.

Daugherty had to wait fourteen years before he was able to visit Ozette a second time. This time he took two students with him. They dug carefully into the black soil. Within a few hours, Daugherty was admiring two smooth bone-whale harpoon barbs. Perhaps Ozette was the ancient whaling village he had been looking for. Four years later, Daugherty returned with adequate research funds and plans for a thorough investigation of Ozette. He has been involved with the site ever since.

Daugherty realized at the outset that he was dealing with a complex site whose history was linked to the vast ocean that lapped against its shore. How, for example, had changing sea levels over the years affected the inhabitants of Ozette? Wisely, he invited geologist Roald Fryxell to study Ozette. In addition, Carl Gustafson, a zoologist, was on hand to examine the many animal bones that Daugherty expected to uncover in the trenches.

The extensive occupation levels at Ozette lay above the high tide mark on top of a series of low platforms or terraces overlooking the beach. Fryxell determined that Ozette had flourished at the water's edge for a long period of time, but the occupants had moved their houses several times as the high-tide fluctuated. The highest terrace was about forty feet above the present beach. Presumably this was occupied first, while the lower, later terraces were still under the Pacific.

Daugherty began by laying out a 240-foot trench across the deepest and widest part of the site to intersect the terraces. The excavations proceeded slowly at first, for dense vegetation masked the rich occupation deposits. But once the twenty students on the crew reached the soil of the ancient village, they dug faster. The diggers worked in teams, some carefully shovelling out the soil, others sifting the damp earth for minute fragments of bones, stone tools, and shells. The

Excavation of the first trench through the terraces at Ozette, with screens for sifting soil at the end of the beach. Note Cannonball Island close offshore.

Meri Flinn, Makah student at Evergreen and member of the Ozette summer crew, cleans a cedarbark basket from House 2.

uppermost levels of the trench yielded rusty nails and broken glass, some coins, and parts of a muzzle-loader rifle. Most of these nineteenth-century finds belonged to historic Makah villages. The lower levels yielded no European trade goods or traces of contact with foreigners. They were obviously earlier than the eighteenth century.

As the students dug deeper into Ozette, they came across bone fish hooks, stone and shell knife blades, and the whetstones used to sharpen them. One student discovered a bone comb decorated with a human face. Many of the fish hooks lay close to the stone sinkers that once carried the fishermen's lines to the ocean bottom. Thousands of fish bones were scattered through the midden, many of them from deep-water species that could only have been taken with nets or by line fishing from offshore canoes. The hundreds of Ozette artifacts lay alongside the remains of thousands of ancient meals. Clam and mussel shells were piled in heaps. The Ozette people also had feasted on shallow-water fish, on sea birds like gulls, and on geese, ducks, and land birds. But sea-mammal bones were the most common food remains of all, far more abundant than deer and elk, who, even today, feed near Ozette.

Why were sea mammals so common? Daugherty wondered. As the excavators dug deeper, whole layers of the site composed almost exclusively of whale and seal bones were revealed. Enormous whale bones blocked parts of the trench, indeed passed right across it. Daugherty carefully recorded the location of the bones, then told the students to saw them up so they could dig deeper. Whale bones came not only from the historic levels, but from the very lowest, prehistoric depths of the settlement. People had been hunting whales for centuries at Ozette, far back into prehistoric times. Clearly the locality had some special attraction for people who lived off the sea, one that kept them tied to Ozette for centuries.

Anyone camped at Ozette in a gale can quickly see one good reason why the site was situated where it was. Cannonball and Ozette islands lie close offshore, the former joined to the beach by a sandspit at low tide. These natural features shelter the beach, breaking the full force of the Pacific swells that batter this remote coast. Ozette was a natural canoe landing, possible even in pretty severe conditions. It also lies on the westernmost point of North America south of Vancouver island, close to fur seal and whale migration routes. A reef teeming with fish eaten by fur seals can be seen just three miles off the coast. Most migrating seals stay at least ten miles offshore. Between March and May, however, many seals migrating to the Arctic are drawn to this plentiful food supply off Ozette's shore. Thus, they can be killed by the dozens without venturing too far into deep water. Over 80 percent of the sea-mammal bones found at Ozette in the first season were those of fur seals. When Gustafson started identifying the more than 80,000 bones from the site, he found a similar pattern of hunting from the oldest to the most recent levels of the site. The Ozette people were obviously skillful seamen. Fur seals could only be hunted from a canoe. And whales never come into the shallow water off the Washington coast except when washed ashore or unable to fend for themselves.

By July 1966, the Ozette trench was over sixty feet long and penetrated deep into the midden. The superimposed layers of successive villages were revealed one after another, a jumble of hearths, charcoal fragments, broken bones, and piles of shells. In one place, a careful student unearthed a cluster of whale barnacles. These golf-ball–sized barnacles grow only on whale skin. Presumably, they were all that remained of a hunk of skin and blubber carried back to the village hundreds of years before. In other places, too, it was possible to identify the packed earth floor of ancient houses, even the dark post holes of the wooden frames. But all the wood had decayed. Clearly, many of the people's tools had vanished forever.

Roald Fryxell spent many hours poring over the complicated geology of the settlement. Dozens of occupation layers, over ten feet deep, could be pieced together to form a continuous history of Ozette life. And this long occupation had to be tied to the complex history of the retreating seashore and of movements of the earth's crust, both intricate puzzles to sort out.

How old was Ozette? The most recent layers could be dated by the coins and other familiar modern objects found in them.

And Daugherty knew that the site had been used as recently as the 1920s. The archaeologists recovered charcoal fragments from the lower level of the beach and sent them off for radiocarbon dating at Washington State University. The radiocarbon laboratory dated the lowest levels of Ozette to around two thousand years ago. Since there was every reason to believe that Ozette had been occupied continuously throughout its long history, Daugherty was now able to say that the Makah had been whale hunting on the Washington Coast for at least two thousand years. At the end of the 1966 season, Fryxell used a powerful core augur to bore below the deepest levels of the excavation. He recovered not only beach sand from a long-buried shore but traces of whale bones and perfectly preserved wood as well. The buried midden seemed very fresh. Fryxell noticed that it was covered by a thick mud slide. Had the slopes of the site slid onto the beach year after year? Had Ozette houses been buried by sudden inrushes of liquid mud? More excavations were needed to solve this and other problems.

In 1967, Daugherty and Fryxell returned to Ozette. Their objectives were to learn more about the recent village and to dig the midden that lay perched on the summit of Cannonball Island close offshore. The foundations of the historic houses yielded a wealth of broken dishes and bottles, as well as the usual seal and whale bones. The Indians had salvaged valuable iron for axes and wedges from the wreck of the barque *Austria* which ran aground off Ozette in 1887.

Cannonball Island was surprisingly interesting, too. The Indians had laboriously carried seal meat and clam shells to the summit over many centuries. Perhaps the island served as a refuge in times of war or as a lookout for migrating whales. But the most interesting finds of all came from a muddy area on the mainland. A test pit dug to test the extent of the ancient village penetrated ten feet into wet mud. Just as Daugherty was about to fill in the hole, a student's shovel hit a solid object in the muck. It proved to be a cedar plank in perfect condition, covered with a cedar-bark mat. Other planks, even some baskets, lay nearby. The probe had hit upon a perfectly preserved house buried beneath a thick layer of sticky mud. Fryxell looked at the pit and checked his measurements of the present slope. It was still oozing slowly toward the beach. The Makah themselves remembered catastrophic mud slides that had buried entire houses, even people, without warning. Regretfully, Daugherty had neither the time nor the money to investigate his remarkable find more fully. So with great reluctance, he was forced to abandon Ozette for the time being.

Ozette lies in the Makah Indian Reservation. Daugherty, with characteristic sensitivity, had not only obtained permission from the Makah Tribal Council to dig at Ozette but had kept the Indians informed of the progress of the excavations. He had developed a close rapport over the years with Ed Claplanhoo, then Tribal Chairman. Claplanhoo, like Daugherty, had connections with Washington State University, where he had majored in forestry. In February 1970, Daugherty received an urgent call from Claplanhoo, urging him to drop everything and come to Ozette at once. A severe winter storm had undercut the bank where the site lay. The precious midden had slumped onto the beach, exposing deep layers of the site. Passersby were astonished to find a wooden canoe paddle, fish hooks, and all sorts of other treasures oozing out of the mud. Could Daugherty come at once and take over? Daugherty could indeed. A day later, he was at the site with the Makah.

The slump was only a small one, from a fifteen-foot-high bank. Groping blindly, but with extreme care in the sticky mud, Daugherty grasped some cedar planks and bone harpoon heads, parts of a carved wooden box, and a complete basketry hat in perfect condition. The mud slide had exposed a collapsed house. Daugherty was thrilled by the new finds, but also worried. Ozette was obviously a unique site, one where ancient Makah life was likely to be preserved in all its fascinating complexity. But how could he obtain the money to dig the site?

At this point, the Makah Tribal Council stepped in. To them, and to Daugherty, Ozette was far more than a fascinating archaeological site. Ozette was a critically important archive of Makah history, equal in importance to the written records of other societies. An emergency meeting of the Council appealed to Senator Henry Jackson of Washington for help. Within a short time, Jackson arranged for a $70,000 grant from the Bureau of Indian Affairs to cover the costs of a new field season at Ozette. From this work, the Makah hoped, their long-lost history would see the light of day.

Daugherty soon realized that the wooden houses could never be excavated by conventional means. The delicate cedar planks would crumble to pulp if even touched with a trowel. The wood was so waterlogged that it had the consistency of soft mud. A thick mantle of dense clay several feet deep covered the wooden objects. This had to be removed before the difficult task of extracting the houses could begin. Some years before, Daugherty had successfully used pressure hoses to clear some ancient baskets from a river bank a few miles away. He decided to try the same technique at Ozette, but on a much larger scale. Jerry Grosso, the Conservator for the Project, devised an elaborate pumping system for the dig, one that enabled the diggers to use jets of varying intensity for different tasks.

The pump rigs were flown in by U.S. Marine helicopter and pipes were extended into the ocean. After a long period of trial and error, Grosso managed to maintain a steady 250 pounds of pressurized water through the hoses. Diggers used the torrents of water to wash away the thick clay above the wooden houses. The upper levels explored in 1966 were removed as quickly as possible. It was urgent to get to the older wooden objects before high tides washed them away. The students on the crew worked in pairs, one watching the mud flow as it was hosed away, the other operating the hose. Apparently, the

Timbers of the old houses are washed free from the mud that has held them for centuries. A whale scapula is just to the right of the upper archaeologist. The cabins are used by the archaeologists; they are not part of the ancient village.

liquid had rushed down the hillside very suddenly, burying within a few moments the houses lying at the foot of the slope. No one knew when the slide had occurred, but it was probably long before whites visited the coast. No European trade goods were found among the many household possessions recovered. Daugherty estimated that the house was buried four hundred years ago.

An extraordinary prehistoric story awaited Daugherty under the clay. It took two years to work from the south wall of the buried house across to the north side of the building. Foot by foot, the students hosed away the clay overburden with pressure hoses. They then used garden hoses to dissolve the mud and free the planks with fine jets and careful brushing. The plank house was nearly seventy feet long and forty-five feet wide. Everything was still in place, including the sleeping benches where twenty to forty people had once slept in the communal dwelling.

Never had archaeologists in the Northwest faced such a formidable challenge of recovery and preservation. Hundreds of small household items lay jumbled among the collapsed walls, everything from bones and storage boxes to baskets and cooking hearths. It took months to sort out the mess, to distinguish the roof and wall planks from the wooden boxes and layers of delicate fiber materials and nets that festooned the collapsed foundations. Some wooden planks were four feet wide and two-and-a-quarter inches thick, split laboriously from huge cedar logs. Every wood fragment had to be lifted with infinite care and treated with the proper chemicals to prevent it from drying out and cracking. Grosso set up a treatment system at the site itself, so that the wooden objects could be taken straight from the waterlogged dig and placed in solutions of polyethylene glycol. The Makah Tribal Council converted a heavy-equipment garage in Neah Bay into a laboratory, where Grosso set up equipment to store the wooden objects as they arrived from the site by helicopter and to treat artifacts that needed special, experimental preservative measures.

The initial excavations yielded over 13,000 wood and fiber objects, many of priceless scientific value. Some of the larger objects will be immersed in polyethylene glycol for years as the chemical replaces the water that has soaked into the wood cells over the centuries. This treatment technique has been commonly used all over the world, especially with the

Swedish warship *Vasa*, whose timbers were recovered from the bottom of Stockholm harbor and preserved in a special museum.

The Ozette conservation operation is probably the largest of its type after the *Vasa* project and, like all projects of this type, involved some real headaches. One was keeping track of the artifacts as they passed through the conservation process. Grosso developed a record system and a log that tracks the artifacts right through the laboratory to storage. Another problem was the conservation of wooden vessels heavily impregnated with seal oil. One vessel was airfreighted to Australia for preservation using a new, freeze-drying technique. Others were treated over long periods in an attempt to break down the seal oil. The task of preserving the unique Ozette finds will take even longer than the excavations.

The Ozette house had evidently stood for several generations, for its planks had been eaten by termites and been repaired on several occasions. The roof timbers were bevelled at the edges, so they overlapped to drain off rainwater. One huge, fragile wall plank over twenty feet long took ten students to lift it from the mud. Its underside bore a carving of a whale with backbone and baleful eye clearly shown.

The dominance of whales in Ozette life was reflected in many ways. One day in 1971, one of the crew unearthed a piece of carved wood covered with sea-otter teeth. For four days, the crew labored to free the carving. When they were at last successful, everyone clustered around to admire a truly unique find—a wooden whale's fin inlaid with no less than seven hundred sea-otter teeth. The rear edge bore a row of sharp canines to give it a jagged edge. Not even the Makah elders had seen such an object before. Daugherty finally remembered an etching of a similarly carved fin in an Indian village on Vancouver Island; the etching had been made by an artist with Captain Cook's expedition. Could the two objects be related?

As the excavations proceeded, the students uncovered hundreds of small wooden objects never before found in early Northwest Indian sites. Carved wooden bowls that once held seal and whale oil still carried the smell of their odiferous contents. One was carved in the form of a man with a braided hair style. The Ozette people also made wooden boxes of every size by grooving and steaming single softwood planks in seaweed and then bending them into squares. Each was carefully assembled with wooden pegs.

With the enthusiastic assistance of surviving Makah craftsmen, the students experimented with carpentry techniques, learned how to duplicate the basketry found in the excavations, and tried their hand at traditional wood carving.

Effigy of a whale's fin carved of red cedar and inlaid with over 700 sea otter teeth. Here Richard Daugherty looks at the reassembled sculpture, which was found in several pieces within one of the buried houses. The teeth at the base form the design of a huge bird carrying a whale in its talons.

An oil bowl from Ozette
carved in the shape of a man,
complete with braided hair.

The incomplete picture of Ozette culture that came from the 1966–1967 excavations was now transformed. The Makah who worked on the dig could admire seal, human, and owl heads carved on heavy wooden clubs and large storage boxes decorated with ornate stylized and geometric designs. Even some sleeping platforms bore shell studs arranged in simple decorative patterns.

Three complete looms and the remains of several others were found in the house. The Ozette weavers used dog wool on their looms to weave fabric for their coats, a wool shorn from a special breed of wooly fleeced dog. Early explorers to Ozette noted that the Indians bred such now-extinct dogs and segregated them from other breeds to preserve their woolly coats. The weavers also made blankets of wool and cattail fluff. One fine example found in a broken box bore a plaid pattern.

The Ozette house contained hundreds of baskets and boxes, many of them still holding the special tool kits originally stored in them. Some baskets held dried foods, others carried fishing gear and equipment. Baskets and mats were woven from rolls of cedar bark which were stored in the house, ready for use. A weaver's kit, complete with spindle whorl, awls, combs, and fiber lay near one of the walls. When the archaeologists opened another storage box, they found a woven pouch containing a complete tool kit for making fish hooks. One whaler's basket held mussel-shell harpoon heads, each carefully wrapped in a sheath of cedar bark. Daugherty and Grosso opened one package by brushing on hot water to saturate the bark. Inside lay the barbed harpoon head, exactly as originally stored away. Even the wooden wedges for the harpoon barbs lay in perfect alignment.

The Ozette excavations are still in progress, for the remains of at least five other houses are known to lie under the mud slide. Daugherty plans to dig two more houses, leaving the rest for future generations of archaeologists to investigate when perhaps even better excavation methods have been de-

veloped. In the meantime, the contents of the single completely dug house give us a fascinating glimpse into the remote past of a community whose livelihood depended on the
sea.

The discoveries at Ozette are, of course, of incalculable
scientific value. They have given archaeologists a unique opportunity to study the rich prehistoric culture of the Makah,
an intricate culture that was enjoyed, with variations, by
thousands of other Northwest Indians. Exceptional preservation conditions have revealed almost the entire range of
Makah technology and a magnificent art tradition without
parallel in North America. The conservation methods used in
the Ozette laboratories will be copied by other archaeologists
fortunate enough to recover wooden objects in their excavations.

But the excavations have also had an impact that extends
far beyond the field of archaeology. Ozette lies just outside the
boundaries of a national park. Tens of thousands of visitors
have walked out to the site since its discovery. Over 80,000
people came to Ozette in 1976 alone. Archaeologists conduct
guided tours through the excavations for tourists and organized school parties by the dozen. No one leaves Ozette
without being stirred by the vivid story of the Makah past that
is emerging from the excavations. The educational value of
the site is enormous.

Ozette has had its strongest impact on the Makah themselves. During the excavations dozens of Makah of all ages
shared in the excitement of discovering their long-lost history. Now, with the aid of federal funds, the Makah Tribal
Council is building a magnificent historical museum at Neah
Bay. The museum will become not only a special place to
display their newly discovered history but also a major economic boon for the local community. The Makah Indian staff
for the museum is already under training in Seattle. The
admission fees paid by the thousands of tourists who visit the
museum will not only pay salaries and operating expenses,

they will yield a profit for the Indians as well. The story of their past will benefit many future generations of Makah in a unique way.

All too often archaeologists forget that the Indian sites they dig and record for posterity are part of the cultural heritage of peoples who are discounted in our Western society. Their technical reports appear in learned publications that few people other than specialist archaeologists ever read. Frequently, the scholars don't bother to disseminate their findings to a wider audience, to the very people whose ancestors inhabited the sites centuries ago. The story of Ozette is one of exceptional cooperation between archaeologists and Indians. As a result, Ozette is far more than a remarkable archaeological site. Thanks to Richard Daugherty's skill and sensitivity, the Makah have not only recovered new chapters of their lost history, they have also shared in the work and excitement of discovery. And that is what good archaeology is all about.

A whale harpoon head with its mussel shell blade, bone barbs, and lashings, intact inside its storage pouch.

# 4

# RENÉ MILLON AND THE CITY OF TEOTIHUACÁN

SOMETIMES ARCHAEOLOGISTS' EFFORTS SEEM PUNY in the face of the achievements of the ancients. A small team of laborers digs for months under the shadow of a great, brooding pyramid, their trenches yielding handfuls of broken potsherds and long-buried house foundations. These finds seem insignificant compared to the vast structures that surround the diggers. One can almost hear the mocking laugh of the long-dead architects and engineers who built the ancient city. They cannot help but be amused by the archaeologists' humble attempts to understand the magnitude of their own works.

Nowhere do the archaeologists seem more puny than in the magnificent city of Teotihuacán outside Mexico City, where, for centuries, a teeming metropolis ruled much of Mesoamerica, only to vanish into oblivion a thousand years ago. This chapter tells the story of Teotihuacán and of the archaeologists who have pitted their abilities and their meager resources against one of the greatest cities of antiquity.

Teotihuacán is now a household word, a prehistoric city familiar to thousands of camera-toting tourists. Its faithfully reconstructed pyramids and plazas—today thronged not by priests, warriors, and merchants, but by busloads of tourists from all over the world—reflect the city's former glory. The Mexican government has spent millions of pesos on the restoration of Teotihuacán, determined to turn the ancient city into a major source of tourist revenue. But they have a deeper motive as well: a desire to foster a sense of nationalism throughout Mexico as the nation moves into the last quarter of the twentieth century. The achievements of the ancient Mexicans are becoming a symbol for the modern nation; their influence can be seen in public architecture, in education, and in philosophy as well. Teotihuacán is a dramatic reminder of Mexico's long and glorious prehistoric past, of a time when the ancient Mesoamericans enjoyed a brilliant and long-lived indigenous American civilization. This symbolism may be lost on the foreign tourist, preoccupied as visitors to the site often are with the city's mysterious past and with the extraordinary authority that brought Teotihuacán's great pyramids into being. Like the Pyramids of Gizeh in Egypt, Teotihuacán has a forceful impact on the casual visitor. The scale of its architecture is simply overwhelming, the magnitude of the achievement stunning.

Fifteen hundred years ago, Teotihuacán was already known the length and breadth of Mesoamerica. Every traveler to the Valley of Mexico would take time to visit the great city, if only to admire its brightly painted public buildings and stroll down the wide and imposing Street of the Dead that traversed the city's center. Teotihuacán was the largest human settlement in the Americas, with a population of at least 100,000 people. The Mesoamerican world shopped at Teotihuacán, traded with its merchants, and worshipped at its temples. Thousands of scattered villages in the Mexican highlands relied on its markets and specialist manufactures. At certain times of the year, the entire countryside would flock to Teotihuacán's plazas to participate in the annual public ceremonies that ensured the future prosperity of the great city and

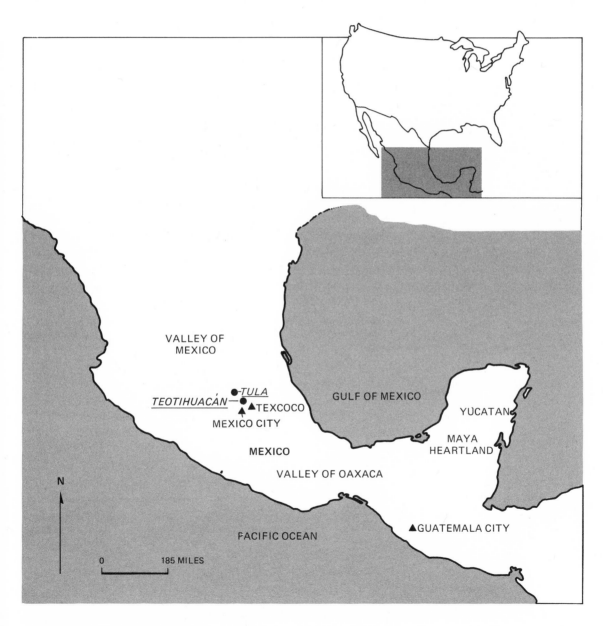

Locations and sites mentioned
in Chapter 4.

Temple of the Plumed Serpent, Quetzalcoatl, Teotihuacán.

the people of the Valley. Yet, within a few short centuries, the city had vanished forever. Only a few crumbling pyramids and temples remained as testaments to its former glory.

The earliest ceremonial buildings were erected at Teotihuacán about 100 B.C. Within a few centuries, Teotihuacán had mushroomed into a huge city dominated by the great Pyramid of the Sun. This sacred, truncated edifice stood 210 feet high and 650 feet square, a vast pyramid of rubble, adobe mud, and earth all faced with stone. A wooden temple on the summit of the pyramid afforded a spectacular view of the sprawling city below.

The priests who served this temple had a panoramic view of a remarkable urban complex. In the morning, they could look westward, down to the long plaza in front of their pyramid and to the Street of the Dead, an avenue that seemed to stretch for miles into the far distance north and south. Its north end opened onto a large plaza in front of another huge pyramid. In the rising sunlight, this vast structure cast long shadows below. The priests could see the small temple at its summit, but the figures of their colleagues there were dwarfed by the scale of the pyramid under them.

Southward, the Street of the Dead led through another plaza and, as the sun rose higher, the priests could gaze even further in this direction. Their eyes would light on the Temple of the Plumed Serpent Quetzalcoatl. The elaborate serpent carvings on its facade were barely discernible in the dark shadows. But the gigantic, open square in front of the temple already teemed with bustling life. From their lofty porch, the priests could dimly hear the noise of the busy city below.

The Street of the Dead was lined with fine civic and religious buildings. Beyond these, the priests could survey a mass of densely packed houses and apartment complexes interspersed with courtyards and separated by winding streets. A lingering pall of smoke from innumerable domestic hearths generally hung in the morning air. Outside the ceremonial precincts, numerous paths led into the surrounding countryside. Small villages of thatched huts dotted the distant landscape. From the heady elevation of the pyramid, Teotihuacán was truly a wonderful sight.

Any traveler to Teotihuacán first made a beeline for the market. There were several markets in the city, but the largest flourished in a huge open compound off the Street of the Dead, opposite the Temple of Quetzalcoatl. The markets supplied the needs of the entire city, a teeming urban population estimated to have once been as high as 100,000 people. While the priests and craftsworkers lived in dwellings built around small courtyards, the less privileged dwelt in large compounds of rooms connected by narrow alleyways and patios. Most of these people were urban dwellers who bought their staple diet of maize, squashes, and beans in the market. There were few farmers within the confines of Teotihuacán itself, but we know that many rural villages flourished nearby. Most of them were compact and expertly planned settlements whose

The Street of the Dead at Teotihuacán, viewed from the top of the Pyramid of the Moon. The Pyramid of the Sun is the large structure on the left.

agricultural activities were carefully supervised by city rulers. These were the villages that produced the enormous surplus of agricultural produce necessary for Teotihuacán's survival. Although we have no definite proof, we can be certain that the villagers used irrigation agriculture, harnessing swamps, lakes, and rivers to fertilize the large acreages of land that were brought under cultivation to feed the nearby urban population. Most of the products of the harvest were sold in the large market off the Street of the Dead.

This market was the center of Teotihuacán's daily life, the place to meet with friends and hear the gossip of the city. Only the market area would provide a visitor with a true measure of Teotihuacán's incredible range of activities. The market itself was organized into sections. In one part, hundreds of stalls displayed ripe maize and every type of food stuff, from fish and game to the most delicate of vegetable

relishes. Teotihuacán lay at a hub of the far-flung obsidian
(volcanic glass) trade of Middle America. A visitor could pause
to handle hundreds of delicate blades and fine knives displayed in the obsidian traders' part of the market. Then there
were the potters, whose booths were thronged with strangers
buying fine bowls and painted pots in large numbers.
Teotihuacán's potters were famous far beyond the confines of
their city. Their wares have been found in the lowlands and as
far west as the Pacific coast. Feather headdresses, cloaks, live
birds, and jewels of every form could also be purchased in
Teotihuacán's bustling daily market. The variety of goods
must have been truly bewildering to the stranger.

If the market was bewildering, the city itself must have
seemed enormous. Today's tourist is exhausted after travers-
ing the Street of the Dead, climbing several pyramids, and
wandering through the huge plazas and temples nearby. So

great is the city that public buildings at one end are barely discernible from the other. Many of the buildings are identical, laid out in monotonous array. Every religious structure bore a terraced facade embellished with similar painted and sculptured motifs, usually elaborate renderings of feathered serpents and other gods. The artists and architects were not being unimaginative, they were simply responding to a rigid religious symbolism. As a result, Teotihuacán seems dull, until one realizes that the buildings were once ablaze with fresh paint, a vivid counterpoint to the repetitive religious symbolism.

Teotihuacán was a highly organized city rigidly governed by religious and secular leaders who had complete control over the minds, spirits, and bodies of their subjects. The priests, an intellectual elite, were skillful astronomers who kept track of the ever-changing cycles of public life, of the seasons for religious ceremonies, and of the endless procession of days, months, and years. But the tentacles of religion extended into every household; domestic altars were commonplace even in humble dwellings. Teotihuacán's art was intensely religious, depicting the feathered serpent deity Quetzalcoatl and other gods. However, some wall murals do depict trade and traders; distant foreigners like the Maya from the lowlands are portrayed with slanting eyes and distinctive dress styles. As Teotihuacán reached the height of its powers and warlike leaders began to assume major roles in public life, warriors and priests also began to appear in the murals.

By A.D. 500, Teotihuacán had established a unique position for itself in the Valley of Mexico and possessed a prestige and power unprecedented in Middle American history. But just as its art and architecture were reaching their full climax and trading activities were at a peak, the political, economic, and religious fabric of the city began to unravel. The first strains appeared about A.D. 650. A century later, Teotihuacán was a shadow of its former self. The population had declined so rapidly that the once-proud city was now little more than a series of hamlets extending over an area of about a square kilometer. Some great catastrophe apparently struck the city in A.D. 700, reducing its population to below 70,000. Many of its people moved eastward. The city was deliberately burnt and destroyed. Over the years, its buildings collapsed and the pyramids became overgrown with dense vegetation. Teotihuacán's decline was almost as rapid as its rise to prominence. Even so, eight centuries later, Teotihuacán was still revered far and wide as an intensely sacred place. But no one remembered who had built it or that tens of thousands of people had once lived there.

Today, Teotihuacán is receiving visitors again. It ranks as one of the world's most famous archaeological sites, attracting almost as many visitors annually as the Egyptian pyramids. It has taken generations of scholars to reveal its mysteries. Their inquiries culminated in some of the most intensive archaeological researches ever undertaken anywhere.

The Spanish *conquistadores* first came upon Teotihuacán six centuries after its final collapse. Hernando Cortés and his followers arrived at the site in 1520—hotly pursued by thousands of angry Aztec warriors. They were in desperate straits and, understandably, had little time to contemplate their surroundings or the high earthen mounds that surrounded their exhausted camp. But only a year later, Cortés laid siege to the nearby Aztec capital for seventy-five days. Tenochtitlán, with its great palaces and imposing temples, was no match for 450 Spaniards and thousands of Indian allies who hated the Aztec. Cortés ordered Tenochtitlán razed to the ground. Within a few months, Mexico City was rising from the rubble of the Aztec capital.

The newly arrived Catholic priests of Mexico City now had a chance to learn more about the remarkable countryside around them. But Teotihuacán was a complete mystery. According to the local Indians, the great pyramids of the city had been overgrown with dense vegetation as long as they and their forefathers had lived there. No one knew who had built them, although great idols still stood on the summit of the two largest pyramids. Perhaps ancient giants had erected the temples in the long-distant past. The local Indians still revered the idols on the greatest mound, known to them as the Hill of the Sun. In an effort to eradicate any competition to their own Christian beliefs, the Spaniards eventually toppled the silent idols. With savage and systematic care, the missionary friars who brought the Cross to Mexico destroyed priceless Aztec archives and historical records, as well as thousands of idols and shrines. Teotihuacán slept on, consigned to an historical oblivion that lasted for centuries.

Only a handful of dedicated priests tried to find out something about the history of the Aztec and their predecessors. They learned that the Aztec remembered arriving in the Valley of Mexico about two hundred years before the Spaniards. They had overrun the remains of a great Toltec civilization that had flourished in the Valley of Mexico before them. When the sixteenth-century friar Bernardino de Sahagun had sifted through a mass of historical data on the Aztec, he was convinced that a great civilization had flourished near the Valley of Mexico for over two thousand years. The logical capital for this vast empire seemed to be the deserted city of Teotihuacán. This city, wrote Sahagun, was "very rich and well ordered, very wise and powerful, which suffered the adverse fortune of a Troy." Sahagun's conclusions were quietly suppressed by the church and the government.

The few foreign travelers who reached Teotihuacán added little to the legends that surrounded the ancient city. It was difficult, at best, to study ancient Indian cities in a country ruled with repressive severity by the Catholic authorities. When the Italian world traveler Giovanni Francesco Careri reached Mexico City in 1697, he was favorably impressed by his reception. Of course, his reaction is hardly surprising, for he had just completed a harrowing five-month voyage in a crowded ship all the way from Manila to Mexico. One hundred thousand people lived in Mexico City by this time. Careri reveled in the company of civilized gentlemen, among them a scholarly priest named Don Carlos de Siguenza y Gongora. Siguenza had a passionate interest in ancient Mexico. His friendship with Indian nobles gave him access to both oral histories and priceless historical documents. He learned some of the secrets of Aztec hieroglyphs and, with this knowledge, managed to reconstruct a chronology of their kings. All these activities were risky at best, for the slightest breath of heresy—and Indian history was a great heresy—meant the Inquisition. One of Siguenza's most important contacts was a family named Ixtlilxochitl, the nominal lords of Teotihuacán. He visited the city's remarkable ancient pyramids on several occasions and even dug into one of them in a vain attempt to find an internal treasure house.

Careri had one priceless asset as a traveler—he was insatiably curious. So one day he rode out in search of Teotihuacán's past. Armed with introductions from Siguenza, Careri had no difficulty obtaining a noble Indian guide to take him around. Laboriously, the curious Italian climbed two great pyramids, the first named after the moon, the second and much larger one named "The House of the Sun." Careri was immediately reminded of the Egyptian pyramids. Both Siguenza and his hosts told him that great idols had once stood on the summits of these mysterious structures. It was obvious that Teotihuacán had once been an enormous city. But no one could tell Careri who had built the silent pyramids or who had lived in the crumbling palaces and houses that stretched for miles toward the horizon.

When Careri returned to Europe, he sat down to write a six-volume travelog that contained, among many other nuggets of information, a sketchy description of Teotihuacán. Most writers dismissed Careri as a fraud who had never left his native Naples. How could such primitive people as the Mexican Indians ever have built great temples or designed a vast city? The eighteenth-century Scottish historian William

Robertson summed it up in no uncertain terms. According to him, ancient Mexican palaces were a myth; it was unlikely that "men just emerging from barbarity" would dwell in such splendid structures. Further, he found it incredible that such elaborate cities as those reported by the Spanish and Careri could have vanished so quickly and with so little trace. "The Spanish accounts appear highly embellished," he noted. To cap it all, when Don Carlos de Siguenza died, his priceless manuscripts were scattered or destroyed by his superiors.

Although some travelers visited Teotihuacán in the early nineteenth century, among them the English merchant Bullock, who described the Pyramid of the Sun as being "as perfect as the great pyramid of Egypt," little firsthand information was available. When the Boston historian William Prescott wrote his immortal *History of the Conquest of Mexico* in 1843, he of necessity relied solely on tourist accounts. "The traveler, who will take the trouble to ascend its bald summit, will be amply compensated by the glorious view it will open up to him," he wrote. There was nothing much he could say, however, about the people who built the Pyramid of the Sun. He could only comment that "a nation has passed away—powerful, populous, and well advanced in refinement, as attested by their monuments—but it has perished without a name. It has died and made no sign." It was some time before archaeologists could expand on the worthy Prescott's speculations.

Archaeological research into the mysteries of Teotihuacán remained sporadic during the remainder of the nineteenth century. Claude Joseph Desire Charney, a French traveler and writer, visited Mexico in 1858 and spent three years journeying from Mayan site to Mayan site, taking the first photographs of the ruins ever made. Twenty years later, he returned for another visit, this time to Mexico City and Teotihuacán. Unlike most travelers, he was now determined to dig for the secrets of the pyramids. He started by excavating at the ancient capital of the Toltecs at Tula. He found traces of a palace and of a pyramid topped with giant statues. His discoveries were treated with skepticism. It was not until many years later that Tula was firmly identified as the Toltec capital, built about A.D. 900 and destroyed by the Aztec two centuries later. All this happened long after Teotihuacán was abandoned, but Charney was not to know this.

Armed with his Tula excavating experience, Charney now turned his attention to Teotihuacán. He climbed up the overgrown Pyramids of the Sun and Moon, admired the view, and then set about finding a place to dig. There were so many fragments of prehistoric life on the surface that it was difficult to know where to start. Eventually he sank some small trenches in the middle of the modern village of San Juan Teotihuacán and promptly recovered a number of ancient graves, containing over a dozen children and several adults. The children had been buried in pots. Convinced that he had struck the poor quarter of the great city, Charney turned his attentions elsewhere. He moved to the opposite bank of the San Juan River and set his men to work at a spot where walls appeared to outcrop on the surface. Within three days, the excavations revealed a complex of ten rooms that formed part of a large building with courtyards, pillared roofs, and several levels. The thick walls were constructed of stone and mortar, sometimes covered with decorated plaster. Some of the painted frescoes on the chamber walls were still bright with multicolored designs. Charney quietly removed several of the frescoes for exhibition in his native Paris. After numerous adventures in the Mexican lowlands, he returned home, never to come back to Teotihuacán.

The political upheavals that beset Mexico in the late nineteenth century prevented archaeological investigations by foreigners for many years; President Porfirio Diaz's harsh dictatorship discouraged any archaeological activity by non-Mexicans. Thus it was no coincidence when the dictator gave the son of one of his henchmen a permit to dig at Teotihuacán. Leopoldo Batres, son of a military man, had himself

Leopold Batres's view of
Teotihuacán.

appointed Inspector and Protector of the Archaeological Monuments of Mexico. This imposing title gave Batres *carte blanche* to excavate anywhere in Mexico he wished. And, if there was gold at the end of the rainbow, so much the better.

Batres excavated at Teotihuacán for two long periods: 1884–1886 and 1905–1911. His first season was financed by the government at a time when much of the country's population was suffering severely from hunger and poverty; his second used up more money than the entire social-welfare budget for Mexico at the time. Batres spent his first months at the site poking around randomly. He dug near the Pyramid of the Moon and discovered a huge building decorated with striking murals. The paintings depicted brightly painted flowers and animals, gods and priests, as well as elaborate geometric designs. He also dug through numerous large, single-story dwellings that were divided into many small rooms and roofed with stout timber beams and stucco-plastered ceilings. Wherever he dug, Batres came across beautifully finished aqueducts that still brought water from natural springs to all parts of what, he now realized, was once a great city.

Batres estimated that Teotihuacán had extended over an area of at least seven square miles. He also determined that much of the city had been destroyed by fire at some late period in its history. Many dwellings Batres dug had collapsed. Their walls were charred and the rafters had settled into the foundations. Some, he said, even contained the skeletons of the inhabitants, lying where they had been trapped in the holocaust. Yet other homes were still perfectly preserved, buried in fine clay. What had happened to Teotihuacán? Batres was puzzled by a question that has still not been satisfactorily answered.

After an interval during which he tried to find treasures at other sites, Batres persuaded President Diaz to fund another long series of excavations on his mysterious city, under the pretext of restoring Teotihuacán as a great national monument, one that would enhance Mexico's image in the world. Diaz provided ample funds in 1905. Batres started on an ambitious project: the complete restoration of the Pyramid of the Sun.

He began by organizing his workmen in teams. Aided by a steam locomotive and a length of track, they removed thousands of tons of earth from the overgrown pyramid. When Batres started, the Pyramid of the Sun was little more than a huge pile of earth. He realized that no half measures were possible. Either he had to leave the pyramid as it was or expose the huge masonry structure that lay, he thought, under the soil. To achieve the latter, it would be necessary to remove several hundred thousand tons of earth.

It was an extraordinary undertaking, one that took four years and cost the then-colossal sum of $45,000. Batres stripped all the earth and rubble from the great mound. When heavy rains started to erode the adobe, Batres was forced to introduce lime and cement to stabilize the outer surface of the pyramid. He found it was a huge, stepped structure with a temple on the summit dedicated to Quetzalcoatl, the Plumed Serpent god. Clay figures and numerous ornaments lay under

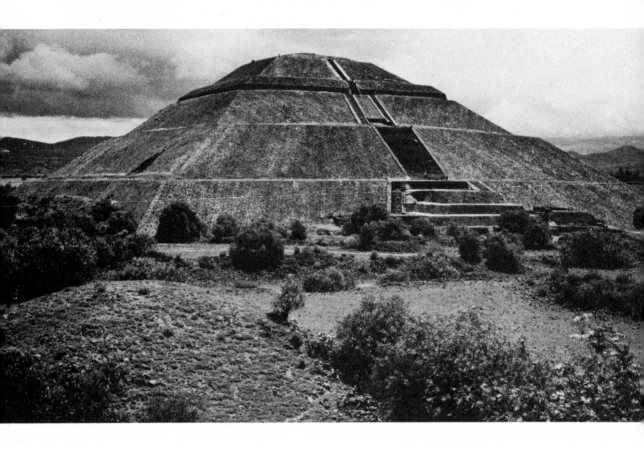

Pyramid of the Sun,
Teotihuacán, as it appears
today.

the surface of the uppermost platform. Child sacrifices had
been placed at the corners of each level. They crumbled to
dust upon exposure to the air. The pyramid was surrounded
with a great platform nineteen feet high and one hundred
twenty-six feet wide. Beautifully decorated houses lay nearby.

Just as Batres was nearing the end of his work, political
unrest caused him to abandon Teotihuacán forever. By that
time, he estimated he had removed between twelve and
twenty feet of earth from the outer surface of the pyramid.
Batres's version of the Pyramid of the Sun was 203 feet high
and 745 by 684 feet at the base. His many enemies were
appalled at the damage. They accused him of having stripped
off the outer layers of the pyramid as if it were an onion and of
having mangled it beyond repair. When President Diaz was
abruptly deposed in 1910, Batres fell from grace, leaving the
field open to better-qualified archaeologists.

Batres's successor, a man of very different caliber, had been
specially trained at Columbia University under the great an-

thropologist Franz Boas. Manuel Gamio was a museum man, in charge of antiquities at the National Museum in Mexico City. Powerful American backers paid for his training in the hope that he would one day make scientific excavations at Teotihuacán and elsewhere. Gamio was a talented archaeologist who spent the years of civil war between 1910 and 1917 quietly digging into the huge piles of rubbish under Mexico City. Unlike his predecessors, Gamio was interested in the minutest of finds, which he dissected layer by layer into a complex chronology of occupation horizons. He found at least three major phases of prehistoric occupation of the Mexico City site—the latest Aztec, preceded by Toltec, with an earlier "Archaic" civilization that had flourished before either Toltec or Aztec. But how did the vast city of Teotihuacán fit into this pattern? Had the Toltecs built it, as Batres and his predecessors believed? Or had an unknown civilization erected its vast pyramids and plazas? Gamio was determined to find out.

Manuel Gamio started serious work at Teotihuacán in 1918. The excavations were conducted along the principles he had followed with success in Mexico City. His first effort was an attempt to establish the chronology of Teotihuacán by studying the architectural styles of the buildings. After sixteen test excavations, Gamio felt confident enough to tackle an even larger project, the excavation of a mysterious quadrangular area of earth-covered mounds known as the Ciudadela, lying to the south of the Pyramid of the Sun.

This was a formidable project, for Batres had already found traces of elaborately decorated temples in the Ciudadela mounds. Like his infamous predecessor, Gamio realized he would have to preserve the temples as soon as he uncovered them; otherwise they would disintegrate in a few days of rain. This part of Teotihuacán was obviously unique and should be preserved as a tourist attraction and as a monument to Mexico's new national spirit. Wisely, Gamio employed the services of an expert architectural draftsman named Ignatio

The carved facade of the Temple of Quetzalcoatl, Teotihuacán.

Marquina. Marquina's drawings of the newly excavated temples gave Gamio the information he needed to anchor masonry and to replace mortar where necessary as the buildings were uncovered. He uncovered only the inward facing sides of the Ciudadela buildings, so that the facades were stabilized by the earth mounds that covered the rest of the masonry.

The Ciudadela excavations began in 1919. Within a few weeks, the earthen mounds were yielding sculptured serpents' heads. When the diggers started work on the large mound in the center of the Ciudadela, they found it consisted of two pyramids, built one against the other. The rear pyramid of the two was the earlier, a vast structure that rose in six steps to a height of seventy-two feet. Gamio had to destroy part of the first pyramid to get at the better-built rear one. But the effort was worth it. As the diggers uncovered each successive stage, Gamio was able to admire the vast, sprawling serpents, some with glittering obsidian eyes, that protruded from each level. These feathered serpents represented the ancient god Quetzalcoatl. A beautifully designed staircase lined by watching serpents led to the summit of the pyramid, where six burials were found.

The entire Ciudadela was a vast complex of buildings over a mile in circumference, covering an area of thirty-six acres. Gamio soon realized that millions of pesos would be needed to excavate the whole of Teotihuacán. And, at best, it would be a controversial undertaking. Already he was being attacked by the aged Batres, who accused him of "grotesque" reconstructions and of being a man "without understanding or conscience." But, while Batres' strictures were ignored, the worldwide depression of the 1930s postponed any further work on a large scale. Although the Swedish archaeologist Sigwald Linne excavated at Teotihuacán in the 1930s and discovered extensive complexes of residence quarters, ball courts, and other public buildings, his work, and that of Pedro Armillas and others who succeeded him, was sporadic. The

The Ciudadela at Teotihuacán as it appears today.

combined work of these men did show, however, that the mysterious site had, in fact, been far more than a complex of temples. It was a great city with a flourishing market and a vigorous artistic tradition that was reflected in brightly colored wall murals of gods and priests. Still, as late as 1960, no one had any idea who had lived in the city or when it had been built.

Teotihuacán languished until 1960, when the Mexican government was looking around for new sources of revenue. They decided to carry out a major excavation at Teotihuacán and to reconstruct the central part of the city to its former glory as a tourist attraction close to Mexico City. The project ended up costing seventeen million pesos and employing over six hundred workmen. The dig was under the direction of José Acosta and Ignatio Bernal, both experienced archaeologists. Within a few months, they had cleared the plaza in front of the Pyramid of the Moon and started work on the buildings on either side of the Street of the Dead, their objective being to restore the central part of the city. As many of the buildings were in a late and inferior architectural style, Acosta and

Bernal boldly decided to tear many of them down to reveal the superior, older buildings that lay behind the later facades. Their efforts were brilliantly successful. Teotihuacán, of course, has become one of the great archaeological tourist attractions of the world and the costs of the excavation have been recovered many times over.

The most ambitious part of the excavation was an effort to reconstruct the Pyramid of the Moon, still an earthen mound that only Batres had tried to excavate—and he had left a huge crater in the middle. Acosta and Bernal were determined not to repeat the mistakes made by Batres. Proceeding with great care, they soon discovered there were at least five stages to the pyramid, linked by a great staircase. Fortunately, one of their colleagues found a cornerstone of the original stairway still in place, so they were able to reconstruct the angle of the steps and replace forty-eight courses. The north side of the pyramid was left in its original state to stabilize the structure.

When all of the work was completed, the visitor could gaze down on the vast complexity of Teotihuacán from the summit of the Pyramid of the Sun and walk up the Street of the Dead to the Pyramid of the Moon. One could obtain a vivid impression of a great ceremonial center, of the great avenue lined by fine temples and palaces. But the city, even when full of tourists, seemed dead. Where had the inhabitants lived? How many people had dwelt in the shadow of the pyramids and temples? Was Teotihuacán just a ceremonial center, or was it a city as well?

The Mexican excavations finally threw some light on the date of the site. When Acosta and Bernal sat down to examine the thousands of pottery fragments and art objects found in their digs, they established that the site had been occupied over a very long time, from about 100 B.C. until as late as A.D. 800. Teotihuacán reached the height of its prosperity around A.D. 500. After that time, the city began a gradual decline and, by the end of the first millennium, was deserted. The Toltec peoples who took over political power in the Valley of Mexico made their headquarters at Tula, abandoning Teotihuacán altogether. The Teotihuacanos came under new rulers.

In 1950, a young American archaeologist name René Millon visited Teotihuacán for the first time. He was fresh out of Columbia University, where his lecturers had waxed eloquent about this extraordinary site. Immediately, he came under the spell of the Pyramid of the Sun and the Street of the Dead, silent under the Mexican sun. How had such a center arisen, he wondered? Had it really been an enormous city? Millon decided then and there to devote his career to solving the mystery.

Millon realized at once that he had undertaken an enormous, almost mind-boggling project; the mapping operations alone would take years. The only plans of Teotihuacán had been prepared by a scientific commission appointed by Emperor Maximilian in 1865 and by Manuel Gamio in 1922. Both concentrated on the center area of the site. Millon wisely spent some years becoming more familiar with archaeology in the Valley of Mexico. He studied with Mexican archaeologists and investigated ancient irrigation systems near Teotihuacán. It was not until 1957 that he felt prepared enough to tackle the city itself.

Millon's preliminary surveys convinced him that Teotihuacán had been a vast and highly complex city. Other archaeologists violently disagreed, insisting it was merely an elaborate ceremonial center of pyramids and temples. There was only one way to solve the problem: the entire site must be mapped in detail. Millon blithely took on the task, a research campaign supported by the National Science Foundation. The project is only now in its final stages. "Depending upon one's point of view," he remarked years later, "it is fortunate or unfortunate that I did not realize the implications of what I was undertaking, for surely I would never have taken it on."

In order to record the full extent of Teotihuacán's twelve-and-a-half square miles, the mapping project covered an area of twenty-two square miles around the site. The first stage of

An interior patio at Teotihuacán. The columns were carved in relief and the cornice of the building has been repainted in its original colors.

the work began in 1962, when a complete air photographic record of the site from 4,000 feet was made on a cloudless April day. Then the archaeologists took the photographs into the field. It took them five years to transform the air photographs and field surveys into a finished map.

The results were astonishing. Teotihuacán was revealed as an orderly, carefully thought-out city that had been laid out on a grandiose scale. Nearly all its buildings had been erected on a north-south axis, an orientation that gave Teotihuacán a planned appearance, in spite of the many thousands of people crowded into its houses and apartments. The orientation of the city was extended to the east-west axis as well, presumably by means of astronomical observations. No one knows why the north-south orientation of the Street of the Dead was chosen.

The city was divided into four quadrants; the northwest quarter was by far the most densely settled. The southern parts of the settlement impinged on extremely fertile agricultural land. Most of the earliest buildings were erected on the northern edge of Teotihuacán. Apparently, the orientation and length of the Street of the Dead were decided early on, perhaps as early as the second century A.D. The three-mile street seems to have been part of a master plan, but it is unclear to what extent the rulers of Teotihuacán kept to any original plan in later centuries. Probably what happened was that the limits of the city were decided on as Teotihuacán grew into a dense complex of closely spaced, walled compounds.

Teotihuacán was far from an open city. Millon found the remains of walled precincts and large compounds that served to restrict entry into certain parts of the settlement. There do not seem to have been defensive walls, nor are there traces of fortifications enclosing the entire city. But anyone wanting to attack Teotihuacán would have had a difficult time. The narrow streets between the apartment complexes could be covered by rooftop arches, and dense thickets of cactus and deep, irrigated swamps would hinder a large army of attackers. In addition, the teeming *barrios* of Teotihuacán would have been a strategical nightmare for any raiding party.

Teotihuacán was divided into many neighborhoods. When Millon came to examine the houses in each neighborhood more thoroughly, he found that groups of apartments were set off into distinctive clusters. There were more than two thousand residential compounds in the city. Each consisted of sets of dwelling units, often with a communal shrine and a central patio. The surface finds from the clusters of compounds indicated that people with the same occupations tended to live in the same apartment complexes. Obsidian knife makers, potters, and merchants all seem to have lived in their own precincts.

In the western part of the city, there was even one enclave where people from faraway Oaxaca lived and worked. Millon found numerous potsherds from this area of Mexico on the surface of a residential complex. When the compound was excavated, it was found that the Oaxacan apartments were first occupied around A.D. 400, and the occupation continued for centuries. No one knows what the Oaxaqueros were doing in Teotihuacán. Perhaps they were merchants, although there is no evidence to suggest this. Although the foreigners lived in the standard Teotihuacán houses and compounds, they preserved their own burial customs for centuries. The vessels they used were comparable to those from the great ceremonial center of Monte Alban in the Valley of Oaxaca. Was there a special relationship between the two centers? Were the Oaxaqueros but one of several foreign enclaves in this cosmopolitan city? This is just another of the many tantalizing questions posed by Teotihuacán.

Once the Teotihuacán map was complete, René Millon sat down to compute the population of the city. He began by examining the excavated apartment buildings in an effort to estimate the number of sleeping places in them. Millon devised a series of estimates for apartments of various sizes. Then he measured compounds throughout the city, using his map as a basis for the calculations. The result was a conservative, minimal estimate of 75,000, with perhaps as many as 125,000 people at the height of the city's prosperity. Millon believes these figures are far too conservative, that Teotihuacán may have housed over 200,000 people. But any population figures for the city are little more than intelligent guesses.

Why did this enormous settlement arise in the first place, a city with over five hundred craft workshops, many of them engaged in obsidian-tool manufacture? Millon points out that the Teotihuacán Valley is semiarid today. Its agricultural potential would be by no means exceptional were it not for the springs at the southwestern edge of the city that provided abundant water for irrigation, agriculture, and domestic purposes. Water supplies were canalized throughout the city. But the valley contained another vital resource as well—obsidian. This volcanic glass was widely prized for toolmaking, and we know that obsidian working was a major activity throughout

Teotihuacán: an early classic effigy vessel from a site near the city. It is about twelve inches high.

the city's history. Teotihuacán Valley lies near the shore of Lake Texcoco, the largest lake in the Valley of Mexico, important both as a communication route and as an economic resource in itself. Thus Teotihuacán occupied a key geographical position and possessed valuable economic resources, both elements of potential political importance. Certainly the Teotihuacanos exploited the potential of their valley brilliantly.

By analyzing both the Teotihuacán map and the thousands of potsherds found at the site, Millon showed how the original settlement a few centuries before Christ consisted of a handful of villages, at least one of which may have specialized in obsidian manufacture. By 100 B.C. Teotihuacán had begun to expand rapidly. The scattered villages became a settlement covering more than three and a half square miles. There were obsidian workers in the city and several public buildings with walls of stone. Much of this early settlement, the home of six thousand or more people, is covered by later buildings. Perhaps the people lived in small clusters of houses. We do not know. But Teotihuacán was already an important center of obsidian trading and of production and marketing. Perhaps its religious ceremonies were known far and wide, too.

By A.D. 150, Teotihuacán extended over eight square miles and contained some twenty thousand inhabitants. By now, the Teotihuacanos could worship at several temple complexes on either side of the Street of the Dead. The Pyramid of the Sun and the Pyramid of the Moon, begun at this time, formed the focuses of two major religious complexes. Obsidian trade and manufacture was expanding fast. So was agricultural production, for a rapidly growing urban population had to be fed. Teotihuacán was now so large that anyone seeking to pass through the valley had to traverse the city. It was a city with a diverse population of specialists, priests, and distinct social classes. A revolution in the structure of Mexican society was under way.

Between A.D. 150 and 200, the Ciudadela was erected and became the religious and political center of the city. What is more, the city's rulers seem to have realized that they could now exert religious and political influence over a much larger area of Mexico. By this time, too, the Street of the Dead, with its vast structures, would serve to impress both local dwellers and visitors with the incredible prestige and power of the city's rulers.

The next two and a half centuries saw the erection of hundreds of standardized apartment complexes and a steadily increasing social distance between the Teotihuacán rulers and those they ruled. Thousands of people had now moved into the city, where their activities and living arrangements were closely regimented. It is likely that they were discouraged from ever returning to the countryside, for, within the confines of Teotihuacán, they could be more easily organized and taxed.

Between A.D. 450 and 750, Teotihuacán was at the height of its powers. The city was actively engaged in trading with communities hundreds of miles away, on the Gulf Coast and in the Mayan lowlands, as well as throughout the Valley of Mexico. The city was now not only an important obsidian workshop, but an international marketplace as well, a place of pilgrimage for Teotihuacanos and foreigners alike. Significant numbers of outsiders now resided permanently in the greatest city Mexico had ever seen.

Then, with an arresting suddenness, Teotihuacán collapsed. Many of the central buildings were burnt during the eighth century A.D. and never rebuilt. Up to this moment, the city was prospering; there were no obvious signs of decline. The city proper was as populous as ever, although the surrounding countryside supported fewer people as more and more rural dwellers flocked to the city. Was Teotihuacán sacked and burned by foreign invaders? Or was the center of the city destroyed by a tremendous fire? If so, why was it not rebuilt? What happened to the thousands of people in the city? Did they disperse to live elsewhere? Why, if the city was besieged, were its inhabitants unable to resist attack? Did more and more people move into the city for defensive reasons? So far, no one has been able to answer these questions satisfactorily.

Millon did determine, however, that Teotihuacán was prosperous up to the very end, although its sphere of political domination appears to have contracted somewhat. Were other centers beginning to challenge Teotihuacán's dominance? The city may have faced a severe ecological problem as well, perhaps generated by a series of dry years and more frequent crop failures. The irrigated fields may have been unable to produce the huge food surplus needed to maintain an urban society. To what extent did the rulers of Teotihuacán over-reach themselves and place intolerable strains on the food supplies available to them? We do not know.

Conceivably, those who ruled Teotihuacán were so set in their responses to the city's difficulties that they were unable to act rationally and effectively to solve the critical ecological problems that faced the city. Their society may have faced major internal stresses too, strains that the rulers sought to contain by force and military curbs. Perhaps it is significant that military figures appear with increasing frequency in Teotihuacán's later art styles. Did the Teotihuacanos turn on their rulers in bloody revolt? Did they destroy the temples and gods that oversaw them in a massive act of desanctification that left the mighty city in smoking ruins? Again, we do not know.

There is but one certainty. By the time the Spaniards came to Mexico, Teotihuacán was a silent ruin, a mystery that generations of archaeologists have puzzled over. But, despite the ancient questions it poses, Teotihuacán leaves us with a strangely relevant thought for our own times. Did the city, by its great and spectacular successes, sow the seeds of its own failure by overreaching the limits of its resources? Conceivably it did. In that case, the lesson of Teotihuacán is indeed timely.

# CHAPTER

# 5

# LAYARD OF NINEVEH

"ARISE, GO TO NINEVEH, THAT GREAT CITY", SAID THE Lord to Jonah. "Cry against it; for their wickedness is come up before me." And Jonah obeyed orders and duly rebuked the city, which repented of its sins and was spared from destruction. Jonah's mission to Nineveh is but one of thousands of allusions to great cities and mighty kings in the Scriptures. But did these cities and monarchs actually exist? Was the Old Testament based on historical fact? These questions have preoccupied not only theologians and archaeologists for generations, but many lay persons as well.

A hundred and fifty years ago, at a time when scientists were challenging the historical truth of the biblical story of the Creation, this preoccupation became almost an obsession. Had Nineveh actually been a great city? Where were Joseph's huge granaries by the banks of the Nile? Did the Assyrians and the Hanging Gardens of Babylon actually exist? This chapter is the story of a man who proved that many of the cities and kings of the Old Testament actually existed and who helped discover the unique and long-lost civilizations of the Assyrians and Sumerians.

Long before Englishman Austen Henry Layard started digging in the desolate plains of Mesopotamia between the rivers Tigris and Euphrates, the area had evoked intense interest among biblical scholars because of its associations with the Garden of Eden and Noah's Flood. As early as the twelfth century, the celebrated Jewish rabbi Benjamin of Tudela gazed on the desolute mounds of Nineveh and commented on the utter destruction around him. Another traveler, the Englishman John Shirley, referred to Nineveh as a "witnesse to God's judgement." When the seventeenth-century Italian explorer Pietro della Valle returned from the mounds of Nimrud with a few mysterious square bricks bearing strange written characters, scholars from all over Europe flocked to see his find. Yet, until the middle of the nineteenth century, the secrets of the Assyrians and Sumerians remained buried deep in the huge *tells* of Mesopotamia. Nineveh was little more than a shadowy city of legend, marked only by a few dusty mounds and desolate palace foundations.

Even a century and a half ago, Mesopotamia was a wild and dangerous place for European travelers. The territory between the Tigris and Euphrates was under the nominal jurisdiction of the sultan of Turkey, part of the huge and slowly decaying Ottoman Empire based in Constantinople. Local rulers held uneasy sway over huge tracts of desolate landscape, under sporadic supervision from far-distant Ottoman officials. The real political force was exerted by nomad tribes who fanned out over the dry plains in constant search of grazing land for their flocks. A long tradition of raiding and tribal warfare, of family feuds and princely hospitality was observed. Woe betide the rash foreigner who ventured into this wild land without either a powerful escort or the money to buy himself out.

Despite its remoteness and legendary wildness, the Great Powers kept a keen eye on this distant land, strategically

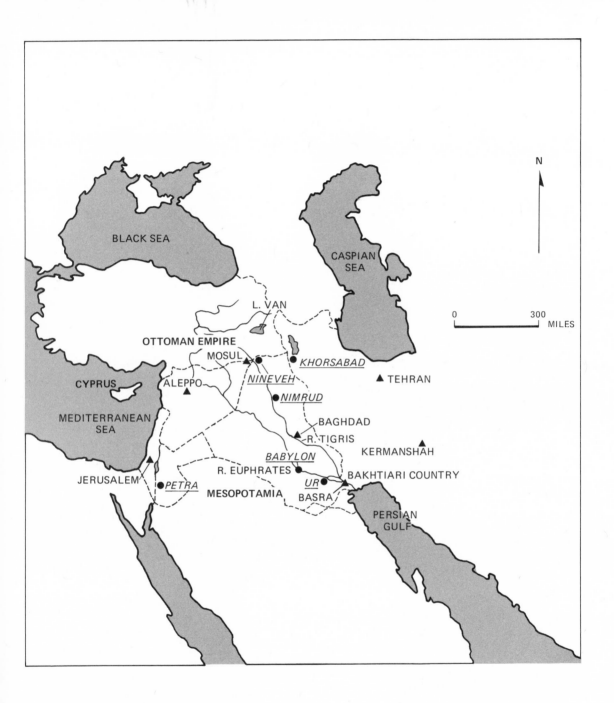

Locations and sites mentioned
in Chapter 5. Some earlier sites
can be found on the map for
Chapters 6 and 7.

placed as it was to regulate overland commerce to the British possessions in India. Its great rivers presented tantalizing prospects for new, navigable trade routes into untapped markets for foreign wares. The European nations maintained embassies in Constantinople, where they competed for the favors of the sultan. Diplomatic missions were constantly on the move into unknown territory, scouting for military or commercial advantage. Britain and France were farsighted enough to post consuls in Baghdad and other remote cities famous in biblical times. These officials ministered to the needs of the occasional traveler, kept an eye on local conditions, and attempted to keep abreast of volatile Mesopotamian politics.

In 1840, this harsh and little-known land was still a region of mystery, considered by Westerners to be the cradle of humankind, the most ancient part of the known world. Archaeologists like Austen Henry Layard were among the first to draw aside the curtain of mystery that shrouded Mesopotamia. In so doing, they gave new life to parts of the Old Testament and generated keen public interest in ancient biblical stories.

"My life has been, in some respects, an eventful one," wrote Austen Henry Layard in his old age. His modest remark grossly understated the truth. By the time he was thirty-five, Henry Layard was not only a traveler of world renown, but he had also discovered a long-lost Near Eastern civilization. In addition, he had made his mark as a brilliant popular writer. But this was only a beginning. In later life, Layard was to become a politician, art connoisseur, and diplomat of high repute. He crammed more into one lifetime than most of us could manage in six, giving up archaeology before he was forty.

Austen Henry Layard was born in Paris on March 5, 1817, the son of English parents who enjoyed living on the Continent. Young Henry grew up in an atmosphere of cultured leisure, for his parents were friendly with many writers and artists. By the time he was seventeen, Layard himself was ambitious to move up in the world. His family was so poor, despite their culture, that he was unable to go to college. Instead, he was articled as a clerk to a relative's law firm in London. For a few years he led a miserable life, going without food to buy the hundreds of books he read in his chilly lodgings. Henry hated being a lawyer. The dull and predictable career that lay ahead of him filled his heart with gloom; his bubbling ambition seemed doomed to die under a mountain of legal briefs and dry court decisions. The family worried about what to do with their unconventional son who seemed intent on rising to the top as quickly as possible by blithely ignoring all normal steps on the ladder to success.

During vacations, Layard abandoned his arid studies and traveled all over Europe. He visited Russia and Poland, ventured as far north as Finland, and fell in love with Italy, a country he was to visit again and again. In his diaries and letters, he poured out his feelings, expressing excitement over his many new friends and adventures. He did most of his traveling on foot, with occasional railway journeys, at a time when travel around Europe was far more difficult than it is today. Fortunately, just as Layard's ambitions were getting the best of him and creating family tensions, salvation came along in the form of Henry's Uncle Charles.

In his early life, Layard's father had worked in Ceylon for a while, until forced to return to England because of ill health. Henry's Uncle Charles had gone to Ceylon at the same time and was now a high government official there. When Charles came home on leave, he suggested that Henry consider practicing law in Ceylon. Layard was interested, so Charles introduced him to Edward Mitford, a young businessman of thirty-two who had just returned from a business venture in Morocco and was about to go coffee planting in Ceylon. The two men took to each other immediately and agreed to travel out together.

The normal route to Ceylon was to take a steamer to Alexandria, then travel overland via the Isthmus of Suez (the

Suez Canal did not, of course, exist), and then continue on by ship to Colombo. But Mitford was subject to chronic seasickness and was determined to go by another route—overland from Europe to Constantinople, then through Syria, Jerusalem, and Baghdad to Persia, India and Ceylon. Although one can now go by bus from London to Calcutta, the journey can still be eventful and beset with unexpected complications. In 1839 such a journey was not only dangerous, it was literally an expedition into the unknown. To further complicate matters, Henry Layard had never been to the East, spoke no Oriental languages, and, worst of all, had never ridden a horse. Even Mitford was a little doubtful as to whether Layard would survive the journey.

With feverish eagerness, Layard threw himself into preparations for the trip. He passed his law examinations, took lessons in surveying, and consulted the few English diplomats and travelers who had visited Persia. The family thought he was crazy and said so in no uncertain terms. But they soon realized their objections were falling on deaf ears. So a small sum of money was scraped together to pay for supplies. Finally, the two travelers left London in July 1839 on a journey that was to change the course of archaeological history. Had Mitford not been chronically seasick, Layard would never have found a lost civilization and would probably have led a life of respectable anonymity.

Layard and Mitford traveled by horse bus, Rhine steamer, and light carriage across Germany to Italy. Layard was so entranced by Venice on this first visit that, many years later, he chose to retire there. A few weeks later, they were deep in Jugoslavia, where they bought saddles. Layard learned how to ride the hard way, but loved it. "The first day we rode 16 hours, the second 14, and the third 26 without stopping except to rest and change," he wrote home in delight. His body, apparently, was constructed of steel.

The Balkans, although fascinating, involved the travelers in some bloodcurdling episodes. At one point, they found themselves surrounded by Montenegran soldiers who smoked long pipes and calmly lounged in the men's lodgings while, just outside the window, they had full view of a circle of forty-five gory heads stuck on poles, trophies from a skirmish with the Turks a week before. Layard seems to have been unmoved by the spectacle. He wrote his nervous, sensitive mother a vivid account not only of the smell, but also of the blood that dripped from the decaying heads. Such chilling details can hardly have reassured his family back home.

By the time the two young men had reached Constantinople, Layard had fallen in love with the East. He was so fascinated by the sights and the cosmopolitan peoples they encountered in official resthouses and on the streets that the trip's hardships seemed insignificant. Fortunately the two men got on well together, despite marked differences in temperament. Mitford was conservative, careful, and a devout Christian. Layard was liberal, rash, and highly impulsive. Mitford watched the birds and animals; Layard visited every Greek and Roman temple he could find. Their diet was simple in the extreme—fish roe, carob beans, and unleavened bread. It cost them about four shillings a day to live as they made their way on horseback down the centuries-old route through Syria to Jerusalem. The Romans had traveled the very same way.

The Holy Land was in such a state of political confusion that Layard's hastily formed plan to travel eastward from Jerusalem to explore the lost city of Petra was regarded by local officials as crazy. Mitford refused to go with him. But Henry's newly acquired enthusiasm for antiquities could not be subdued. Eventually he left Jerusalem with only two camels and a very young Arab to cross country where most travelers survived by buying off the local chiefs.

Layard harbored the romantic notion that the Bedouin nomads of the desert offered hospitality to every stranger passing through their territory. How wrong he was! As soon as Layard entered the narrow defile that led to the mysterious city of Petra, a place hitherto rarely visited by Europeans, a crowd of suspicious Arabs surrounded his camel, demanding money. Fortunately, the chief arrived just as Henry was about to draw his pistol. Otherwise, he would certainly have been killed.

The Arabs looked on suspiciously as Layard poked around in the rock-cut temples of Petra and finally allowed him to depart for the mountains of Moab. There his luck ran out. He was attacked and robbed of everything by a group of tribesmen. Incredibly, Layard managed to grab the sheikh as a hostage in the nick of time. After lengthy bargaining, his supplies and simple possessions were restored to him, but the sheikh then "sold" him to another chief, who simply did not believe that Layard had no money or valuables. Layard's new owner was so surprised at his folly in traveling without ample "buy-off" money that he let him go free. After numerous adventures, Layard rejoined Mitford in Aleppo, where they made preparations to journey to Baghdad. Their arduous route would take them to Mosul and through the flat, harsh terrain of the Mesopotamian delta. It would be essential to travel light and sleep in their clothes. On March 18, 1841, the two men set out on a stage of the journey that was to change Layard's entire life.

Mosul, which the travelers reached at the beginning of April 1841, is situated on a flat floodplain of the Tigris River. Across the river lies a range of low hills, some four miles in circumference. These man-made mounds were all that remained of a vast ancient city. Layard rode over to look at the deserted hills and found them littered with a profusion of potsherds and mud-brick fragments. Unlike most of his educated contemporaries, he had never been captivated by the spell of ancient Greece and Rome. Their classic temples left him relatively cold. But the deserted mounds of Kuyunjik, alleged to be ancient Nineveh, sent him into raptures. "Desolation meets desolation," he wrote in his diary that night. "A feeling of awe succeeds to wonder; for there is nothing to relieve the mind, to lead to hope, or to tell of what has gone by." These huge mounds made a deep impression on Henry Layard. "A deep mystery hangs over Assyria," he said to Mitford. He insisted on staying in Mosul for two weeks while he brooded over the mounds and visited other sites in the vicinity.

By far the easiest way to reach Baghdad from Mosul was to float down the Tigris on a wooden raft supported by fifty sheepskins. The three-hundred-mile journey took them down a river route that had been in use for thousands of years. Twenty miles south of Mosul, they passed the ruins of another great city, Nimrud, their raft careering over some rapids that, according to the boatman, marked the remains of a dam built by ancient kings. Layard decided at that moment that he would one day explore these ancient mounds. By the time they reached Baghdad, a vague notion had become a fixation.

Colonel Taylor, the British agent in Baghdad, received the two travelers kindly. For two months Layard stayed in a guest house near the British residency. He spent hours poring over the books and manuscripts in Taylor's fine library. Henry was particularly interested in cuneiform, the mysterious ancient script that seemed to crop up everywhere—inscribed both on clay tablets and on great cliffs at Bisutun near Kermanshah. Everything he read increased his determination to dig at Nimrud and find out more about this strange writing.

At the end of their stay, Layard and Mitford joined a caravan that took them to Kermanshah and deep into Persia. At this point the two men parted company. Mitford was concerned about their delays and was anxious to reach India after a year on the road, while Layard wanted to press on into unknown country. Mitford, therefore, left along a safe route to the southeast, leaving Layard to venture off on his own in search of ancient cities and lost civilizations. Layard never reached Ceylon.

An extraordinary interlude in Layard's life followed. He decided to visit the country of the Bakhtiari nomads and attempt to locate the site of the ancient city of Susa. For over a year, Henry lived alone among the fierce and proud Bakhtiari, a tribe of warrior herdsmen. He seems to have been content to wander with them and was adopted by Mohamed Taki Khan as a member of his family when he cured the chief's son of fever. Layard became deeply involved in the Bakhtiari's constant quarrels with Persian officialdom. He took part in their skirmishes and political intrigues and, at one point, was captured by a cruel shiekh named Manuchar Khan who had a reputation for inhuman torture and indiscriminate use of the bastinado. Layard managed to escape and started the ride back to Baghdad, only to be robbed in the desert of his horse and possessions. His life was spared simply because he was English. Eventually he managed to reach the British residency in Baghdad, dressed as an Arab right down to the skin.

Layard was now in deep trouble with his family. His long silences kept his mother in a state of constant frenzy. Finally, Henry's father persuaded the Foreign Office to make inquiries about his son's whereabouts. When the British ambassador in Teheran inquired of Layard from the vizier, the latter replied, "That man! Why, if I could catch him, I'd hang him." This was hardly reassuring to the Layards.

But young Layard was regarded quite favorably in some circles. Colonel Taylor and others were deeply impressed with his knowledge of local affairs and sent him to see the British ambassador in Constantinople, Sir Stratford Canning. Layard was delighted to be off on his travels again and journeyed up the same route to Mosul, where he met Paul Botta, the new French vice-consul. Botta was a charming man, sent out by his government to look into reports of ancient cities in Mesopotamia. Layard spent hours poking around the mounds of Kuyunjik with Botta. The latter had already started to dig into them, but had, so far, found almost nothing.

The diplomatic world of Constantinople was a far cry from the wilds of Bakhtiari. Layard was received with scant courtesy by the British embassy staff, so, leaving an indignant letter for the ambassador, he stormed off to find a ship to England. The ambassador, on reading Layard's angry letter, received him promptly and listened to his tales of the Bakhtiari with great interest. Sir Stratford Canning, a formidable diplomat with tremendous prestige with the Turks, took an instant liking to Layard and retained him as an unpaid personal assistant for many months. Many of his assignments were confidential and dangerous and, true to character, Layard relished the secrecy and intrigue.

But always at the back of Layard's mind were the silent mounds of Mosul, especially when Paul Botta sent him drawings of some of his new and extraordinary discoveries at the ancient city of Khorsabad and elsewhere. He showed the drawings to Canning, in the hope that the ambassador would send him to Mosul and Nimrud in search of the ancient Assyrians. Eventually Canning gave in. He dispatched Henry to Mosul with instructions to spy out the land. The ambassador was prepared to pay for two months' excavations. Layard, acting as Canning's agent, was to keep his investigations as secret as possible. It's difficult to understand why

Layard's sketch of "An Arab Tent." He visited many such encampments.

Canning agreed to pay for the excavations, unless, of course, he felt he could make money from Layard's finds.

On November 8, 1845, Layard slipped away from Mosul on a raft. The departure was intentionally inconspicuous, for the French vice-consul, Botta, was both suspicious and anxious to keep a monopoly on all excavations in Mesopotamia on his own behalf. Fortunately, since the British vice-consul in Mosul was a contractor, Layard was able to have his excavation tools secretly made in the vice-consul's workshop.

Nimrud was deserted when Layard reached the site. His foreman went to look for laborers while the others slept. All night Layard tossed and turned on his hard mattress, visions of vast treasures, buried palaces, and great warriors floating through his dreams. At dawn, his dreams gave way to reality and Layard, accompanied by six laborers, confronted the huge and silent mounds of Nimrud.

The site consisted of a long line of narrow mounds, dominated by a conelike pyramid. The pyramid, once the great *ziggurat* temple, had been worn over the centuries into a conical earthwork of mud brick over a hundred and forty feet high. The first problem was to decide where to start digging.

Layard chose a spot where a fragment of limestone stuck up above the ground. Within a few hours, the workmen had cleared the remains of a chamber about twenty-five feet long, with an inscribed marble floor covered with cuneiform writing. The room was filled with rubbish and yielded some magnificent ivory figures of a king, some crouching sphinxes, and beautiful flowers. Another trench on the southern side of the site revealed a long, inscribed wall that obviously formed part of another huge structure. In his first few days of excavations, Layard found not one, but two, royal palaces. Several years were to pass before Layard was to know that the North West Palace, where he first excavated, had been built by the great Assyrian King Ashur-nasir-pal II (883–859 B.C.). No one had yet deciphered cuneiform writing, nor could anyone read Assyrian inscriptions.

Since there were over nine hundred acres of Nimrud to be excavated, Layard wisely decided to concentrate on the western side of the site. He also decided to concentrate his search on sensational sculptures and art objects. These, he realized, were the sorts of things that excited popular interest and generated future financial support.

As the excavations went on, Layard heard rumors of avid curiosity among local officials in Mosul. Every local ruler was on the lookout for treasure, and treasure seemed to be what Layard was digging for. When a workman smuggled a tiny piece of gold leaf found in the North West Palace into a Mosul bazaar, rumors of major caches of gold spread like wildfire. So, while Layard continued to look for sculptures, others were after his gold.

After three weeks of work, the workmen in the South West Palace unearthed a wall covered with elegant bas-reliefs of battle scenes and a siege. These were executed in an even finer style than those that Botta had found at Khorsabad. Layard glowed with excitement. Every detail of the siege was represented in astonishing detail. There were long-haired women begging for mercy, a warrior setting fire to the gates of the city, a wounded man falling from the walls. The charioteers and regal horses that pranced across the slabs were ample reward for the months of frustration and uncertainty Layard had experienced. He realized now that he had found a flourishing ancient civilization fully as important as that of the ancient Egyptians.

At this crucial moment, Layard received news that the suspicious and gold-hungry local ruler had withdrawn his permission for Layard to excavate at Nimrud. Instantly Layard galloped to Mosul and sought audience with the pasha. The pasha was evasive. "I have learned that your site is a Moslem burial ground," he said. "The law forbids anyone to dig into ancient burial places."

In vain, Layard argued that there were no signs of recent burials on the mounds. But the pasha, who feared the French vice-consul, was adamant. "Your life is more valuable than old stones. What grief would I suffer if anything happened to you?"

There was nothing Layard could do but return to Nimrud and make drawings of his discoveries. There he was confronted with a startling sight: his men were busy moving modern gravestones onto the site at the pasha's order! A local chief with whom he had become friendly was supervising. "We have destroyed more real tombs of the true believers in making sham ones than you could have defiled," bemoaned the chief.

The sympathetic locals let Layard do some quiet digging on the grounds as he was recording the sculptures already uncovered. These surreptitious excavations led to more exciting discoveries, including some gigantic winged bulls and nine-foot-high human figures. Wisely, Layard left these figures in the ground until his relations with the authorities improved.

Just as Layard had begun to despair over the possibility of any future progress, the sultan of Turkey abruptly replaced the pasha with a new governor who was not only pro-European, but a just and efficient administrator as well. The new pasha encouraged Layard to excavate and issued instructions that every assistance be given to him. This, since the local tribesmen had contemplated raiding the excavations, was a distinct advantage. Layard pressed on with the dig as fast as he dared, despite sporadic troublemaking by other Mosul bureaucrats who were convinced that golden treasure was slipping out of their grasp. In the intervals between making further discoveries of sculptures in the South West Palace, Layard carefully cultivated the local nomad chiefs to protect himself even further. It was a wise move, for rumors of treasure had spread fast and Layard's small huts on the mound were a tempting target.

One day as Layard was returning from a diplomatic visit to a local sheikh, he was overtaken by two horsemen riding at a frantic pace. "Hasten, oh Bey," they cried, "they have found

Nimrud himself." Layard spurred his horse to a gallop as the riders sped on to spread the word. He found his workmen clustered around an impromptu screen of cloaks and baskets that they gleefully lifted as he approached. An enormous human head sculptured in alabaster rose out of the ground to greet the astonished Layard. "The expression was calm, yet majestic," he wrote in his diary. The workmen were terrified when they first came across this astonishing apparition, half human, half bull, emerging from the ground like a strange monster. At least one man took to his heels, never to return. When he burst into the bazaar at Mosul, the town began to seethe with strange rumors of a new god and of heresy emerging from the earth. The pasha eventually summoned Layard with some concern and suggested he slow the pace of excavations for a while.

Meanwhile, Layard had found a second bull opposite the first, obviously the two sides of a great gate, and was quite content to take it easy for a time. Thousands of Arabs converged on the mound from miles around to stare at the strange bulls with human heads that guarded the gates of Nimrud. Layard himself admitted he spent hours contemplating "these mysterious emblems, and musing over their intent and history."

The discovery of the great head.

Layard knew that his discoveries would amaze the world and that much more lay under the ground. But he lacked the financial backing to finish the work. He had now been excavating for nearly six months at a total cost of eighty English pounds. To pass the time, he threw a huge spring party for all his Arab friends. The tribesmen flocked from all directions to the mound, which at that season was covered with green grass and wild flowers, to gaze at the great figures and dance to the sound of drums and pipes. Over five hundred Arabs joined Layard in dancing and feasting for five days. Although people in Constantinople considered such conduct "immoral," Layard was wise enough to know that the goodwill of the locals depended on such displays of hospitality. And, unlike many of his archaeological contemporaries, Layard never had any trouble with his laborers.

In May of 1846, Layard finally received a permit from the sultan of Turkey that allowed him to excavate freely wherever he wished. At last he was able to proceed with his discoveries. He drew on family funds to continue and tunneled deep into the North West Palace. The deeper he dug, the more exciting and perfect the sculptures became. The rooms of the palace were decorated with bas-reliefs of kings and horsemen, with servants and scenes of the chase. As each figure came to light, the Arabs would dart forward and either curse it or kiss it, depending on its sex. Slowly Layard began to saw away the bas-reliefs and to pack them in padded crates. They were then carried to the river on buffalo carts and floated downstream to Baghdad.

Layard himself worked frantically, making drawings of sculpture after sculpture in intense heat that often exceeded 110° in the shade. Gone were the spring flowers of a month before; the plain had shriveled under the relentless sun. Layard realized it would be necessary to move to the cool highlands for the summer months, but, before leaving, he paused to look at the human-headed bulls once more. "Their meaning was written upon them," he wrote. "They had awed and instructed races which flourished 3,000 years ago. Through the portals which they guarded, kings, priests and warriors had borne sacrifices to their altars, long before the wisdom of the East had penetrated to Greece." Now all that remained were desolate piles of rubbish covering a long-lost civilization.

When Layard returned to Mosul in October 1846, he found letters from the British Museum awaiting him. It had taken over the financing of the excavations from Canning, but on a scale so niggardly that Layard gasped with horror. The trustees of the Museum made no offer to send out an artist or other experts as the French had done. They had a bargain in Layard and they seemed to know it. He was working with minimal resources at a time when all the European nations were racing to dig up as much as they could in the Near East, many of them with abundant funds. It was sheer luck that the British Museum obtained as many finds as it did. With its backing, Layard was able to raise his labor force to one hundred thirty men. He built a mud-brick house for himself and barracks for his laborers on top of the Nimrud mound. He now headed a considerable party and was often sought out to mediate disputes among quarreling tribes.

By this time, tales of Layard's wisdom and bravery had spread all over Mesopotamia. He was almost an uncrowned ruler amonger the nomad tribes. His main labor problem was simple worker boredom. To relieve the monotonous routine, the workers devised strange forms of amusement. One day Layard found a group of horsemen driving a large flock of sheep from Nimrud village across the plain at full speed. To his great surprise, the men were emitting bloodcurdling war cries and flourishing swords. One of the men explained that they were bored with digging. "An Arab is an Arab," he cried. "We should be with our swords and mares in the desert. We are pretending that these sheep are taken from the enemy and we are driving them to our tents!"

The excavations continued to yield astonishing discoveries. Layard now realized he was dealing with two periods of occupation. The new finds included a black obelisk erected by Shalmaneser III, the son of Ashur-nasir-pal II, which was decorated with two hundred and ten lines of cuneiform. As the finds were dug out, they were packed for shipment downriver. One day, however, the valuable ropes and packing materials needed to prepare the shipments were mysteriously missing. Layard promptly called on the shiekh he felt sure was responsible for the theft, refused to believe his protestations of innocence, and boldly abducted him. By the time the uncooperative chief arrived at Nimrud, he was ready to confess. The packing materials were returned without delay and the shiekh released. There was no more trouble.

The black obelisk of Shalmaneser III in the British Museum.

Considerable numbers of visitors were now making their way to Nimrud. The news correspondent J. A. Longworth wrote a memorable account of the excavations for the London *Morning Post*. He wrote of the awe he felt at seeing the ancient kings and viziers who had emerged into daylight after centuries of darkness. Layard was soon a famous man as the public eagerly began to follow the progress of his excavations. Longworth encouraged him to think about writing a book on the digs.

While he contemplated this proposition, Henry decided to move the great human-headed bulls from their centuries-old resting place. He had no illusions about the difficulty of the task, for each weighed more than ten tons. After examining some bas-reliefs of Assyrians hauling huge statues with ropes and levers, he decided to follow their example. When everything was ready, Layard climbed to the summit of the mound,

Lowering the winged figure
onto its rollers.

high above the exposed bulls. The straining Arabs levered one of them on its side with innumerable ropes. As it tilted toward the waiting rollers, the ropes broke and the bull crashed onto the timbers. Layard, seized with fear, rushed to the pit. But, marvel of marvels, the bull was still intact. Overjoyed, the Arabs danced until dawn, gaily prancing back to work the next morning with no apparent ill effects. After further strenuous efforts, the bull reached the river safely and was levered onto a waiting raft, finally ready for its long journey to the British Museum.

The Nimrud excavations were closed down as Layard turned his attention to the secrets of the mound of Kuyunjik near Mosul, still believed to be the site of ancient Nineveh. The Frenchman Paul Botta had worked there for some time. Since his departure, the French consul had hired laborers to put down some haphazard pits. They had found nothing. But

Layard was now wise in the ways of Assyrian palace architects and, within a few days, he located a huge palace. Its long and narrow chambers rested on a large platform of mud brick, similar to those that Layard had contemplated for months at Nimrud. The bas-reliefs from this palace were larger than those from Nimrud, although of somewhat inferior workmanship. Winged bulls stood at the entrance to the palace. Layard had only enough time for a cursory examination of this remarkable structure before he hastened home to England, where fame and fortune awaited him. He was certain he had found ancient Nineveh itself and all of its ancient glories.

The once-unknown law student and family black sheep was now a national hero. During two years' arduous excavations, Layard had not only identified the sites of Nimrud and Nineveh, he had also excavated the remains of no less than eight Assyrian palaces. Hundreds of tons of sculpture from the excavations were already on their way to England when Layard himself arrived with his drawings and notebooks. At the age of thirty-one, Layard was well on the way to satisfying his ambitions. The sculptures caused a sensation when they were first displayed and Layard's public lectures were enthusiastically received. The idol of the moment, he was wined and dined. All these popular successes encouraged him to sit down at last and write a book about his discoveries.

Regrettably, Layard's popularity with the public did not seem to extend to the trustees of the British Museum. Although polite, they were rather indifferent to his sculptures and gave no sign of being willing to send him back for more excavations. So he departed, disgruntled, back to a post as an unpaid attaché at the British embassy in Constantinople.

No sooner had Layard arrived in Turkey than his *Nineveh and Its Remains* appeared in the bookstores. It took the public by storm. Layard had the gift of a vivid pen and *Nineveh* proved to be one of those books that every cultured person had to read, if only to say he or she had done so. The printer couldn't keep up with demand. It was a remarkable achievement, for Layard displayed a considerable academic talent and depth of knowledge, far more than might have been expected of a man with no formal training. The London *Times* described *Nineveh* as "the most extraordinary work of the present age." Yet its talented author was stuck in a foreign embassy without pay or work of importance.

This deplorable situation did not last long. Soon Layard was appointed as a paid attaché, then invited to head a new archaeological mission to Mesopotamia. The new expedition was more elaborate and included both an artist and a doctor. In September 1849, Layard and his party finally reached Mosul. His workmen greeted him rapturously; the very same horse was ready for him to ride. Layard felt as if he were coming home.

This time the excavations focused on the great Kuyunjik mounds of ancient Nineveh, which Layard had barely touched two years before. In his absence, the British vice-consul had kept a few men at work to prevent looting. A hundred men were now hired to look for more bas-reliefs. Layard then based himself at Nimrud, where excavations continued for most of the winter. The North West Palace continued to yield important finds, including some magnificent copper cauldrons. The excavators at Nineveh uncovered an ancient roadway, deeply rutted with chariot-wheel tracks.

Layard's main preoccupation, however, was with a pair of lions he had uncovered at Nimrud two years before. It was now time to move them to the British Museum. The night before the move took place, Layard and his companions rode to the mound to take a last look at the two guardians in their ancient resting place. Moonlight dramatically highlighted their fine heads. "It seems almost sacrilege to remove them," muttered Layard quietly. Later he wrote, "They had guarded the palace in its glory, and it was for them to watch over it in its ruins."

Both lions were heavier than the sculptures moved two years before. Layard shifted them by tilting each one over on soft mounds of earth which were slowly removed by quarrying underneath the recumbent animals. Just after the first lion was placed on a cart, the heavens opened and, in the heavy downpour, the cart's wheels bogged down in fresh mud. It took three hundred men and a week of hard labor to free the giant creature.

Meanwhile, the excavations at Nineveh were proceeding smoothly, so much so that Layard was able to slip away for a visit to new mounds in northern Mesopotamia. The country was in a state of considerable unrest and his workmen refused to dig in strange territory. Undaunted, Layard collected a mass of information about the nomads who lived in this remote area and had himself lowered over a steep cliff to read some

The great lion passes the mounds of Nimrud.

famous Assyrian inscriptions near Bavian. The huge bas-relief of King Sennacherib seemed to sway in the wind as Layard, suspended at the end of a fragile rope, tried to copy the inscriptions. He was highly relieved to return to solid ground.

After two months of exploration, Layard returned to Nineveh to find that a whole new series of bas-reliefs had come to light in the depths of the Kuyunjik mound. Among the discoveries was a great gate bounded by two human-headed bulls and some enormous, incomplete human figures. The sculptures had been damaged by fire and a collapsed wooden gate lay between them. Apparently, the city had suffered some awful calamity. On each side, the deep walls of the excavation seemed to crowd in on the huge gateway, more than fourteen feet wide. Layard was deeply moved by these silent figures. "Between them," he wrote, "Sennacherib and his hosts had gone forth in all their might and glory to the conquest of distant lands, and had returned rich with spoil and captives. . . . Through them, too, the Assyrian monarch had entered his capital in shame, after his last and fatal defeat."

The southeastern side of the same palace yielded another imposing entrance, lined by ten huge bulls and six colossal human figures. The bulls bore inscriptions that linked them to Sennacherib. The same palace contained a series of magnificent bas-reliefs that told the story of the king's siege of the city of Lachish. Layard immediately recalled the biblical siege of Lachish by Sennacherib's generals, which took place when Hezekiah refused to pay the Assyrians tribute. As more and more clues came to light, historians were able to link Layard's Assyrians and their palaces with the biblical kings who had tormented the Hebrews. The public interest generated by these and other Mesopotamian discoveries was immense, for Nineveh and other excavations were living proof that the biblical stories had, indeed, been based on historical fact.

By this time Layard's funds were again running low. Just as he was contemplating closing the digs, the workmen at Kuyunjik uncovered a room in the palace that contained a

Layard, at the end of a rope, records Sennacherib's inscription.

vast collection of terra-cotta tablets covered with minute cuneiform. Layard realized that this was a treasure house of vital information, probably the archives of the kings of Nineveh. Within a few weeks, he had filled six packing cases with tablets. There were still many more awaiting shipment. History has judged these archives to be one of the most important of all Layard's finds, for they were literally packed with vital information about the day-to-day concerns of the Assyrian kings.

The political situation was now so unsettled that it was obviously wise to scale down the excavations. Layard himself accompanied several rafts to Baghdad. En route, one of them was suddenly attacked by marauders, but the men put up a strong resistance and Layard and his precious cargo reached the city safety.

Although conditions were very difficult, Layard was allowed to do some digging into ancient Baghdad itself. All he found were masses of mud bricks, hardly worth the expense of excavation compared with Nimrud. What was the use of continuing, questioned Layard, "if Alexander the Great, after employing 10,000 men for ten months to clear away rubbish from the ruin, was obliged to give up the attempt?" So he contented himself by traveling around the neighboring country and observing the Marsh Arabs tunneling their way through dense reeds in their tiny wicker boats. He recalled the Kuyunjik sculptures with their scenes of Assyrian wars conducted in small wicker boats just like those he now observed. Truly, Mesopotamia had deep roots, extending back thousands of years into prehistory.

Layard at work in the archives at Kuyunjik.

Unfortunately the unhealthy swamps gave Layard a fever that seriously weakened him. By April 1851, he had had enough and made his way back to London. Although Layard himself felt he had achieved but little, his excavations, conducted with minimal financing, had resulted in quite extraordinary discoveries. "I had opened no less than seventy-one halls, chambers, and passages, whose walls, almost without exception, had been paneled with slabs of sculptured alabaster recording the wars, the triumphs, and the great deeds of the Assyrian kings," he wrote of Nineveh. "By a rough calculation about 9,880 feet, or nearly two miles, of bas-reliefs, with twenty-seven portals formed by colossal winged bulls and lion sphinxes, were uncovered in that part alone of the building explored during my researches."

Thousands of drawings, an entire Assyrian archive, and magnificent bas-reliefs and sculptures were on their way to the British Museum. But Layard was frustrated, for only a small portion of his discoveries could be shipped home. The rest were left to the mercy of looters and the local people. Had the British government been prepared to spend more, the

Drawing of warriors hunting
a lion.

discoveries sent to England would have been even more spectacular and much more could have been saved for posterity.
Nevertheless, the clay tablets from Nineveh alone were
sufficient to lay the foundations for the modern study of
Assyriology.

Henry Layard received a hero's reception in London. It was
the year of the 1851 Great Exhibition, a symbol of Britain's
emerging preeminence in the world of industry, trade, art, and
culture. He was a man of the hour, feted everywhere and
welcomed in the homes of the great and famous. The only
people who did not seem to approve were the trustees of the
British Museum, with whom Layard argued passionately
about his finds and the future of the excavations. He consid-

ered the authorities niggardly and shortsighted. They, in turn, distrusted their maverick former employee and his enormous popularity.

The public adored Layard. Within two years, *Nineveh and Babylon* followed Layard's earlier book as a best-seller. Everyone read it and all the reviews were favorable. A large folio of drawings of bas-reliefs from Nineveh was published at the same time and is now a rare collector's item. Layard had the gift of literary eloquence, an ability to write moving and evocative descriptions of excavations and personalities, crises and great discoveries. He ranks among the most remarkable of all early archaeologists, not only because of his discovery of the Assyrians and Sumerians, but also because he was able to make these ancient peoples accessible to the general public through his writings and drawings. Londoners could now imagine Assyrian kings strutting to war or sitting in judgment over their subjects. Further, they could gaze on drawings of Ashur-pani-bal as he went hunting or of Assyrian boatmen crossing the Tigris in wicker and bitumen boats. A shadowy biblical civilization had suddenly come alive through archaeological excavation. Perhaps Layard's greatest achievement was that he laid the foundations for the great excavations that were to take place in Mesopotamia later in the nineteenth and twentieth centuries, excavations that could only build on his astonishing finds.

*Nineveh and Babylon* was Layard's last archaeological book. In 1852, powerful friends persuaded him to pursue a political career, a profession in which he was far from comfortable. Some time later, Henry became a much-admired diplomat, serving in both Constantinople and Madrid with great distinction. He never returned to the brooding mounds of Nimrud or Nineveh and seems to have taken little interest in archaeology. His life was now consumed by great affairs and by an ambition to succeed in other, less academic spheres. Still, by the time Layard died in 1894, he ranked among the archaeological immortals. He lent an eloquence to archaeology that has yet to be surpassed. In his own memorable words: "The great tide of civilization has long since ebbed, leaving these scattered wrecks on the solitary shore. Are those waters to flow again, bearing back the seeds of knowledge and of wealth that they have wafted to the West? We wanderers were seeking what they had left behind, as children gather up the colored shells on the deserted sands."

CHAPTER

# 6

# HEINRICH SCHLIEMANN AND ANCIENT TROY

"WHAT MEMORIES THE NAME OF TROY BRINGS BACK! The miseries we Achaeans put up with there! Raid after raid across the misty seas in search of plunder at Achilles' beck and call, fight after fight round the very walls of royal Priam's town. . . ." The occasion was a royal banquet. Veteran King Nestor was entertaining noble visitors from the island of Ithaca off the west coast of Greece. Inevitably, the conversation turned to fresh memories of bloody campaigns, to raids and wars fought over the lush plains of distant Troy, hundreds of miles to the north. Nestor himself had played a prominent part in the wars. His memories and those of thousands of his fellow soldiers were soon enshrined in folklore and song, passed on from generation to generation of traveling minstrels who would recount these much-loved stories the length and breadth of Greece, in royal palaces and remote farmsteads alike.

Hundreds of years later, in the tenth century B.C., the epics were written down for the first time. The long poems that made up the story were grouped into two great works: the

*Iliad* and the *Odyssey.* Popular legend ascribes the authorship of these magnificent works to the poet Homer. But whether he was a single individual or a group of poets is unknown. Homer's stirring tales of the long siege of Troy, of heroic deeds by brave chieftains, and of divine plots and human frailty became a cornerstone of classical Greek literature.

The *Iliad* tells the story of the final stages of the ten-year siege of the ancient city of Troy, situated in northwest Turkey. Many years before, the Trojan prince Hector had abducted and himself married the lovely Helen, wife of King Menelaus of Sparta. Menelaus and his brother Agamemnon, intent on recovering Helen, formed a holy alliance of dozens of Greek chieftains to wage war against King Priam's Troy. The *Iliad* opens with the Greek camp in turmoil. The mighty hero Achilles, a warrior essential to the Greek cause, is sulking in his tent after a quarrel with Agamemnon over a slave girl. As long as Achilles refuses to fight, the Greek forces are seriously weakened. The dramatic stanzas of the *Iliad* relate how the gods intervene in the war and recount the battles that bring the Trojans to the fences of the Greek camp. Achilles finally emerges from isolation when his friend and lover Patroclus is killed by Hector. To avenge his friend, Achilles slays Hector in single combat. The book concludes with the funeral of Hector, some time before the fall of Troy.

The blow-by-blow battle descriptions of the *Iliad* are richly embroidered with detailed accounts of weapons, customs, ornaments, and dress—all the panoply of a fully developed civilization. The sequel to the *Iliad,* the *Odyssey,* begins some ten years after the fall of Troy. All the heroes have returned home, with the exception of Odysseus of Ithaca, a crafty and skillful warrior-politician who has inadvertently angered Poseidon, the god of the sea. It was Odysseus who invented the brilliant stratagem of the wooden horse, the means used to smuggle Greek soldiers into Troy. As soon as the Trojans had dragged the massive horse into their city, Greek soldiers emerged from its cavernous depths and opened

Locations and sites mentioned
in Chapters 6 and 7.

the gates to their comrades waiting outside. Troy fell soon thereafter. When the *Odyssey* opens, we learn that Odysseus is now condemned to wander aimlessly on the oceans of the world, after all his companions have perished. Odysseus' final adventures and his secret return to his beloved Ithaca are related in the *Odyssey.* Once in Ithaca, Odysseus kills off the suitors who are courting his faithful wife and, of course, lives happily ever after.

The *Iliad* and the *Odyssey* contain all the crowd-pleasing ingredients a good epic needs—bloodshed, scheming gods, lust, sex, high living, and, best of all, a wonderful narrative. It's not surprising that, a century ago, both volumes could be found on most educated people's bookshelves. But were the epics true? Had the Trojan War ever taken place? Did Agamemnon, Achilles, and Odysseus ever exist? Was there once an actual city of Troy? These questions intrigued everyone who read the poems. Although expert scholarly opinion leaned toward the belief that Homer himself probably had not existed and that the epics were compiled by the combined efforts of many bards, some classicists fervently believed that Troy was a real place and that Homer had been writing true history.

Now we turn to the story of Heinrich Schliemann, a man so firmly convinced of the existence of ancient Troy that he set out to find it.

Heinrich Schliemann ranks as one of the most extraordinary archaeologists of all time. He was born in 1822, the son of a Protestant minister in a rural parish in northern Germany. As he later wrote, even as a child he possessed "a natural disposition for the mysterious and marvellous." The village of Neu Buckow abounded in legends and folktales that Ernest Schliemann often told his children. The Schliemann house itself was haunted: a ghostly maiden would rise each night from a small pond nearby. Then, of course, there was the terrible robber baron buried in the churchyard. He had killed a cowherd by frying him alive in an iron pan. When cornered,

Henning Bradenkirl had committed suicide. For centuries, the story went, his left leg, clothed in a black silk stocking, had protruded from his grave. The young Schliemann, when not planning where next to dig for buried treasure, spent hours contemplating the tombstone.

Ernest Schliemann was deeply interested in the classics. He was fond of a good story, especially the tale of the Greeks and the Trojans, which he often repeated round the fire on a winter's evening. His excitement rubbed off on his son, and young Heinrich became a champion of the Trojan cause. When the pastor gave his eight-year-old son a copy of Georg Ludwig Jerrer's *Illustrated History of the World*, Heinrich pored over the illustrations for hours, returning repeatedly to a picture of Troy in flames.

"Father," he cried, "Jenner must have seen Troy, otherwise he could not have represented it here."

"My son, that is merely a fanciful picture," replied his father.

"Father, if such walls once existed, they cannot possibly have been completely destroyed—vast ruins of them must remain," insisted Heinrich. Ernest Schliemann quietly disagreed, but Heinrich was persistent.

"One day, when I grow up, I will find Troy and dig it up." Thirty-nine years later, Heinrich Schliemann found the site of Homeric Troy.

The astonishing story of how Heinrich Schliemann became a world-famous archaeologist, as well as a millionaire, is as remarkable as his discovery of Troy. The Schliemanns were so poor that Heinrich was apprenticed to a grocer at the age of fourteen and was therefore unable to complete his schooling. For five and a half long years, Schliemann sold provisions from five o'clock in the morning to eleven at night. Grinding poverty and long work hours slowly sapped his once-strong desire to continue his learning. One day, however, a drunken miller shopping in the store absentmindedly began to recite a hundred lines of Homer in the original Greek. Schliemann

leaned on the counter entranced and, when the miller came to the end of his recital, bought three whiskies for the drunkard so he would repeat the lines.

Things went from bad to worse when a chest ailment cost Heinrich his job. In 1841, he wandered to Hamburg, where, in desperation, he boarded ship for Venezuela, selling his only coat to buy a blanket. En route, the *Dorothea* was wrecked in a North Sea gale off the island of Texel. Schliemann and his companions were lucky to reach shore alive. Destitute, frozen with winter cold, ever hungry, he obtained a humble clerking position in Amsterdam. The hours, at least, were not as savage as those at the grocer's. With astonishing single-mindedness, Schliemann set out to educate himself, setting aside half his annual salary of sixty-four dollars for self-improvement. First, he learned to write properly. Then he settled down to learn English and French. He accomplished his objective in a year by the simple expedient of reading the original languages and learning as much as he could by heart. An extraordinary memory and ability for languages encouraged him to tackle Dutch, Spanish, Italian, and Portuguese next: he mastered each in six weeks.

Schliemann's luck was now turning. His original employers were unimpressed by his new learning, but he was hired by the Schröder brothers, prosperous merchants with extensive connections in the indigo trade with Russia. Schliemann promptly sat down to learn Russian, a formidable task, for there were no qualified teachers in Amsterdam. He learned the Russian alphabet from a dictionary and recited the adventures of the Greek hero Telemachus aloud in Russian. His loud discourses could be heard clearly through the partitions of his cheap lodging house, so he was obliged to move. Desperate for a teacher, Schliemann hired a poor Jew to listen to him for two hours a day. His visitor earned four francs a week for suffering through hours of unintelligible recitation. But, within six weeks, Schliemann was conversing fluently with Russian merchants at the indigo auctions.

In 1846 the Schröders sent Schliemann to St. Petersburg to act as their firm's Russian agent, a task he fulfilled brilliantly. Within a year he had set himself up as an independent, wholesale indigo merchant. He was now applying himself to money-making with the same intensity he had exhibited in learning languages. His fluency in Russian and other European languages enabled him to conduct business all over the Continent. In 1850 he ranged even further afield, sailing to California at the height of the gold rush. Schliemann promptly set up a banking agency in Sacramento and accumulated a substantial fortune. Returning to St. Petersburg two years later, he married, had three children, and made another fortune in war materials during the Crimean War. He took time off to learn Swedish and Polish and, later, mastered Latin and Arabic during an extensive tour of the Near East that took him to Petra and the Holy Land.

Classical Greek was next on the list. He began by mastering the modern language in six weeks. Then he spent two years on classical Greek, learning it ungrammatically as if it were a living language. The *Iliad* and *Odyssey* now came alive, as Schliemann learned their mellifluous lines by heart. His obsession with Troy sharpened with time. "In the midst of the bustle of business," he later wrote, "I never forgot Troy, or the agreement I had made with my father to excavate it." In 1863, a fluent classical scholar with years of preparation behind him, Heinrich Schliemann retired from business at the age of forty-one. The rest of his life was to be devoted to Troy and archaeology. "I loved money indeed," he once remarked, "but solely as a means of realizing this real idea of my life."

While most people would have dashed off to Greece at once, Schliemann took the long way around. He set off on a world tour that took him to Carthage, Egypt, India, China, Japan, and finally North America, where he stopped to visit friends in California before settling in Paris to study archaeology seriously. All the energy that Schliemann had devoted to languages and indigo was now diverted to the search for Troy.

In 1868 he set out on a leisured inspection of ancient Greece, the first time he had set foot in the land of Homer.

The energetic newcomer was an archaeologist with a difference. He believed with a fanatical intensity in the absolute truth of the *Iliad* and *Odyssey*. When the *Iliad* told how Achilles had chased the doomed Hector three times around the walls of Troy, Schliemann had no doubt that the chase was historical fact. The Troy described by Homer was a substantial fortress, with "wide streets" and "lofty towers." The walled town possessed at least two named gates. There was a marketplace and a great palace. If Homer's description is at all accurate, there were perhaps as many as 50,000 people living in or near the fortress. The description of Troy in the *Iliad* is by no means detailed, but Schliemann believed that every bit of information in the Homeric poems could be discerned in the ground.

This was not the first time that Schliemann had flown in the face of established opinion. Most classical scholars were firmly convinced that the *Iliad* was nothing more than the product of poetic imagination. Homer himself was probably a fictional character, the Trojan War part of a world that never existed. The Greece of Homer was depicted as a sophisticated land. But, pointed out the learned classicists of Schliemann's day, the earliest Greeks to appear in recorded history were an unsophisticated, poverty-stricken people. How, therefore, could one square the Homeric account with historical fact? They concluded it was useless to look for the actual site of the Homeric city. But Heinrich Schliemann was a dreamer, a romantic at heart who was so wrapped up in the *Iliad* that he was certain the site of ancient Troy could be found. This faith, nurtured from childhood, brought him archaeological immortality.

Schliemann began his search for the lost city far to the north of Greece, near the mouth of the Dardanelles. He reached the Troad—the territory surrounding ancient Troy—by ship, then hired a Greek guide to take him out to the

Trojan plain on horseback. Riding bareback in his smart business suit, Heinrich Schliemann gazed for the first time on the land of his childhood dreams. The problem was to locate the ancient city.

Henrich Schliemann was not the first person to look for Troy. A few explorers had ridden out to the village of Bunarbashi at the south edge of the plain, famous for its springs and overshadowed by the rocky heights of Bali Dagh. Some people thought this was the site of Troy, although Austrian excavations in 1864 had yielded nothing. Schliemann was unconvinced. Instead of a cold and a hot spring rising by the banks of the river Scamander, as Homer had described, he found forty cold springs. Furthermore, Bunarbashi lay eight miles from the sea, whereas the Greeks had obviously camped far closer to Troy than that, for they traveled to and from the besieged city several times a day from their coastal camp. Hasty test excavations near the springs and on the citadel confirmed his hunch. Bunarbashi was not Troy.

Next Schliemann wandered through the hills on either side of the Trojan plain, looking for old town sites. The search was fruitless until he came to a hill named Hissarlik, three miles from the Hellespont. At this point Schliemann was introduced to Frank Calvert, the United States vice-consul at the Dardanelles. Calvert not only owned half the mound, he had also dug into his property in search of Troy. Calvert and Schliemann soon became fast friends, partly because each had made a fortune out of the Crimean War. The consul, however, was in deep trouble with the British, who had accused him of profiteering and condemned him to death in his absence. So, unable to return to England, Calvert lived in great style in the Troad, devoting some of his leisure to archaeology. He had been convinced for some time that Hissarlik was Troy. Most exciting of all, his excavations had revealed traces of stone walls deep in the Hissarlik mound.

Schliemann wandered over the deserted mound, looking for confirmation of Calvert's theory. The topography was flat enough for substantial buildings, the town mound small enough for Achilles to have run around it thrice without undue effort. There were no springs, but, as Calvert pointed out, these could have dried up since the town was abandoned.

Impetuously, Schliemann rode down to the sea and reconstructed the battles that raged between the city and the Hellespont. Homer in hand, he marshalled his arguments in favor of Hissarlik, dismissed the speculations of his contemporaries as irrelevant, and decided to dig into the mound.

It was not until two years later that Schliemann returned to Hissarlik. His marriage had been a complete failure and, with characteristic efficiency, he visited the United States and obtained a quick divorce in Indianapolis. In April 1870, he returned to Hissarlik, sank a trial trench at the northwestern corner of the mound, and discovered the remains of a huge stone wall sixteen feet below the surface. Nothing more could be done until he had received a permit from the sultan of Turkey allowing him to excavate on a large scale.

Schliemann was now a man possessed, perhaps because he realized he was on the threshold of immortality. Now totally in love with Greece, he sought a Greek wife to help in his work. Old Greek friends, among them his language tutor, Father Theokletos Vimpos, were importuned. Soon he was interviewing likely candidates, finally settling on the young and beautiful Sophia Engastromenos, the daughter of a shopkeeper. She was seventeen, Schliemann forty-seven, yet the marriage was a success. Sophia was set to work to learn the classics and several languages. Together they waited impatiently for the sultan's permit. To Schliemann, his lovely wife may have been the living embodiment of the lovely Helen of Troy, so often in his dreams.

The Sublime Porte in Constantinople was not to be hurried. Schliemann's permit finally came through in September 1871, leaving barely enough time for any excavations that summer. Immediately the Schliemanns set out for Hissarlik, only to encounter more frustrating delays at the hands of local of-

Sophia Schliemann wearing
part of the treasure of Priam.

ficials who insisted on property maps and other minor formalities. Finally, on October 11, 1871, the excavations began.

Conditions were far from comfortable. The only accommodations were in the village of Chilak, over a mile from Hissarlik itself. But bedbugs, poor food, and the ever-present threat of malaria could not deter Schliemann from the task ahead. Eighty laborers recruited from nearby villages set to work with pickaxes and wooden shovels at the northern side of the mound. Six weeks later, with the onset of winter, excavations had to be halted. Even with inadequate tools, the diggers had quarried a large trench thirty-three feet into the mound. Quarrying was an apt description for the digging. Schliemann let nothing stand in his way; stone walls and foundations were ripped out piecemeal. Thousands of pottery fragments, stone implements, and grinders were excavated in the lower levels of the trench. A jumble of stone blocks, perhaps signs of a great city, came from the bottom of the huge cutting.

The 1871 excavations were just the beginning. In March of the following year the Schliemanns were back at Hissarlik with an enormous arsenal of shovels, pickaxes, and wheelbarrows. They built themselves an excavation house on top of the mound. Three foremen and a surveyor were retained to supervise a labor force of a hundred men that grew at times to one hundred and fifty. Large teams were deployed to uncover the successive layers of the mound like layers of a cake. At times the weather was so cold that the Schliemanns shivered in their plank-built house as the wind whistled through the walls and the temperature fell to 23 degrees. Even pots of water near the fire froze solid. Although they were able to keep warm in the trenches by day, the evenings were chilly indeed. "We had nothing to keep us warm except our enthusiasm for the great task of discovering Troy," recalled Schliemann later. But their efforts were richly rewarded.

As the excavations penetrated ever deeper into the mound and finally reached bedrock at a depth of over forty-five feet, a fascinating picture of an evolving settlement slowly unfolded.

Schliemann had started by assuming that King Priam's city was the original town on the hill. Therefore, its ruins were bound to lie at the base of the mound, below the later occupation levels. With characteristic thoroughness, he marshalled his labor force and started to cut a huge trench some 130 feet across through the mound from north to south. Even with modern equipment this would have been a stupendous undertaking. Eventually Schliemann was obliged to scale down his operations, but not before more than 325,000 cubic yards of earth had been excavated from the mound.

Schliemann's great trench through Hissarlik, showing exposed "Trojan buildings." Some people believe that his excavation methods were influenced by the digging of the Suez Canal.

The results of the excavation were astonishing. City after city had flourished at Hissarlik, each succeeding series of buildings erected on the foundations of earlier settlements. The debris did not form a single homogeneous mass, but had accumulated in superimposed layers that represented different chronological periods. By the end of the 1873 season, Heinrich Schliemann had recognized no less than seven cities of Troy. By 1890, he had added two more. The earliest city was but a crude and tiny settlement, far too poor to have been Homer's Troy. So Schliemann revised his thinking and proudly announced that the third city from the base was Priam's Troy. What clinched his verdict was the existence of a dense layer of burnt masonry and ash that contained "many treasures" of copper, gold, and silver. This city had been burnt down. Obviously, said Schliemann, this was the Troy that was destroyed by the Greeks at the end of the war. Cities found higher in the mound were obviously more recent.

At this stage in his mercurial career, no one could call Schliemann an expert archaeologist. But archaeology was hardly a science at all in the 1870s. The average excavation was little more than a glorified treasure hunt. People were still looting the ancient tombs of Egypt wholesale, with little concern for conservation or accurate chronology. The Troy excavations were started on a large scale without any firm plan beyond a copy of the *Iliad* and some indications from the surface of the mound as to where digging might be most richly rewarded.

The sheer scale of the Schliemann operation is mind boggling. His methods were drastic, direct, and costly. The cost was both monetary—the best equipment and a team of workmen that rarely numbered below a hundred—and, re-

Schliemann's trench near the Great Tower of Ilium. His excavation houses can be seen on top of the mound.

grettably, archaeological. The narrative account of the excavation reads like an army campaign. "The great extent of my excavations rendered it necessary for me to work with no less than 120 laborers," Schliemann notes. A few pages later he blithely admits, "I was forced to demolish many interesting ruins in the upper strata." Temples, fortification walls, burials, and vast quantities of occupation debris were shoveled aside in the search for Homer's city. Nothing was allowed to stand in the way of Schliemann's objective. Without any archaeological experience at all, the Schliemanns tackled the large-scale excavation of an ancient mound with no vast stone structures to guide them. Schliemann was, however, quick to learn. He observed the complex layers of the mound and soon sought out experts to help study the finds.

By June of 1873, the pace of excavation and the difficult living conditions were beginning to take their toll. The Schliemanns had nearly perished in a fire that threatened to engulf the base house, the constant stiff north wind blew dust into their food, and, most nights, they were kept awake by hundreds of shrieking owls and millions of croaking frogs in the surrounding marshes. It was time to call a halt. Besides, the material uncovered so far needed to be studied before excavations could proceed profitably.

As this stage of the excavations drew to a close, efforts were concentrated on the third city. One hot morning, the diggers were working twenty-eight feet below the surface when Schliemann suddenly stiffened. Gold glittered in the morning sunlight, gleaming from a pile of loose earth. The workmen had not yet spotted it. Schliemann rushed for his wife and told her to send the men home for the day on some pretext. She demurred. "Pretend it's my birthday," he whispered. As soon as the delighted men had left, Schliemann jumped down in the trench with a large knife. Oblivious to the huge stone blocks that teetered above him, he cut into the soft earth. Sophia stood close by with her shawl at the ready. Quickly Heinrich shoveled the priceless finds and the earth containing

The treasure of Priam: Schliemann's own illustration of the hoard. The treasure was destroyed in World War II.

them into the red shawl. No one witnessed this climactic moment of the Troy excavations. "The sight of so many immeasurably priceless objects made me foolhardy," wrote Schliemann later. "I did not think of the hazard."

The laden shawl was soon carried safely to the base house where, breathlessly, the Schliemanns spread their treasure on a rough wooden table. There were gold pendants and earrings, ivory and buttons, chains and brooches. Inspired and ebullient, Heinrich Schliemann decked his twenty-year-old wife in part of the golden treasure. "You are truly Helen of Troy," he cried. Schliemann never doubted that he had found King Priam's own treasure. "Apparently someone in Priam's family had hastily packed away the treasure in boxes," he reported. "Then, on the walls, this person met his death either directly at enemy hands or when struck by a flying missile. The treasure lay where it fell, and presently was buried under five or six feet of ashes and stones from the adjacent royal house."

At this crowning moment in his career, Schliemann was downright unscrupulous. One condition of his permit was that he had to give half of his finds to the Turkish government and, of course, the treasure came under this condition. But, determined that European scholars should have access to the treasure, Schliemann quietly smuggled it out of Turkey with the help of his wife's relatives. The priceless gold pieces were hidden in a garden shed in Greece.

For days the Schliemanns quietly studied and cataloged the find, bringing the collection to their house in small lots. Every piece was photographed separately. Then, on a feast day when the streets were quiet, the whole collection was brought to the laboratory. The photographer took portraits of the treasure and of Sophia decked out in the ornaments of prehistoric Troy. Then, six months before his book on Troy was to appear, Schliemann wrote a full account of the discovery of the treasure for a German newspaper. In the article he freely admitted that the treasure had been smuggled out of Turkey. The gold pieces, he announced, would be housed in a new museum to be built in Athens at his expense.

The Turks were incensed by the announcement. Rumors of smuggling by the Schliemanns had already been circulating in Constantinople. Official protests were lodged in Athens. The Greeks, anxious to avoid a confrontation with the sultan, rejected the offer of the museum and refused Schliemann the permit to dig at Mycenae that he had requested. Local newspapers accused Schliemann of forging the treasure. Heinrich and Sophia were ostracized by their friends.

The furor was at its height when Schliemann's *Trojan Antiquities* appeared in January 1874. It was a handsome and comprehensive narrative of the Schliemann excavations. *Tro-*

*jan Antiquities* received mixed reviews. The British were enthusiastic, but the German scholars, who refused to believe that Troy existed, murdered the book. Schliemann was castigated for being unscientific and for pulling down priceless temples. Some reviewers openly theorized that Priam's treasure had come from the bazaars of Constantinople. But the general public was captivated.

Despite all the protests of conservative scholars, Heinrich Schliemann was now an international celebrity, accepted as a first-rate archaeologist in his own right. The destitute grocer's clerk was the darling of Europe, his every move observed and duly reported in the press. Some men would have been content to rest on their laurels, but not Schliemann.

The scandal over the treasure dragged on for months. Schliemann wrote to Constantinople offering to pay all the costs of the new excavation season at Troy. He received no reply. Then the Turks resorted to the courts, claiming half the treasure. After prolonged maneuvering, the court fined Schliemann two thousand dollars. He promptly offered the Turks eight thousand as well as the fine, an offer that was only accepted in April 1875. Needless to say, his future relations with Constantinople were never easy.

For some time now, Schliemann had had his restless eyes on Mycenae, anxious to dig into the palace and burial place of the legendary King Agamemnon, leader of the Greeks at Troy. Mycenae lies at the north corner of the plain of Argos, a fertile area famous in Homer's time for its horses. The giant stone blocks of its vast fortifications had long been a familiar landmark. In A.D. 170 the Greek traveler Pausanias visited Mycenae. He marvelled at the massive walls and the entrance gate with its carved lions. Nearby lay great subterranean structures that, wrote Pausanias, were the treasuries of the kings. Agamemnon and his royal companions reposed in royal tombs inside the walls of the citadel.

Agamemnon had inherited the wealthy kingship of Mycenae from descendants of Atreus. Such was the prestige of

Mycenae that Agamemnon was the logical person to lead the expeditionary force against Troy. His prolonged absence of a decade left his queen Clytemnestra alone at Mycenae. She was promptly seduced by Aegisthus, son of one of Agamemnon's nephews. Aegisthus now plotted to inherit Agamemnon's kingdom. When warned of the king's return, the queen and her seducer invited the returning warriors to a great banquet. Agamemnon and his companions were slaughtered at the table. Aegisthus survived as ruler for seven years before Orestes, Agamemnon's son, killed the usurper and the queen as well.

Schliemann had such faith in Homer that he believed that Agamemnon's bones actually lay inside Mycenae's walls. Once again he put his trust in ancient writers rather than modern authorities. Accepting Homer as historical truth and Pausanias as his guide, Schliemann applied for a permit to dig at Mycenae. After long delays, the Greeks agreed. The famous husband and wife team settled in at Mycenae for a large dig in 1876.

No one expected Heinrich Schliemann to repeat his spectacular Trojan discoveries; he had been too successful already. Surely, for once, he would fail. Two years before, the Schliemanns had sunk some discreet trial pits to see where the deepest deposits lay. They had noted that the thickest accumulations of occupation deposit lay inside the citadel, where the inhabitants withdrew in time of war. All Schliemann's archaeological instincts, well developed by many months of digging at Troy, sent him inside the citadel.

While the experts shook their heads, sixty-three men were put to work in three parties. Twelve men began to clear the lion gate; forty-three dug a huge trench immediately to the southwest of the entrance inside the walls; a further eight cleared a "treasury" near the gate, whose entrance was partly exposed.

The excavations inside the gate soon turned up thousands of painted vase fragments. Then a curious, circular structure,

The Lion Gate at Mycenae (see photo at left).

General view of Schliemann's
excavations at Mycenae.

built of a double row of stone slabs set on edge, came to light.
Nearby were nine "tombstones," several of them decorated
with armed charioteers. Immediately Schliemann remembered the Greek playright Euripides' description of Agamemnon's grave. According to Euripides, the circle of stones was
an assembly place for the elders, built in such a way that the
heroes' graves were in the middle of the circular arena. With
an astonishing and highly unscientific faith in his ancient
sources, and even before he had dug below the grave stones,
Schliemann announced that he had discovered the burial
places of Agamemnon and Atreus.

The first grave was uncovered four months almost to the day after the excavations began. For days the Schliemanns labored inside the stone circle. They found five graves containing fifteen bodies lying in soft earth and ash. Sophia spent hours on her knees separating delicate ornaments from the soil. The fifteen skeletons were literally smothered in gold ornaments, the greatest archaeological treasure ever found until the discovery of the tomb of Tut-ankh-Amun in 1921. The wealth and variety of the Mycenae ornaments far exceeded that of the treasure of Priam. Delicately hammered embossed plates of gold, delicate crowns and vessels, and dozens of small ornaments were found in the graves. Several gold death masks with clipped beards and mustaches came to light. Schliemann and the world were excited. In a torrent of articles and books, the discoveries at Mycenae were revealed to a delighted public. Almost daily, the London *Times* carried detailed descriptions of the Mycenae excavations. When the graves were finally unearthed, Schliemann promptly telegraphed to the King of Greece: "It is with great pleasure that I announce to Your Majesty that I have found the graves which, according to tradition, are those of Agamemnon, Cassandra, Eurymedon, and their companions."

And the public believed him. Even those who scoffed at his finds, who thought them to be Byzantine or the work of "Orientals," were forced to take Schliemann's researches seriously, even if he was apt to jump to sensational and controversial conclusions. The excavations did far more than bring Homer to life: they brought prehistoric archaeology into the public consciousness to a degree never before deemed possible. The entire world vicariously participated in the Mycenae excavations; two ruling monarchs and a prime minister were kept posted on every phase of the dig. The king of Brazil himself visited the dig and dined in the treasury of Atreus. "I want the world to experience our excavations," Schliemann once said. "If I find I am wrong, I admit it, so people can see me thinking." He succeeded brilliantly.

There seemed to be no end to the wonders from the Mycenaean graves. One of the bodies was so well preserved that some of the nonskeletal parts still remained. The body was squashed almost flat and much compressed, but the gold ornaments were perfectly preserved. News of this unusual discovery spread like wildfire. From miles around the local people arrived to gaze on the long-dead warrior. Schliemann was at a loss to know how to preserve the mummified remains before they crumbled to dust. He commissioned an oil painting of the grave while a local druggist mixed some alcohol and gum arabic to harden the body. After great efforts,

Gold mask of the bearded
man from Shaft Grave V at
Mycenae.

the body was lifted out in a block of soil. The laborers insisted
on carrying the precious find to the storeroom on their backs,
followed by a large crowd. So much gold came from the excavations that the Schliemanns lit watch fires at Mycenae to
prevent looting and warm the soldiers who were guarding the
excavations around the clock. These were, Schliemann was
fond of saying, the first watch fires to be seen at Mycenae
since Agamemnon's time.

Schliemann completed his account of the dig within a few
months of returning to Athens. *Mycenae* was little more than
a diary of the excavations and an essay on Schliemann's conviction that he had found the bodies of Homer's heroes. His
claims were immediately disputed by German experts. They
felt that the burials—and, indeed, both Mycenae and Troy—

predated the time of the Homeric epics. We now know that Schliemann had, in fact, discovered the prehistoric Mycenaean civilization, a society that provided many of the ingredients which later went to make up classical Greek culture. The magnificence of the Greek Bronze Age was revealed to a delighted world for the first time.

It would be years before the true significance of Heinrich Schliemann's discoveries at Mycenae was fully understood. In the meantime, the world was ready to admire and praise his achievements. British Prime Minister William Gladstone ac-

Sophia Schliemann poses in front of the beehive tomb which she excavated at Mycenae.

cepted with alacrity an invitation to write a preface to *Mycenae,* in which he spoke of his "strangely bewildered admiration" at the discoveries. It never occurred to Schliemann that his theories might be wrong. One has the impression that he felt he was God's messenger, sent to bring the truth about Homer to a waiting world.

Heinrich Schliemann himself remains a somewhat enigmatic figure. He has been characterized as a megalomaniac who was, perhaps, also a mythomaniac. His admirers called him a genius, his enemies, a lunatic. But behind the facade of ruthless, single-minded dedication was a kindly and thoughtful man. His second marriage was apparently a real love match. Sophia helped him become a warm and loving person with a lively enthusiasm for life and for people. The Schliemanns' house in Athens was a comfortable, hospitable place. Guests were greeted by the great man himself and were entertained by his gentle and gracious wife. It was only when the talk turned to archaeology that Schliemann's fanaticism would bubble to the surface. A glint would come to his eye as he spoke of Troy or of long days at Mycenae under the hot sun. The trivia of archaeology and the controversies of Homeric scholarship could easily engross him for hours.

Hissarlik now beckoned, for the way had been cleared for further excavations just before the Mycenae dig began. A short 1876 season had been unproductive. The local governor was highly uncooperative, delaying Schliemann on flimsy grounds for two months and then grudgingly allowing him to start work under the eagle eye of one Izzet Effendi. Izzet was so obstructive that Schliemann returned to Athens in despair. In disgust he wrote a furious letter to the editor of the London *Times* in which he denounced Ibrahim Pasha's conduct before, as he aptly put it, "the tribunal of the civilized world." The Constantinople papers picked up the story and the governor was abruptly transferred to another province.

The two eventful years of Mycenae turned Schliemann into a respected elder statesman of archaeology. Other scientists were now glad to work with him. The 1878 Hissarlik excavations started in bitterly cold March weather. "It was only possible to keep warm by exercise in the trenches," wrote Schliemann in his diary. But the chill did not prevent him bathing in the sea every morning before dawn, returning to Hissarlik on horseback before the day's work started. This, he claimed, prevented him from catching cold. He was now working with the great German scholar Rudolf Virchow, who studied the geology of the Trojan plain and the mound. His awesome scholarly knowledge helped Schliemann greatly as he struggled with the details of the excavations. Virchow, too, was responsible for Schliemann's giving Priam's treasure to Berlin after his plans for a museum in Athens were aborted. The treasure vanished during Hitler's war.

In later seasons, from 1882 to 1890, Wilhelm Dörpfeld, an archaeologist and architect trained in the German excavations at Olympia, worked alongside the master. Dörpfeld was of a new generation of archaeologists who had grown up with the pioneers and were now improving on their methods. Together the two men decided initially that the so-called third city was, in fact, part of the second city. Toward the very end of their work, Dörpfeld produced irrefutable evidence that the sixth city coincided most closely with the Homeric settlement, a conclusion that Schliemann was planning to test with a huge campaign of excavations in 1891.

Schliemann has often been criticized for his large-scale excavation methods. To reach his ultimate objective, he would not hesitate to plough through buildings and delicate strata. In his defense, it should be noted that he was a pioneer in mound excavation. Dörpfeld refined Schliemann's methods, techniques that had evolved through the application of common sense, as well as sound organizational.and business principles, to the excavations. He preserved not only valuable gold objects, but also simple, prosaic items, such as pottery. These artifacts often shed more light on the past than the more spectacular, headline-making finds. Above all, Schliemann was never afraid to take expert advice in the field.

Hissarlik remained a dominant theme in Schliemann's archaeological career for the rest of his life. But the demands of Troy did not prevent him from excavating elsewhere as well. His last great excavation was at another famous citadel, that of Tiryns on the plain of Argos, not far from Mycenae.

The stone fortifications of Tiryns, like those of Mycenae, had been known for centuries. Greek archaeologists had considered them medieval and of no particular interest. But classical writers, Schliemann's prime source of inspiration, were familiar with Tiryns. Pausanias had referred to it as one of the wonders of the world, a place built by giants. Schliemann believed it was related to Mycenae, took Pausanias as his guide, and started digging.

The 1886 digging season saw the sixty-four-year-old archaeologist attacking Tiryns with such zeal that he unwittingly destroyed the local farmers' crops. The excavations had hardly begun when the foundations of an elaborate palace came to light on the summit of Tiryns, a palace that far surpassed the grandeur of others of its type already discovered. Schliemann had done it again, this time with an architectural treasure.

The foundation stones of the palace itself were up to eleven yards thick and sixteen yards high. An outer courtyard with stores and workshops also lay inside the massive, fortified walls of the great citadel. The palace itself had been graced with a pillared main hall, various courts, antechambers, even a bathhouse. Its walls had been decorated with fine wall paintings. Thousands of clay vessels bore designs similar to those found at Mycenae and elsewhere, especially on Crete. The geometric designs on this pottery even turned up on vessels found in far-away Egypt and over wide areas of eastern Greece and the Aegean. Schliemann was now convinced that he had found the traces of a widespread culture, perhaps of Asian origin, that had been centered on the Aegean and especially on the large island of Crete.

His thoughts now turned to that island, the legendary home of the terrible King Minos and his fabled Minotaur, part man, part beast. It was to Crete that the Athenian Theseus had journeyed to slay the Minotaur. The palace of the Cretan king was thought to lie at Knossos, a rubble- and pottery-strewn hillside planted with olive groves.

A permit to excavate on Crete was relatively easy to obtain, but the landowners were reluctant both to sell their land and to have Schliemann digging around in their olive groves. Strenuous bargaining brought the price for the land down from ridiculous levels to a more realistic price of about 50,000 piastres. It then transpired that the land was owned by several Turks, only some of whom wanted to sell. One landowner tried to play Schliemann off against another.

In disgust Schliemann called off any deal and returned to Athens. For the rest of his life he was planning to return. "I want to crown my career with one great project," he wrote, "namely with the excavation of the prehistoric, royal palace at Knossos, on Crete, which I believe I discovered three years ago."

He was never to realize his dream. In December 1890, Schliemann was alone in Italy, preoccupied with his plans and in pain from an ear infection. On Christmas day he suddenly collapsed in a Naples piazza. Fully conscious but deprived of speech, he was carried to a hospital where he was turned away. Never a fastidious dresser, Schliemann did not look like the millionaire he was. He was dumped at a police station where the officers found a scrap of paper in his pocket with a doctor's name on it. The physician was summoned and made arrangements for his transfer to a hospital. No one believed that such a poorly dressed man could afford hospital fees. In exasperation, the doctor exclaimed, "He is very rich," and pulled a purse of gold coins from Schliemann's pocket. It was too late: Heinrich Schliemann died several hours later.

Schliemann's death marked the passing of an era in archaeology. Royal personages, diplomats, politicians, and dozens of scholars paid tribute at his funeral. His archaeology had always seemed an intensely private crusade, conducted with the precious books of Homer in one hand and a spade in the other. The sheer force of his enthusiasm had seemed to wrest great discoveries from the ground. A whole new generation of archaeologists had been inspired by his work, men like Arthur Evans, soon to discover the Minoan civilization, and Flinders Petrie, one of the greatest Egyptologists of all time. One archaeologist wrote, on hearing of Schliemann's death, that "the spring had gone out of the year." The once-controversial figure was now a man universally beloved and admired.

Schliemann's achievements were awesome: the discovery of Troy and of the glorious Mycenaean civilization of Bronze Age Greece. He died believing that he had proved the historical accuracy of Homer, that the *Iliad* was real history. To Schliemann, archaeology was simply digging to find history in a systematic way, using the best people and resources available—and no one can fault that way of looking at the field. Perhaps the best epitaph we can give Schliemann comes from Homer himself: "It is almost as though you had been with the Achaeans yourself or heard the story from one who was." Schliemann's greatness lay in his unique ability to turn prehistory into public property.

# 7

# ARTHUR EVANS AND THE MINOANS

HEINRICH SCHLIEMANN'S DEATH PREVENTED HIM FROM fulfilling his final dream: to excavate on mysterious Crete. Archaeological genius that he was, he recognized that its olive-covered hillsides harbored the secrets of yet another lost civilization. Fortunately, another great archaeologist carried on where Schliemann left off. Arthur John Evans, an Englishman who never set foot on Crete until his fortieth birthday, followed a Greek legend and a handful of ancient seals to find the Minoan civilization.

Like the excavations at Troy and Mycenae, Evans's explorations on Crete were inspired by Greek legend, in this case by the romantic myth of Theseus and the dreaded Minotaur, a terrible half-human monster kept by King Minos of Crete. According to legend, King Minos sent his son Androgeus to compete in the Athenian games. Androgeus won so many laurels in the competition that, in a fit of jealousy, King Aegeus had him murdered. Minos exacted a terrible revenge for his son's death. After his fleet sacked Athens, he demanded a ghastly tribute. Every nine years the Athenians were to send seven youths and seven virgins to be sacrificed to the Minotaur. Regular as clockwork, the king's messengers arrived each ninth year and demanded this tribute from the cream of Athenian youth. The third time they appeared, however, Aegeus's son Theseus was in town after a long absence abroad. Already famous for his heroic deeds, Theseus boldly joined the party and offered to kill the Minotaur. Amidst great lamentations the black-sailed ship departed for Crete. Theseus arranged with his father that his ship would carry white sails on the return trip if he managed to kill the Minotaur.

Upon their arrival, Theseus and his companions were imprisoned in the Palace of Minos. As the story goes, King Minos's daughter Ariadne fell helplessly in love with the handsome young Athenian and managed to smuggle a sword to the prisoner. Then, while Ariadne held one end of a ball of wool, Theseus unrolled the other and made his way into the depths of the dreaded Cretan labyrinth where the Minotaur lived. A terrible battle between Theseus and the monster ended in the Minotaur's death. Theseus made his way out of the labyrinth by rewinding the ball of wool and, with Ariadne by his side, hastily set sail for Athens. In his elation he forgot his promise to Aegeus to carry white sails. When King Aegeus saw the black-rigged ship approaching, he jumped off a cliff in despair.

Schliemann's excavations at Troy and Mycenae had convinced many that the Homeric epics were true. Now they wondered about Theseus and the Minotaur. Had King Minos and the Minotaur actually lived? Was there a great palace with a labyrinth where human sacrifices were performed? The only way to find out, as Schliemann had realized, was to undertake an excavation on Crete to find the fabled palace. Fortunately, the task fell into the hands of a trained and exceptionally gifted archaeologist.

Arthur John Evans was born in 1851 into a family that revered archaeology. His father, a prosperous paper manufacturer and early champion of prehistoric archaeology, collected prehistoric artifacts and was a respected geologist. He embodied the best type of Victorian patriarch, for, as he often stated, he firmly believed in "Peace, Prosperity, and Papermaking." But while John Evans was content to stay at home in England, his son Arthur was ever restless, eventually spending much of his time in the Balkans and the Mediterranean.

Young Arthur Evans was familiar with archaeology from his earliest years. At age seven he was drawing coins. (At the same time, he announced he would become a poet and an astronomer.) At ten, he accompanied his father on geological excursions. Teenage Arthur, although a familiar sight at learned lectures in London, was a far from ideal student. At school he was considered "dirty" and "untidy." Arthur, in return, found his teachers equally objectionable and complained that his Oxford University lecturers were dull. During summer vacations, to dispel the tedium of school, he wandered all over Europe, mostly on foot. An incurable romantic, he once bought a red-lined cloak that made him look like a revolutionary. A friendly customs officer advised him to take it off if he valued his safety.

Soon Arthur was venturing far off the beaten track. He reached the Balkans, a politically volatile country, after a "most weird journey beside people in sheepskin mantles and hats like Cossacks." He walked high mountains, wandered through deep forests, and encountered "wild looking Wallachs" dressed in shaggy skins. As he knowingly told a friend, "The women may be readily distinguished from the men by showing more of their legs and less of their hair."

For the rest of his life, Arthur Evans was never happier than when miles from anywhere and deeply immersed in local society. He fell deeply in love with the Balkans, both with the people and with their complex politics. It was hardly surprising that such an experienced traveler should feel at loose ends after graduating from Oxford in 1875. Arthur, although he had made some reputation for himself as an adventurer, was generally thought of as his father's son, for John Evans was a man of considerable repute. With typical determination, Arthur resolved to strike out on his own. He envisioned a life of travel and literary pursuits, a career he planned to combine with coin collecting and some archaeological research.

Evans's credentials for such a life-style were impressive enough. Under the tutelage of his father, Arthur had already developed an instinct for style and an encyclopaedic knowledge of archaeology. In addition, he was gifted with clear reasoning and an ability to grasp the wider significance of archaeological discoveries—qualities vital to a man who was to discover a lost civilization.

Lost civilizations were far from Evans's mind when, after spending a postgraduate summer at the University of Gottingen in Germany, he embarked on a long journey by foot through his beloved Balkans. The Balkans had been a concern of European statesmen for generations, for delicate balances of power could be upset by even a trivial rebellion in southeast Europe. Still, few ever bothered to master the intricacies of its volatile politics. Arthur plunged into this political morass with such enthusiasm that he was arrested by the Austrian police as a spy. Such was the power of a British passport that Evans was free within an hour. A few weeks later, he passed deep into Yugoslavia, walking from town to town until he ended up in Dubrovnik on the Adriatic coast. Evans soon made the ancient walled city his headquarters in the Balkans.

Summers do not last forever. When Evans returned to Oxford he was penniless and without a job. To make a bit of money, he wrote a racy account of his Balkan travels that appeared to popular acclaim in 1876. He was now considered an authority on the Balkans, so much so that the *Manchester Guardian* newspaper sent him back to Dubrovnik in 1877 as a special correspondent to report on the unrest caused by Austrian rule in what is now Yugoslavia.

Evans was in his element. Letter by letter he documented the mercurial fluctuations of Balkan politics for the *Guardian*'s readers. The letters further established Evans's literary reputation, especially his dramatic accounts of the suffering caused by the rebellions. He described refugees with "pinched haggard faces, lean bony frames, scarred by disease and bowed down with hunger."

The "mad Englishman" was welcome everywhere, although some suspected him of being an English spy. He visited princes, rebel leaders, war dances, and refugee villages. Arthur's new wife, the daughter of a historian, soon became accustomed to bearded messengers and secret late-night meetings at their villa in Dubrovnik. The smoky crosscurrents of political intrigue flowed through the Evans house. To keep his readers ever intrigued, Arthur, armed with nothing more formidable than a walking stick, would frequently dash off into the mountains in search of new trouble spots or fresh atrocities.

In the intervals between rebellions, Evans collected artifacts omnivorously. He was continually bargaining for himself, for museums, and for his father. In addition, a few surreptitious excavations in cemeteries and abandoned ruins enhanced his reputation as an archaeologist. His microscopic eyesight enabled him to peer at the most intricate inscriptions with ease and, as a result, he began to appreciate small objects in a way not possible for many of his less-keen-sighted colleagues. And it was tiny seals that would eventually lead Evans to the most spectacular discovery of his long career.

Increasingly the Austrian authorities found the *Guardian*'s special correspondent a public nuisance. His anti-Austrian statements sparked official reaction and, in March 1882, Evans was hauled off to prison. For six weeks he languished in jail while his family and the Foreign Office bombarded the Austrians with petitions for his release. He was lucky to escape a long prison sentence. As it was, Arthur was expelled

Arthur Evans in 1907.

from Dubrovnik forever. His reaction to six weeks' imprisonment was typical Evans: "Stone walls do not a prison make / Nor iron bars a cage / But they make a very tolerable imitation of one, I can assure you."

With the Balkans closed to him, Arthur Evans was again without a job and casting about for a career. After an unproductive year and a half in Oxford, Evans managed to get himself appointed Keeper of the Ashmolean Museum in June of 1884. This curious institution was to be his base for the next quarter century.

The Ashmolean was an anachronism in a university that specialized in such things. In 1677 scholar-astronomer Elias Ashmole had presented Oxford with a large collection of "curiosities." The university built a handsome museum for the gift and then entirely neglected the collections for two centuries. Not that they were not of great interest: the Ashmolean owned some of the first American Indian artifacts ever seen in Europe, as well as Captain Cook's South Sea relics and great collections of fish, birds, and mammals from the Pacific.

Traditionally, the Keeper of the Ashmolean was expected to do virtually nothing. But not Arthur Evans. He plunged into the job energetically and began to bring order to the chaos that was then the Ashmolean. Some influential collectors, including John Evans, closed ranks behind the ambitious young curator and helped him create new displays and acquire no less than two thousand new objects in five years. The university was astonished.

The long hours of slow-moving committee work bored Evans to tears. But it was the only way he could save the Ashmolean. Plans for a new building were eventually pushed through innumerable boards. All this dogged administrative work was sandwiched between extended periods of travel, for Evans was always on the move, always off to Mediterranean lands where he collected and geologized. The Assistant Keeper of the Ashmolean answered all queries by saying, "The

Keeper, Sir, is somewhere in Bohemia." Curiously, nobody at Oxford seemed very worried about Arthur's extended absences, presumably because he was less of a nuisance that way.

In 1893, the year Evans finally succeeded in obtaining a new building for his beloved museum, his wife Margaret died of tuberculosis. "She was," he wrote to a friend, "a helpmate such as few have known." Arthur buried himself in his work, feeling increasingly restricted by the monotony of museum routine. He was now a year older than Schliemann had been when he retired from business to look for Troy. A small, pugnacious man, he peered at the world through eyes that were happiest examining the minute artistry of prehistoric craftspeople. Evans's rather insignificant appearance belied his genius, his extraordinary energy, and an intuition that would eventually lead him to the greatest achievement of his life.

No one quite knows when Evans first became aware of Crete and its influential role in Greek prehistory. He had met Schliemann in 1883 and heard him lecture in London. He had peered curiously at the dazzling artifacts that this "odd little man" with a passion for Homer displayed to his learned audiences. Schliemann had always preferred a simplistic explanation for his finds at Mycenae and Tiryns: both were simply Homer come true. Arthur Evans, not content to accept this version, quietly formed a detailed synthesis of the finds from Mycenae in his own mind. He had always thought of Mycenae as a Bronze Age site, a far earlier settlement than the legend of Agamemnon and Homeric times. Exotic imports from all over the Aegean had poured into Mycenae, objects that Arthur had also purchased in antique stores throughout Greece, on the Aegean islands, and in the Balkans. Where had all these objects come from? Had the Mycenaeans fabricated the minute seals and engraved gemstones that were so common in their palaces? What were the origins of writing in the Aegean and who was responsible? Evans resolved to find out.

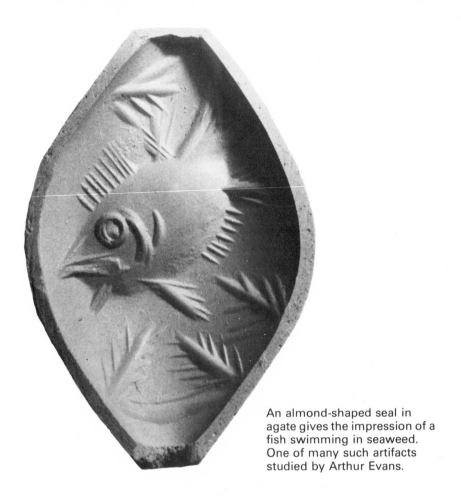

An almond-shaped seal in agate gives the impression of a fish swimming in seaweed. One of many such artifacts studied by Arthur Evans.

Many people believed that the Mycenaeans were illiterate, but Arthur's keen perception caused him to think otherwise. Browsing in the antique dealers' collections in Shoe Lane, Athens, Evans became interested in the dozens of engraved gems and seals so commonplace in these shops. Every one of the three- or four-sided stones bore symbols similar to the scratchings he had seen on jars from Mycenae. More such symbols had been found on Mycenaean vessels discovered in Egypt. Evans haunted the dealers' stores and bombarded them with questions about the seals. "Crete," they said, "they are found in Crete." Like a terrier, Evans quickened on the scent. Perhaps, he speculated, Crete had been a staging post in the gradual diffusion of writing to Mycenae and Europe. There was only one way to find out: he decided he must excavate on Crete.

Arthur Evans visited Crete for the first time in March of 1894, his mind full of seals and complex symbols. He arrived in Iraklion much the worse for wear from seasickness, but felt at home at once. The architecture reminded him of his beloved Dubrovnik, and the villages seemed familiar and friendly. Crete was soon to become his second home. Iraklion's market proved a gold mine. Arthur purchased twenty-two Cretan gems for one and a half piastres each and a fine Mycenaean ring. Three days later he engaged a guide to take him to Knossos, the olive-covered hillside where Heinrich Schliemann had always wanted to excavate.

The road out of Iraklion led through a pleasant landscape of gently sloping hills and scattered olive groves. Soon they came to a low spur of land to the west of the road where Knossos lay, brilliant with purple and white anemones in the spring sunshine. For hours Evans combed the hillside, copying strange marks off of stones he found protruding from the ground. Someone brought him a piece of a stone vessel. To his astonishment, it was of Mycenaean type. His surface finds that day were such that he was certain that spectacular results could be obtained from a dig. Without further ado, the lone Englishman set out to do what many others before him had failed to accomplish: to purchase the site—lock, stock, and barrel.

Knossos was owned by several landowners, some of whom had tried to cheat Schliemann until that astute gentleman went elsewhere. Since that time, a French archaeologist had applied to dig at the site but had never started work. So Evans had a clear field—if he could purchase the land. He promptly succeeded in persuading the owners of a quarter of the property to sell it to him outright. He then boldly formed the "Cretan Exploration Fund," an organization that existed only in his imagination. The fund, he assured the owners, would raise enough money to buy the rest of Knossos. The negotiations dragged on for two years while the landowners tried every scheme in the book to raise the price. Evans finally invoked an obscure legal statute to force them to sell. Eventually Knossos changed hands in 1896 for a sum just under a thousand English pounds.

By then Arthur Evans had ridden from one end of the island to the other in search of antiquities. Accompanied by a muleteer guide, he scrambled up and down hillsides, through rough watercourses, and into small villages. He found seals similar to those discovered at Mycenae for sale in even the smallest of village markets. At one village Evans spent two days trying to buy seals from a woman who wore them as charms, but she quietly refused, pointing to her child. "If I part with the stone," she explained, "he'll die."

Evans returned to England in a rare state of excitement. He had found traces of at least two writing systems on Crete, both preserved on his precious seals and gems. The solution to the ancient writing problem lay, he knew, at Knossos. Crete had nurtured a great civilization that predated Schliemann's Mycenaeans yet had strong ties with the Greek mainland. Determination to excavate Knossos fired Evans to feverish fund-raising activity. Back in Crete again, he haunted the site as negotiations for its purchase dragged on. One day, while eating lunch on a hillside overlooking the settlement, Evans turned to his companions. "This is where I shall live when I come to dig Knossos," he told them firmly. And he did.

Just as Knossos passed into British hands in 1896, the Cretans rose in savage revolt against their Turkish masters. Evans had to leave for his own safety. It was a year before the Great Powers intervened in the dispute. As soon as the revolt died down, Evans rushed to the island. He wrote long letters to the *Manchester Guardian* full of Turkish atrocities and the plight of the villagers. Anxious to help, he traveled all over the island distributing relief supplies and, of course, at the same time buying antiquities. Prince George of Greece, the new ruler of Crete, was so grateful to Evans for his assistance that a permit to dig at Knossos was forthcoming within a few months.

Arthur turned his attention from partisan politics to the greatest intellectual and archaeological challenge of his life.

Knossos was obviously a very complex site, and Evans had never excavated systematically in his life. His digging experience was confined to a few small digs, most of them little more than collecting forays. Fortunately, he had the sense to see that he needed experienced assistants. Architect Thomas Fyfe was engaged to prepare drawings and a Scotsman with flaming red hair and an uncertain temper named Duncan Mackenzie came along as Evans's excavation assistant. Mackenzie was to remain at Knossos for more than thirty years. He dealt with the workmen in a fluent but curious Greek spoken with a strong Scottish accent. Soon he became godfather to their children and a witness at innumerable weddings. Evans also started off on the right foot by insisting on both Christian and Muslim workmen. Although the two groups had been shooting at one another only a few months before, the experiment worked and Knossos was never beset with the labor problems that affected so many digs of the time. Thirty workmen were engaged under Mackenzie's supervision. Evans decided where to dig, examined every find minutely, and kept voluminous notes.

The Knossos excavations began in March 1900 and continued intermittently for thirty years. On the very first day, the excavators came across buildings and artifacts and, on the second, Evans was summoned excitedly to examine an ancient house with faded wall paintings. Within a few more days, the site was transformed into a veritable labyrinth of rooms, passages, and foundations. Evans was ecstatic; obviously, they had found a palace—a very unique palace. "It's an extraordinary phenomenon," he cried, "nothing Greek, nothing Roman. . . . Maybe its greatest period goes back to at least well before the pre-Mycenaean period."

The discoveries had only just begun. A hundred men were put to work clearing the palace rooms. In the process, they

View of the Palace of Knossos as it appears today from the west (see photo on pages following).

THEATRAL
AREA

NORTH
ENTRANCE

ALTAR

ALTAR

WEST ENTRANCE

CENTRAL
COURT

PRIVATE
HOUSES

SOUTH
ENTRANCE

32

■■■■ Walls in use at the time of the destruction: ground floor (central court) level

▨▨▨ Walls in use at the time of the destruction: lower levels

—— Earlier walls and foundations; some may have been in use at the time of the destruction

----- Conjectural walls

Plan of the Palace of Knossos. (From Sinclair Hood, *The Minoans,* London, Thames and Hudson; and New York, Praeger, 1971, p. 69.)

1 Pillared hall
2 Northeast magazines
3 North entrance passage
4 Northwest lustral basin
5 Throne room
6 Lustral basin
7 Stairway to upper floor
8 Triple shrine facade
9 Room with cists in floor (temple repositories)
10 Pillar rooms
11 Corridor of the west magazines
12 West magazines
13 West entrance
14 Corridor of the Procession
15 Monumental doorway
16 Stairway to upper floor
17 Grand staircase to residential quarters
18 East/west corridor

19 Light well, Hall of the Double Axes
20 Anteroom, Hall of the Double Axes
21 Main living room of the Hall of the Double Axes
22 Private staircase
23 Bedroom
24 Bathroom or sleeping place
25 Service room
26 Lavatory
27 Treasure chamber
28 Colonnade
29 Terrace
30 Store of lapis lacedaemonius (Spartan basalt)
31 Schoolroom
32 East entrance
33 Shrine of the Double Axes
34 Loom-weight basement of the earlier palace
35 Court of the Stone Spout

found thousands of artifacts in the foundations. Great storage jars, hundreds of small cups, even a complex drainage system came to light. The dozens of incised clay tablets bearing Cretan writing especially pleased Evans. At the beginning of April a magnificent wall painting of a male cupbearer emerged from the soil. That same night, the nightwatchman's dreams were troubled; he complained of spooks, lowing and neighing. But Evans was entranced by the "noble profile of the face." He admired the figure's full lips and "the waist of the smallest." The figure was carefully backed with plaster and transported to Iraklion's museum in triumph. As Arthur fingered the tablets and gems, the ornaments and frescoes, he was certain that he had located the ancient civilization of Minoan Crete, the historical basis of the Theseus legend, even if Minos and Theseus themselves had never actually existed.

Overjoyed, Evans announced his discovery of the Minoans in a telegram to the London *Times*, at the time the only place to announce a really sensational discovery. The term "Minoan" seemed natural to him—in commemoration of the legendary king said to have lived at Knossos. The Evans family was jubilant. Old John Evans sent his son a welcome gift of 500 pounds with the joyful message: "Dies Creta notanda!—a joyful Cretan day of note."

The site now extended over more than two acres. In April 1900 laborers uncovered a room with a ceremonial bath. Nearby stood a stone throne still upright and intact. Stone benches lined the walls. Fine paintings of wingless griffins formed an imposing background to the royal presence. It was here that the queen of Knossos may have sat, in her personification of the mother goddess who brought fertility to the land. Evans sent for Emile Gillieron, a Swiss artist who had vast experience in ancient inscriptions. Together they set to work to interpret the Knossos frescoes. There was much to piece together: frescoes of people marching in solemn procession, olives in flower, a young boy gathering saffron. A great, painted stucco relief of a charging bull stuck in Evans's mind.

Residential area of the Palace of Knossos, looking down from the central court before the upper floors were restored. The porch of the Hall of the Double Axes is left center, the bedroom is at bottom right.

"What a part these creatures play here," he wrote. Bulls were everywhere—in frescoes, on vases, on gems. Was the Minotaur a great bull? Arthur's mind boggled at the possibilities.

Every day Evans and Mackenzie rode out to the site on mules from Iraklion. Arthur always rode at breakneck speed, spurring his beast along the rough tracks. Eventually he acquired a fast horse, which partially assuaged his lust for speed. The day began by checking the previous day's work. Nothing was hurried or skimped. Page after page of notes in Arthur's tiny handwriting documented every layer, every find, every room. It was just as well that the excavators were careful, for the palace became more complex daily. It was quite an extraordinary structure. The great central courtyard was entered from the north through a huge, pillared hall. Rows of narrow storage magazines lay to the west of the courtyard, each opening onto a narrow passageway. At one time many of them had been lined with lead to house valuables. Huge supplies of grain must have been kept in these storerooms. Arthur estimated that as much as 79,000 gallons of olive oil were once stored in the palace.

The western side of the courtyard also led to the royal staterooms and the ceremonial precincts. It was here that the throne room with its ceremonial bath was found. All the baths in the palace were oddly reminiscent of Victorian hip baths.

Two staircases of imposing design led to the state rooms, which formed a second story above the shrines to the west of the courtyard. A western entrance to the palace led through a paved courtyard past huge pictures of young men leaping over bulls. But the king and queen actually lived to the east of the central courtyard. Here the ground slopes away sharply, so that the palace had three or four stories built downwards onto the slope. A great staircase led from the courtyard to the living quarters below. Since the complex framework of wooden beams and large pillars that formed the staircase had collapsed into the living quarters, it took Evans and Mackenzie months to sort out the jumble of rubble. Fortunately, Fyfe was on hand to prepare architectural drawings. The Knossos excavation was one of the first digs where an archaeologist insisted on having an architect on the site at all times.

The royal living quarters lay below the staircase. In the "Hall of the Double Axes," decorated with Cretan double-axe symbols, traces of wooden thrones were found. The floors were paved with limestone, and sheets of gypsum lined the walls up to a height of eight feet. The rest was plastered and painted. The royal bedrooms, complete with bathroom and toilet facilities, lay nearby, with an elaborate drainage system crisscrossing below them. Many features of the palace seemed remarkably modern, quite unlike the Greek or Roman palaces of classical antiquity.

The residential areas of the palace looked out over the valley of Kairatos, where the royal gardens probably lay. On the northeastern corner of the palace, the craftspeople had their quarters. Great pottery storage jars were found near a jar maker's workshop. The noise, dust, and clay emanating from its busy workbenches must have sometimes bothered the scribes and fresco painters who worked quietly nearby, recording the deeds, policies, and dealings of the king.

Arthur Evans was a celebrity by 1901, the recipient of honorary degrees and a lecturer much in demand all over Europe. The Palace of Knossos was to absorb most of his energies for the rest of his life. A major concern was to keep as much of the site as possible in his own family. A legacy from a relative in 1908 made him financially independent for the first time. "We may as well keep some of Knossos in the family," he wrote. "I must have sole control of what I am undertaking. My way may not be the best, but it is the only way I can work." Still, there were probably times when he regretted Knossos, for the workload was overwhelming, the site was malarial, and the expense simply enormous.

Evans was not content with excavation alone. With typical impetuosity, he resolved to reconstruct at least some of the buildings of the palace. This was, to put it mildly, a controversial undertaking, for many archaeologists believed that nothing should ever be rebuilt for fear of making false reconstructions. Others felt that nothing short of complete reconstruction should be the archaeologist's goal. Evans believed in limited reconstruction. By judicious rebuilding and restoration, he could show both Cretans and tourists something of the marvels of the palace of Minos. One suspects, too, that he wanted a more tangible symbol of his Minoan discoveries, something that would be appreciated by a wide audience, not just readers of learned dissertations.

On the whole, Evans's reconstruction is a fair one. The wooden colonnades were replaced with concrete pillars colored to conform with Minoan decor. Thomas Fyfe was invaluable, for his plans were so accurate that some buildings could be reconstructed at the same time that they were being dug.

The throne room in the Palace of Minos, as reconstructed by Arthur Evans.

Soon, restored walls were rising alongside trenches where workmen still labored. Colonnades and window frames were replaced, other walls set back in place, and the great staircase rebuilt from fragments found in the digs. The frescoes were a harder proposition. In the throne room, for example, Evans made detail changes that some consider to be inaccurate. But such cavilings are academic, for the overall effect of the palace is achieved. For over half a century the reconstructed walls have resisted war and earthquake, heat and storm to bring prehistory alive for the thousands who visit Knossos each year.

As one sits among the colonnades on a quiet summer's evening, time seems to slip away. In a few moments one is back in prehistory, hearing the tinkle of sheep bells and the distant barking of dogs as smoke from evening cooking fires wafts across the palace. It's easy to imagine the soft footsteps of the palace guard, a ripple of laughter from the potter's quarters, quiet talk from a group of young noblemen seated in the cool shade of the great courtyard. Without Evans, such magical moments would be impossible.

The visitor to Knossos is immediately struck by the incredible complexity of its ruins. A remarkable jumble of artifacts came from the excavations. Apart from the frescoes and architecture, Evans had to sort out thousands of potsherds, metal and stone ornaments, clay tablets, seals, gems, even burials to build up a coherent picture of Minoan civilization. When was Knossos founded? What was the chronological framework for the Minoan civilization? What did the people look like and how did they make their living? The answers to these questions was pieced together from the information painstakingly recorded in Arthur's notebooks and from the vast repository of Knossos finds.

From 1900 to 1935 Evans commuted between Knossos and Oxford, where he now began to write up the history of the Minoans, a task that occupied him for the rest of his long life. By 1906 he had wearied of his daily ride from Iraklion to Knossos, so he built a steel and cement house on the very slope he had chosen ten years before as his headquarters. The Villa Ariadne was to be his Cretan home for over thirty years. There he laid out the large collections of Minoan potsherds and began puzzling over Minoan chronology.

Happily for Evans, the Minoans had been aggressive traders and their society had dealt with many nations. The Knossos storerooms contained all types of exotic treasures, including occasional Egyptian vessels of known age that could be matched to vessels found in Egypt itself. In addition, the great Egyptologist Flinders Petrie had dug up Mycenaean pottery at Ghurab near Thebes that he dated to between 1500 and 1000 B.C. By using this important cross-reference, Evans produced a provisional time frame for the Minoans that could be cross-checked against Egyptian chronology. His original classification, a chronology that he refined progressively for the rest of his life, was published in 1905.

The first occupants of Knossos, suggested Evans, were simple farming folk who had no metals. He boldly dated them to ten thousand years ago, a pure guess. These early Cretans lived in small wooden huts and kept cattle, sheep, and goats. Evans did not have access to radiocarbon dating methods. Had he been able to use them, he would have dated the first Knossos people to between 6000 and 3500 B.C.

By 3000 B.C., Evans continued, rapid technological and economic changes were afoot. The "Early Minoan" period of Cretan civilization began with the beginning of the Bronze Age on the island. Immigrant peoples arrived from the eastern Mediterranean, bringing with them metallurgy, new pottery styles, and extensive trading contacts. There were signs of political upheaval. The Cretans seemed to have taken refuge in caves, as if warfare and raiding had disrupted the rhythm of agricultural seasons. The villages of the newcomers were not much different from those of their predecessors. Small, one-storied houses were packed together in tiny settlements. Some of the larger villages soon acquired small palaces, often associated with relatively humble shrines or temples. The Early Minoan period lasted for over a thousand years, as trading activities expanded and the Minoans began trading with other nations.

With the "Middle Minoan" and the "Late Minoan" periods, two eras that Evans dated at between 2000 and 1250 B.C., the Minoan civilization achieved the height of its glory. By this time Crete was densely populated. The Minoans founded colonies on several Aegean islands and, possibly, also on the Greek mainland itself. Wealthy traders and nobles lived on country estates and in elaborate palaces. Luxury, almost to the point of ostentation, was important. Cretan art overflowed with flamboyant color and lushness.

During its heyday, Cretan civilization was completely self-supporting. Wheat and barley were abundant on Crete; meat and milk came from large herds of cattle, sheep, and goats. But olives and grapes were the most important staples on the island. Since these two crops flourish in two different types of terrain, it is possible to grow them alongside one another without wasting land. Both olive oil and Cretan wine were widely exported by the Minoans in their seagoing vessels. The valuable oil and wine were carried far and wide through the Aegean and further afield in gaily painted Minoan jars, perhaps an export in their own right. Cretan jars and pots have been found as far afield as Egypt, Cyprus, and Syria. Many other necessities, such as foodstuffs and cloth, were exported in the same ships. Cretan wool and perhaps timber may have been exchanged for Egyptian papyrus.

As Evans pored over the Knossos collections, he realized what a huge variety of imported luxuries had flowed into the palace storerooms. Tin and copper came from Italy or the Aegean islands, gold and silver from western Turkey. Syrian ivory, Egyptian amethyst, and even lapis lazuli from Afghanistan were worked into ornaments and fine tools. Scarabs from the Nile, beads, pendants, ostrich eggshells, and Mesopotamian gems and seals were stockpiled in the palace treasure houses. All this trade was highly regulated and conducted with the aid of bronze scales used for weighing gold and silver.

Life at Knossos reflected the wealth and power of the Minoans and the cosmopolitan nature of their civilization. But the wall paintings at Knossos convey a strangely pastoral existence. Youths and young girls wander through meadows blooming with flowers. Birds flock by reedy streams, while gentle winds blow through fields of thyme. It seems a peaceful world, one where the Cretans lived in complete security, protected by their rugged island coasts and a powerful fleet. None of the palaces have any fortifications, so different from the massive walls that encircle Mycenae or Tiryns.

The Minoans themselves were literally beautiful people. They placed great emphasis on youthfulness and physical fitness. Palace clothes were, of course, much more elaborate than those worn in the countryside. The men were bare chested, with a small loin cloth around the hips. This was worn in various styles—as a kilt or folded under the groin like a pair of shorts. A codpiece often bulged in front of the kilt. This stylish costume was sometimes replaced by a long kilt adorned with tassels and worn with a wide belt. Skin and woolen cloaks were worn in cold weather.

The women wore long skirts held up by long waist girdles that were knotted down the front. Sometimes priestesses wore flounced skirts with elaborately checkered patterns woven into the cloth. Short- or long-sleeved bodices rose to a high peak at the back of the neck. But the breasts were left exposed, often thrusting forward provocatively from the cut of the bodice. The styles of Cretan fashion changed from generation to generation. Sometimes the women's clothes were cut tight and emphasized every curve of the body; other times, the skirts flowed more easily and were covered with aprons. Lips, cheeks, even nipples were painted with cosmetics.

Arthur Evans puzzled for a long time over the religion and cosmology of the Minoans. The only clues to their religious beliefs were the paintings and sculptures found in the excavations, like a book without a text. The chief deity appeared to be a goddess, perhaps a goddess of fertility. She presided over the cycles of planting and harvest, over the annual death and birth of the natural vegetation. But animal-headed gods were worshipped too. Many seals depict bull-headed humans. Bulls obviously occupied a central place in religious life. At certain times of the year, youths played with bulls, vaulting gracefully over their pitching horns, as depicted on the walls of the palace. Evans was fascinated by the bull rituals. Were they elaborate dances, religious ceremonies, or the very sacrifices commemorated by the Athenian legend of Theseus hundreds of years later? Was the Minotaur a giant bull kept by the king? Unlike Schliemann, Evans refused to link Minoan civilization directly to the legend of Theseus. He remarked only that "the old traditions were true. We have before our eyes a wondrous spectacle—the resurgence of a civilization twice as old as that of Greece." In other words, the legend of Theseus and the Minotaur had some basis in fact. There was a labyrinth, a great Cretan civilization, perhaps a huge bull who was the centerpiece of elaborate annual dancing rituals. Perhaps

A priestess modelled in faience dating from a late period in Knossos's history. She holds two snakes. A lioness sits on her head.

Theseus himself was a legendary symbol of the conquerors from the Greek mainland who finally overthrew Minoan civilization.

The legend of Theseus spoke of the utter destruction of the Minoans. For years Evans puzzled over the sudden ending of this Cretan civilization. The palace of Minos had been rebuilt many times during its long life. Earthquakes and fire had destroyed earlier structures, but each time a new palace rose on the ashy foundations of the fallen buildings. The latest occupation of Knossos, however, ended suddenly and the palace was never rebuilt. Everywhere he looked Evans found signs of interrupted daily life, of a sudden catastrophe. As the excavations revealed more and more of the palace, Evans became convinced that a great earthquake had tumbled Mi-

The bull-leaping scene from the Palace of Knossos. The figures on the left and right appear to be women.

noan civilization, a conclusion that many of his colleagues challenged.

His mind was full of ancient earthquakes as he lay reading in bed at 9:45 P.M. on June 26, 1926. Suddenly, the basement of the Villa Ariadne shook and groaned as a tremor rocked the house. For a minute and a half Evans lay still, feeling almost seasick from the motion. "A dull sound rose from the ground like the muffled roar of a bull," he later wrote, "while through the open window came the more distant jangling of the chimes of Candia [Iraklion] Cathedral." Roofs crashed to the ground, women and children screamed. A cloud of dust rose above the swaying trees. There was widespread damage to local villages, but the reconstructed palace came through well. Evans was fascinated. "It is something to have heard with one's own ears the bellowing of the bull beneath the earth," he told some guests at the Villa. This was the beast who tossed the earth with his horns, the great Minotaur whom the Cretans sought to appease with constant sacrifice. Arthur Evans was convinced he had lived through a reenactment of the death of the Minoan civilization.

Evans was now an old man with but one preoccupation—to publish the results of the Knossos excavations. As the annual dig continued, he started work on a monumental description of his findings. *The Palace of Minos* appeared in several volumes, the first in 1921, the last in 1935 when Evans was eighty-four. It is a chronological survey of Minoan civilization and of the great palace at its center. Stage by stage Evans unfolded his detailed story, pausing in the final volume to bid farewell to his beloved palace. In the book he admits his one great failure: he had failed to decipher Minoan script, the original and ultimate objective of all his Knossos researches. But no one minded, for his achievements at Knossos far outweighed the significance of the four scripts he had found in the palace.

Arthur Evans died in 1941 at the age of ninety. His restored palace was to survive further earthquakes and all the turmoil of the Second World War. Other scholars have carried on where Evans left off. Minoan chronology has been modified by radiocarbon dating and new excavations. But some mysteries still remain. The Cretan scripts, for example, continue to be the subject of considerable controversy. In 1952, Englishman Michael Ventris announced a decipherment of Linear B that indicated these particular tablets were written in Greek. His decipherment is still debated, however, and it is still uncertain whether we can read Minoan writing. Many of the tablets are probably little more than storehouse inventories. Thus one of Arthur Evans's primary objectives in going to Crete is still very much an issue among archaeologists.

The earthquake that shook Evans's house in 1926 led him to believe that Knossos met a violent end. Many people have

argued with his interpretations of the closing centuries of
Knossos, but most scholars agree that a major natural
disaster—perhaps an earthquake and fire—hit the palace in
about 1500 B.C. New credibility has been given to this theory
by the dramatic finds on the island of Thera, eighty miles
north of Crete. Greek archaeologists found a Minoan colony
there, buried under many feet of volcanic ash. Apparently, an
earthquake overwhelmed the settlement in about 1500 B.C.
At that date, they conclude, the center of the island of Thera
literally blew into space in a violent eruption and earthquake
that generated enormous tidal waves and deposited thick
layers of volcanic ash over hundreds of miles of ocean and on
the exposed slopes of northern Crete.

The scale of this great natural disaster beggars the imagination. The only recent analogy is the explosion of Krakatoa in
southeast Asia in August of 1883. Tidal waves from that
cataclysm killed over 36,000 people on the low-lying coasts of
Java and Sumatra. Knossos is less than a hundred miles from
Thera. The effects of the eruption must have been devastating
to coastal settlements, although the tidal waves would not
reach Knossos itself. But the choking ash from the explosion
mantled valuable agricultural land and rendered it useless for
cultivation. Minoan civilization must have been weakened
seriously by the Thera disaster, never to recover its former
vigor. Some scholars believe that the Thera explosion was so
violent that it provided the historical substance for the legend
of Atlantis, a lost continent that sank below the sea and killed
thousands of people in the process. Is the legend of Atlantis a
folk memory of one of the greatest natural disasters ever to
affect humankind—the destruction of Minoan civilization?
Perhaps we shall never know. But the cupbearer and long-
forgotten processions painted on the walls of Minos's palace
remind us not only of one of the world's great civilizations,
but of the remarkable man who rescued them from a historical oblivion that could have been as profound as that of Atlantis itself.

# 8

# PYRAMIDS, PYRAMIDOLOGISTS, AND PYRAMIDIOTS

THE PYRAMIDS OF GIZEH HAVE GRACED THE BANKS OF the Nile for nearly five thousand years. They have withstood wars and famines, the best efforts of treasure hunters and quarrymen, and the onslaught of tens of thousands of tourists. Even today, they remain somewhat of a puzzle. Why did the ancient Egyptians build these vast monuments? And why the pyramid shape with its angle of 51 degrees, 52 minutes to the ground? Were these strangely shaped structures sophisticated astronomical observatories as well as the burial places of the early pharaohs? How did the Egyptian kings manage to recruit the enormous labor forces necessary to erect their huge tombs? Even with unlimited human resources, construction of the Pyramids represents an incredible engineering feat, for they were built without the assistance of iron tools or wheeled carts. These and many other questions have provoked centuries of vigorous scholarly debate.

The sheer scale of the Great Pyramid boggles the mind, for it seems to dwarf even modern Cairo at its feet. It is built of over 2,300,000 large rocks, covers 13.1 acres, and rises to a height of 481.4 feet above the plain. Each side is approximately 755.79 feet long. Our awe is heightened by the long shadows that the pyramids cast at dawn and dusk, when their dark profiles overshadow the settlements at their feet. During the heat of the day they seem to swim in a brown haze like airy structures floating in eternity.

If the outside of the Great Pyramid seems impressive, its interior is downright confusing, a bewildering maze of narrow passages and hidden chambers. The entrance, on the Pyramid's north face, is about 55 feet above the ground and 24 feet to the east of the center of the face, presumably to guard against tomb robbers. A long passage approximately 3.5 feet wide descends from the entrance to the deep core of the Pyramid and then down even further into the basement rock below the structure. Three hundred and forty-five feet further on, the corridor levels out and leads into an unfinished subterranean burial chamber, apparently abandoned in favor of a funerary chamber located in the main body of the Pyramid itself. Some time after the Pyramid was constructed, workmen cut a hole in the roof of the corridor 60 feet from the entrance and then laboriously tunneled their way through the core of the Pyramid toward its center. After 129 feet of arduous quarrying, they widened their passage into the magnificent Grand Gallery, 153 feet long and 28 feet high, a chamber they lined with polished limestone. The Grand Gallery leads to the King's Chamber, obviously the burial place of the pharaoh, for an empty sarcophagus weighing three tons still rests there. Two long, narrow shafts lead from the King's Chamber to the outside of the Pyramid. Five closed compartments above the roof of the chamber apparently serve to relieve the massive weight of the rubble core above it.

If the Great Pyramid seems awesome and mysterious to us today, it's not difficult to imagine how less sophisticated travelers of earlier centuries must have viewed it. Controversies about the Great Pyramid began as long ago as 450 B.C., when the Greek traveler Herodotus wrote an account of the

MEDITERRANEAN SEA

LOWER EGYPT

*GIZEH* ●  ▲CAIRO

▲—MEMPHIS

●—*DASHUR*

●—*MEIDUM*

●*EL-AMARNEH*

SINAI

*NILE R.*

UPPER EGYPT

RED
SEA

DEIR EL MEDINEH ▲—▲—THEBES
●
*VALLEY OF KINGS*

FIRST CATARACT

N

0      150   MILES

Locations and sites mentioned
in Chapters 8 and 9.

building of the Great Pyramid, an account he said he obtained from Egyptian priests. He told how the stones were raised to their places "by means of machines formed of short wooden planks. . . . The upper portion of the Pyramid was finished first, then the middle, and finally the part which was lowest and nearest the ground." We know now that the ancient Egyptians used thousands of laborers with rollers and sledges to move the quarried stone blocks from the Nile to the building site. Huge brick and earth ramps provided a pathway for bringing each block to its proper place on the Pyramid. As construction proceeded, the ramps were raised until the summit was reached. Then the builders started to cover the Pyramid with polished limestone casing stones. As these were added course by course to the exterior, the ramps were slowly removed until the shining Pyramid stood free and clear of ramps and scaffolding. Were the "short planks" Herodotus mentioned the sledges and rollers used to shift the thousands of huge blocks?

In Herodotus's time, the Great Pyramid still bore many of its fine casing stones. When Herodotus, visiting the site, stooped to peer at a hieroglyphic inscription on the casing stones near the ground, his guide informed him that it recorded "the quantity of radishes, onions, and garlick consumed by the laborers who constructed it." The gullible Herodotus was fascinated by this revelation and spent hours more poking around the Pyramids. The tourist guides, recognizing an easy dupe, regaled him with lurid tales. Apparently, they said, Cheops ran out of money to complete the Pyramid, so he sent his daughter out to work as a whore to contribute her share. Not only did she raise the money, she made every client contribute a stone block toward her own personal pyramid, which was eventually erected without incident nearby. The thousands of Roman tourists who relied on Herodotus for their Egyptian history must have thought the pharaoh and his daughter a brazen pair.

The Sphinx and Cheop's
Pyramid at Gizeh.

Century after century travelers gazed on the Pyramids and
speculated about their history. Some early Christians believed
them to be the vast granaries erected by Joseph to store grain
against the seven lean years spoken of in the Scriptures. The
Arabs who followed thought the Pyramids were treasure
houses of long-dead kings. In A.D. 870 Caliph al-Mamun directed his engineers to find the entrance to the Great Pyramid.
Meticulously they searched the exterior. "There is no entrance," they reported. "Then quarry into the boulders," ordered the caliph.

The engineers began to tunnel laboriously into the stones.
Suddenly, a hundred feet in, they broke into a corridor. They
made their way back to the ancient entrance through this
passageway and broke it open. Within a few days, they found

the King's Chamber—but it was bare. While the would-be tomb robbers hammered at its polished granite walls in frustration, the caliph mused on the Pyramid's elusive treasure. "Why," he asked the engineers, "is the interior empty when there are so many obstacles to overcome?"

Not everyone was interested simply in treasure. Others ascribed to the Pyramids a deeper and more mysterious purpose. The Arab chronicler Abu Balkhi thought the Great Pyramid was a place of refuge from divine judgment, a sort of early fallout shelter. Some Christian travelers fell on their knees at the sight of the vast monuments, amazed at what they thought to be a divine revelation. "The Almighty arranged for this great and wonderful plan to be portrayed in symbol long before the Bible was written," cried one astonished observer. As might be expected, extraordinary superstitions surrounded the mysterious structures. The Great Pyramid was said to be full of horrible vermin, and a naked woman with huge teeth supposedly seduced visitors with her spells and drove them insane. Bold was the scholar who dared set foot in the bat-filled chambers of the Great Pyramid.

One of the first people to investigate the Great Pyramid at all scientifically was the Englishman John Greaves, who came to Gizeh in 1638. Greaves was a bookish mathematician, more at home in a library than in a dusty pyramid. But he had become obsessed with the origins of scientific measurement and with techniques that would enable scientists to measure the size of the earth. Ever since Ferdinand Magellan had circumnavigated the globe, people had been searching for a way to measure the earth's circumference. All the stories Greaves had heard of the Great Pyramid convinced him it had been built upon what he called "higher and more weighty considerations"—in other words, he believed the Pyramids had been constructed as an observatory for measuring the earth and as a repository of sorts for the standard units of linear measurement. He decided to test his theory by actually measuring the Great Pyramid.

Armed with a special ten-foot rod divided into ten thousand equal parts, Greaves gingerly lowered himself into the entrance of the Great Pyramid. As he crawled through the piles of dust and rubbish, huge bats, some over a foot long, circled his head. In desperation, he fired his pistols to scare away the creatures, the shots reverberating along the narrow passageway. Cordite mingled with the almost unbearable stench of bat dung and vermin. For several hours, John Greaves crawled through the chambers, marveling at the close fit of the limestone blocks of the interior walls. He laboriously measured the King's Chamber and the stone sarcophagus in it, which he found to be 6.488 English feet long. "The structure," he wrote, "hath been the labour of an exquisite hand." Outside, he climbed to the summit to admire the panoramic view and estimated the summit of the pyramid to be 499 feet above the ground, an almost correct guess. Greaves returned to England convinced the Pyramids constituted a giant observatory.

No one really studied the Pyramids thoroughly until Napoleon decided to conquer Egypt and control the Nile. He set sail for Egypt in May 1798 accompanied by 35,000 soldiers and 175 scientists. Napoleon was bent on colonization as well as conquest, his objective being to civilize the Egyptians with the expert assistance of his savants, a group gathered from all over France. Principal among these were Edné Jomard, a young antiquarian, and Vivant Denon, a skilled artist and diplomat with a reputation for good living, pornography, and vivid writing. It took Napoleon but a short time to defeat the Mameluke Turks in a famous battle waged near the Pyramids and, within a few days, the savants were crawling through the bat-filled chambers of the Great Pyramid.

Denon and Jomard found that the bat population of the pyramid had increased since Greaves's day. Bat dung clogged the narrow passages. As the scientists crawled through the tight corridors, swarms of infuriated bats clawed at their half-naked bodies and flew into the flaring torches, their wings frizzling in the heat. Denon and Jomard fought off the

Napoleon's savants visiting the interior of the Great Pyramid.

striking bats with little success, gasping for fresh air. Finally, pouring with sweat, they paused in the Grand Gallery to discharge their pistols. Thunderous echoes reverberated in the hot, cavernous interior. As soon as possible, Jomard gave the signal to retreat.

When they emerged, young Jomard trotted around the Great Pyramid to examine the huge piles of debris that had collected around its footings. Then he climbed to the summit, taking an hour to get there. After admiring the breathtaking view, Jomard tried to measure the height of the Pyramid by means of a slingshot, but was unable to get the shot near the ground. So he measured each step in turn, coming up with a height of 488 feet.

Meanwhile, the savants had put 150 Arabs to work clearing sand from the base of the Pyramid. Soon the workmen hit a huge paved surface surrounding the foundations and two sockets that marked the ancient corners. Army surveyors measured the base and found it to be 757 feet on each side. Jomard then calculated that the slopes were inclined at 51 degrees, 19 minutes. But what did these measurements mean? Rushing back to Cairo to consult the thick tomes the scientists had brought with them, he decided that the Great Pyramid was a huge metric yardstick used by the ancient Egyptians to calculate the dimensions of the earth. Even when two cynical colleagues remeasured the base of the Great Pyramid and found each side to be two feet longer, Jomard stuck to his guns. The Egyptians were such skilled astronomers, he argued, that they were capable of measuring the circumference of the earth thousands of years before Christ.

Then Napoleon himself got into the act. On August 12, 1799, the general was escorted into the King's Chamber. He had already announced that the Pyramids of Gizeh contained enough stone to build a wall nine feet high and over a foot thick all around France. After a few minutes, Napoleon asked to be left alone in the chamber. When he emerged, he appeared pale and awestruck, but refused to his dying day to describe what he had experienced in the King's Chamber. "What's the use," he said later, "you'd never believe me."

Most of the tomb robbers and antiquarians who flocked to the Nile after the Napoleonic Wars paused only briefly at the Pyramids before sailing south to Thebes and its rich mummy caves and fine temples. But a Genovese sea captain named Giovanni Caviglio was so excited by Gizeh that he abruptly retired from the sea and settled down to explore the mysteries of the pyramid.

Caviglio was deeply religious and single-minded in his pyramidical devotions. After shoveling tons of bat dung from a small chamber, he actually set up living quarters inside the Great Pyramid and began to sell antiquities to wealthy tourists to finance his excavations. Convinced that the Great Pyramid contained a secret chamber full of treasure, Caviglio started to tunnel into the solid rock of the Pyramid's interior. Soon discouraged, he gave up digging and contented himself with studies of magic, magnetism, and other esoteric subjects. Perhaps his profits from grave robbing were a consolation to him.

At this point a singularly humorless Englishman named Colonel Richard Howard-Vyse arrived on the scene. Howard-Vyse, a difficult man, was a constant trial to his family. When he wrote from Cairo in 1836 that he intended to study the Pyramids, his family was relieved, although their relief cost them over ten thousand pounds. Howard-Vyse was not one to spare expense: at times, he was paying over 700 men to work on his excavations.

Howard-Vyse hired Captain Caviglio as excavation supervisor and Caviglio—at least initially—was delighted with the arrangement. But the two men soon quarreled over money, for Caviglio was by this time more interested in profit than serious scientific inquiry. Contemptuously declaring that the Englishman had "nothing but money," Caviglio retreated to Paris, leaving Howard-Vyse camped in front of the Great Pyramid.

There he was visited by a lady who evidently admired this strict and eccentric man. In her words: "He sat down before the Great Pyramid as a fortress to be besieged." Convinced that the Lord had entrusted him with the great task of interpreting the Pyramid, Howard-Vyse braved summer heat and crowds of tourists to continue his labors, always, wrote his female admirer, "preserving the utmost urbanity, but dealing out the strictest justice in a manner that made a most honorable and lasting impression on the tawny Arabs around him."

But Howard-Vyse's excavation methods were far from honorable. He used gunpowder to blast his way into a series of chambers located above the King's Chamber in the center of the Pyramid. When the dust from the gunpowder subsided, Howard-Vyse could decipher the name of the pharaoh Cheops on the walls. Had Cheops built the Great Pyramid? It seemed entirely possible, especially since the same cartouche—i.e., the oblong design enclosing the pharaoh's name—appeared at the stone quarries where the blocks of the Pyramid had come from. Howard-Vyse also unblocked the small ventilation shafts that "air conditioned" the King's Chamber to a constant temperature of 68° summer or winter, a great relief to the many tourists who crowded into the Pyramid during the steamy summer months.

After four long years Howard-Vyse returned home and compiled a massive treatise on the Pyramids. Wisely, he devoted much of the treatise to recording precise dimensions and architectural features of the Pyramids, information that astonished everyone who read his book. The unloved colonel laid the foundations for a new field of inquiry, that of pyramidology, the science of pyramids. And many were the pyramidologists who subsequently descended on Gizeh.

One of the first was John Taylor, a benign and sober gentleman of mature years with an established reputation as a journalist and essayist. Taylor was also a gifted amateur astronomer and mathematician who used these skills to construct scale models of the Pyramids. From these, he derived

The Pyramids of Gizeh.

mathematical formulae that proved, he said, that the Egyptians were familiar with the value of $\pi$ and had constructed the Great Pyramid to "make a record of the measure of the earth." Thus, according to Taylor, the Great Pyramid had been built to express basic astronomical and geometric laws in simple terms and to perpetuate this knowledge for future generations.

Taylor, a deeply religious man who firmly believed in the Ussherian chronology of the Creation and in Divine Revelation, published his findings in *His Great Pyramid: Why Was It Built and Who Built It.* The volume, which appeared in 1859, attempted to prove that the Lord had revealed the arts of advanced mathematics to the ancient Egyptians. Most people laughed at Taylor. Only an eminent astronomer took him very seriously.

Charles Piazzi Smyth was Astronomer Royal of Scotland when he read Taylor's book. His academic colleagues were horrified when Smyth published a paper supporting the theory of Divine Revelation. Smyth further argued that the "sacred cubit" used by the builders of the Great Pyramid was the same length as that used by Noah to build the ark. The British inch was almost exactly the same as a twenty-fifth part of the cubit, so, Smyth concluded, it had a direct ancestry in the Egyptian unit. When everyone ignored his arguments, Smyth decided to go and measure the Pyramids for himself.

Piazzi Smyth and his wife arrived in Cairo in late 1864. They found the sprawling city highly disagreeable—it stank of garlic and human excrement, and barking dogs kept them awake at night. So, their Scottish sensibilities affronted, they hastened to the Great Pyramid.

While his wife unpacked their belongings and tidied the abandoned tomb they called home, Smyth inspected the impressive collection of instruments he had brought along to help him scientifically prove that the Great Pyramid was built by using a special sacred cubit. His measuring bars were specially balanced and constructed with built-in thermometers

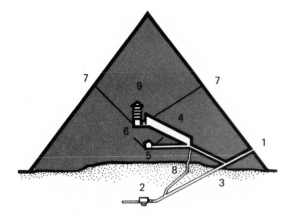

1 Entrance to descending corridor
2 Unfinished chamber
3 Ascending corridor
4 Grand Gallery
5 Queen's Chamber
6 Unfinished shafts
7 Shafts leading to surface from King's Chamber
8 Shaft leading to descending corridor
9 King's Chamber

Plan of the interior of the Great Pyramid. (Adapted from I. E. S. Edwards, *The Pyramids of Egypt,* New York, Viking Press, Studio Books, 1972, p. 8.)

The Pyramids of Gizeh in the nineteenth century (see illustration at right).

designed to record even the slightest temperature differences. Smyth had also designed a special clinometer, an instrument for measuring angles of elevation, and had even brought a camera with him, at that time a revolutionary piece of scientific research equipment.

For weeks on end, Piazzi Smyth measured and remeasured the passages and chambers of the interior of the Great Pyramid. He took particular pains with the coffin in the King's Chamber which, he believed, had served as an absolutely standard unit of measurement for all Egyptian observations. It was, he said, far better than any standard yardstick of measurement kept in London, for its dimensions did not expand and contract with changes in temperature.

Refreshed with copious draughts of Nile water, guaranteed, he claimed, to cure "the windy melancholy arising from the shorter ribs," Piazzi Smyth now turned his attention to the outer slopes of the Great Pyramid. He spent several eventful nights sleeping on the summit, with the tips of the other pyramids floating eerily nearby. With plumb bob and a 500-inch cord, as well as a sextant and theodolite, Smyth carefully measured the altitude, latitude, and longitude of the Great Pyramid. He was amazed at the precise orientation of the structure which, he said, could only have been obtained by a meridian observation of a polar star. But his main preoccupation was with Taylor's conclusions. Was Taylor correct, for example, in believing that "the height of the pyramid was designed to be in relation to the perimeter of its base as the radius of a circle is to its circumference?" After lengthy surveys and profuse calculations, Smyth concluded that the

Egyptians had built a structure whose basic unit of dimension measurement—the inch—incorporated not only a system for linear measurement but also one for measuring time. Smyth went on to claim that the Egyptians were expert astronomers some 1500 years earlier than the Greeks. As soon as Smyth paid off his laborers—the best workers were given copper lamps, the worst, mousetraps—he started revealing his conclusions to the world. The 1,600 pages of his report were described charitably as being "full of strange hallucinations." One colleague said publicly and in front of Smyth that "only a few weak women and a few womanly men believe these theories." Smyth's response is not recorded, but he persisted in his beliefs. Eventually, like Taylor, he turned to divine inspiration as the explanation for the Great Pyramid. "Wisdom and metrical instructions" were imparted, he wrote, "to chosen men, by the Author of all wisdom." Smyth's earthly reward was abuse and academic oblivion. History has come to regard this sincere pyramidologist as a "pyramidiot."

In 1880, tourists visiting the Great Pyramid were greeted by a strange and outrageous sight. Hastily, respectable gentlemen hustled their wives into the Pyramid or back to the mules. An extraordinary figure carrying a theodolite and binoculars was wandering around the Pyramid. This in itself, of course, was in no way strange—many scientists measured and surveyed the Pyramids. But this gentleman was different: he wore nothing but his pink underwear. The Victorian ladies were horrified, but their horror went unnoticed by this remarkable archaeologist. He was caught up in a colossal task—an accurate triangulation survey of the Pyramids of Gizeh and their surroundings, something Piazzi Smyth had never managed to complete.

Flinders Petrie was a newcomer to Egypt who relished ignoring the niceties of Victorian etiquette. His one passion was pyramids, a passion developed at the age of thirteen when he came across a copy of Smyth's treatise on Gizeh. Petrie senior was an engineer with a talent for surveying, and his son

Visiting the Pyramids in 1874.

followed suit. By the time he was twenty-one, Flinders was an
expert practical fieldworker who had surveyed over a hundred
British earthworks. By this time, too, he had read every reference on pyramids he could find. In November 1880 he finally
had the opportunity to visit Egypt. Flinders Petrie sailed for
Cairo to begin a career that would eventually culminate in his
becoming the foremost Egyptologist of recent times.

Petrie felt at home immediately. He set up camp in an
ancient tomb and soon developed a camp routine that he
would observe for the rest of his life. He rose from his ham-
mock early in the morning, ate a simple breakfast, and greeted
Arab visitors. He did most of his own cooking, for he detested
the Arabs' standards of cleanliness. In the evening he wrote up
his notes and, as his sole diversion, read before retiring. Day
after day Petrie worked around the Pyramids. For up to ten
hours at a stretch he peered through his theodolite and laid
out his special steel tapes. A large parasol protected him from
the midday heat. The survey took months. Petrie was determined to make the definitive survey of the Pyramids, one
accurate within a quarter of an inch. He succeeded brilliantly.

By digging at the base of the Great Pyramid, he uncovered some of the beautifully fitted casing stones and found that they had been laid on an absolutely straight line that varied by only 1/100 inch over 75 inches. In many places the mortar between the stones was only 1/50 inch thick.

By the time Petrie turned his attention to the interior of the Pyramid, the tourist season was in full swing. Every day crowds of visitors would swarm into the Pyramid and be pushed and pulled by Arabs up the stepped slopes to the summit. Twenty years earlier, Piazzi Smyth had written disapprovingly of "tobacco-stinking gentlemen from some vulgar steamer" and of "whirling dances performed over King Cheops' tombstone with ignorant cursing of his ancient name." Some tourists took lumps of the Pyramid home as souvenirs, others drank from brandy flasks, shouted and yelled, and generally created bedlam. So Petrie waited each day until dark to enter the interior. There he toiled for hours in fetid heat, "clad," as he said, "in nothing, not even a pair of spectacles." The dust was so thick that he choked and suffered from intense headaches. Vandals had blocked up the ventilation shafts again.

But the results were astounding. The walls of the descending passage were so precisely designed that there was an error of a mere 1/50 inch in 150 feet of wall and only 1/4 inch in 350 feet. The design of the King's Chamber showed considerable mathematical skill, for its dimensions were based on the same proportions as those configurations of $\pi$ that had governed the exterior of the Pyramid. Clearly, the builders of the Pyramid had been expert mathematicians. Petrie concluded that the Egyptians had used a "royal cubit" of 20.63 inches to build a pyramid with a base line of 440 cubits and a height of 280 cubits. He pointed out that Smyth's hypothesis—that the perimeter of the pyramid would give one the number of days in the year and was thus a calendar—was based on faulty measurements of the base length of the structure. But he called the structure itself "a triumph of skill. Its errors, both in length and angles, could be covered by placing one's thumb on them."

When Petrie's survey was published in 1883, people were astonished at his achievement. His book was read from cover to cover by dozens of pyramidologists who promptly launched ingenious experiments of their own with the new measurements. A gentleman named John Schmaltz "proved" that a deck of cards was in fact a symbol of the ancient Egyptian calendar. In a book entitled *Nuggets from King Solomon's Mines*, he argued that the 52 cards in a pack equaled the 52 weeks of a year, "the 12 face cards the months, the 13 cards in a suit the lunations, the suits the seasons, the total face value of the cards (counting jack as 11, queen as 12, and king as 13) 364 days, plus the joker as the magic 1.234, for a total of 365.234 days in the year."

The excesses of other pyramidologists were even wilder. Some sought to interpret the Great Pyramid as a prophetic monument. According to Morton Edgar, Colonel J. Garnier, and others, the Great Pyramid contained a 6,000 year prophetic history of the world which began in 4000 B.C. and extended to A.D. 2045. The prophecies in the Bible were all marked in the stones, the Pyramid's descending passage depicting the gradual decline of humankind toward "ignorance and evil." But there was hope yet. Those who had benefited from Christian teachings would be saved from this fate, for the ascending passage prophesied the ascent of true and humble believers through the Antechamber of Chaos (the modern era) into the King's Chamber, where the Second Coming of Christ would glorify humanity. One pyramid inch on the walls of the passage equaled a year of prophetic time. The first inch represented the biblical Creation and the Garden of Eden, the last inch, the Day of Judgment. All pyramidologists of this school agreed that the modern era began with the World War in 1914, while the Second Coming was timed for 1953.

One American naval officer who dug sporadically at Gizeh summed it up nicely when he wrote, "If a suitable unit of measurement is found—say versts, hands, or cables—an exact equivalent to the distance of Timbuctu is certain to be found in the roofing work of the Crystal Palace, or in the number of street lamps in Bond Street, or the Specific Gravity of mud, or the mean weight of an adult goldfish."

The pyramidologists' debates over the Great Pyramid continue to this day. There are many people who still believe the Pyramids are a mysterious and powerful source of cosmic energy. This energy, according to believers, can perform miracles, provide heat and light, and generally illuminate modern life. But although Flinders Petrie's surveys fueled this kind of nonrational speculation, they also provided for the first time a scientific basis for the study of the Pyramids. Now, nearly a century later, we know a great deal more about the technological abilities of the ancient Egyptians, as well as about their society.

Unfortunately, there are no surviving contemporary records that give us details of the building of the Pyramids. We can merely extrapolate from other, later records that describe public building projects of a much smaller scale. We can be fairly certain that the engineers who laid out the Great Pyramid on a flattened rocky plateau by the Nile at Gizeh were not particularly sophisticated astronomers. They used simple astronomical observations of major celestial bodies to position the four straight sides of the Great Pyramid on the cardinal points of the compass—north, south, east, and west. The surveyors used fiber measuring cords to lay out the ground plan in units of 20.62 inches, Petrie's royal cubit. Unfortunately the strings stretched, so there is an error of nearly eight inches between the various sides.

While many details of how the Pyramids were built are now satisfactorily established, we still do not know why the Pyramids were erected in the first place. Without question, they served as burial places for the pharaohs. But why did the kings of Egypt commission such enormous works, projects that took as long as twenty-five years to complete? Surely royal vanity alone is insufficient explanation. If we reject the idea that the Pyramids were spectacular observatories—and most serious scholars do—then can we develop an alternative explanation?

British physicist Kurt Mendelssohn had little interest in Egyptology until he paid a chance visit to the pyramids in the 1960s and ended up spending many months studying their design and the rationale behind them. From these studies he has developed a pragmatic explanation for the pyramid projects. Mendelssohn was surprised to find out, as are many strangers to Egyptology, that all the Egyptian pyramids were erected over a very short period of time—only about a century, beginning in 2500 B.C. To complete all this work in such a brief period, he concluded, the builders must have been working on more than one pyramid at a time. It was an eventful architectural century, for the builders had to cope with many new engineering problems. The second pyramid they built at Meidum collapsed during construction. The lateral thrusts of the rubble core were such that the buttresses gave way and probably buried thousands of workmen. So the builders modified their designs and started a new pyramid at Dashur instead. By the time they came to Gizeh, the architects had solved the thrust problem by using packing blocks to counteract the forces of plastic flow and had reached the classic angle of 52 degrees that stood the test of time.

Mendelssohn, in addition to discovering that Meidum had collapsed, carefully considered the human engineering of the construction projects. No one, he found, had any real idea of how many people worked on the Pyramids during the three months when agriculture was at a standstill. Herodotus claimed that 100,000 people toiled at their construction, an estimate many authorities felt was not unreasonable. While a relatively small number of skilled artisans worked on the Pyramids all year round, the logistics of organizing and feeding armies of unskilled laborers during the peak construction season must have been an enormous undertaking. A perma-

Tourists at the Pyramids in the
1970s.

nent organization of bureaucrats and overseers must have
been needed to keep the work force in being from year to year.
But as each pyramid rose from the floodplain, fewer and fewer
laborers were needed. The alternatives were simple: either
dismantle the labor organization, a process that would have a
number of far-reaching political and economic consequences,
or divert the many thousands of laborers to another pyramid
project.

Mendelssohn soon realized that once one or two pyramids
had been built, a profound change in the living conditions of
the Nile's rural population would be inevitable. For a quarter
of each year a large segment of Egypt's population was dependent on the country's central government for food and shelter.
The pyramid administration had to stockpile surplus grain to

feed the workers, grain levied by the pharaoh from the scattered villages of the Nile. As the villages became more accountable to the pharaoh and his government, they gradually evolved from a scattering of settlements into a unified state ruled by a divine king. And the towering Pyramids were the awesome symbol of the power of the pharaoh and the gods he represented on earth. Had the pharaohs and their advisors exploited the advantages of this new economic situation, wondered Mendelssohn? Was it the orgy of pyramid building that strengthened their position and built one of the world's most durable civilizations from hundreds of scattered villages on the banks of the Nile? His hypothesis is certainly a sensible one, far removed from cosmic energy and other improbable theories.

No one knows by what means the pharaohs recruited their
labor gangs. The workmen were probably volunteers, for there
are no signs of the huge armies that would have been needed
to discipline the sweating slaves that Hollywood film produc-
ers are so fond of depicting. More likely, speculated Mendelssohn, the Pyramids were built by gangs of peasant volunteers who willingly submitted themselves to the rivalry and
discipline of construction-camp life for the good of the state
and for the gods. The powerful religious and spiritual forces
that motivated this extraordinary army of volunteers will
perhaps always be a mystery.

There can be little doubt that Mendelssohn's conclusion is
correct: the Pyramids very likely did play a unique role in
Egyptian history. Any structures conceived on such a grandiose scale are bound to have had a dramatic effect on the
thousands of people involved in their building. But why the
pyramid form? And why did the pharaohs choose to be buried
under structures that pointed so dramatically heavenward?
Perhaps American Egyptologist James Breasted was right
when he wrote: "The king was buried under the very symbol
of the sun god which stood in the holy of holies in the sun
temple at Heliopolis and when in mountainous proportions
the pyramid rose above the king's sepulchre, dominating the
royal city below and the valley beyond for many miles, it was
the loftiest object which greeted the sun god in all the land,
and his morning rays glittered on its shining summit long
before he scattered the shadows in the dwellings of humbler
mortals below."

Sometimes on a cloudy day a single ray of sun will pierce
the cloud cover and strike the Great Pyramid along the very
angle of its sloped side. Witnessing this, one truly grasps the
meaning of an ancient Egyptian text: "I have trodden these
thy rays as a ramp under my feet whereon I mount up to that
my mother, the living being on the brow of Re." Perhaps the
Pyramids were a colossal and quite logical gateway to heaven.

# CHAPTER

# 9

# HOWARD CARTER

# AND

# TUT-ANKH-AMUN

"I STOOD IN THE PRESENCE OF A KING WHO REIGNED three thousand years ago," wrote British archaeologist Howard Carter half a century ago. He had just opened the burial chamber of an obscure Egyptian pharaoh, Tut-ankh-Amun. Only a few months after the discovery of his undisturbed mummy, Tut-ankh-Amun had become the most famous of all the ancient Egyptian kings simply because, over the years, his tomb had escaped detection by the voracious Egyptian grave robbers. No other archaeological discovery has ever rivaled the golden splendor and magnificence of Tut-ankh-Amun.

The tale of Tut-ankh-Amun centers around the desolate Valley of Kings near Thebes, for centuries the burial place of Egypt's greatest pharaohs. While early Egyptian rulers had been buried under vast pyramids, the later pharaohs were more circumspect. They were buried in elaborate, rock-cut tombs with carefully hidden entrances. Soon the Valley of Kings was honeycombed with secret burial chambers, each, theoretically at any rate, containing the elaborate and costly worldly goods of the departed pharaohs. Only those who worked on the tombs and the priests who guarded the valley knew the secrets of the royal sepulchres. The greatest of all Egyptian kings slept there, men whose names had been known and feared throughout the ancient world—Ramesses II, Sethy I, Thutmose III, and many others.

The funerary rites of the pharaohs, their relatives, and their important officials provided employment for hundreds of people. The guards and workpeople lived in a special village at Deir el-Medineh near Thebes. Contemporary records give us a fascinating glimpse into life in the Deir el-Medineh workshops. We read of absenteeism and of strikes called when rations were issued late. The villagers were kept continually busy—quarrying rock-cut tombs, making grave furniture, preparing the elaborate funerary inscriptions that vaunted the deeds of the dead to heaven and to posterity.

But the people of Thebes not only buried the dead, they robbed them as well. Thousands of richly furnished graves in the necropolis brought untold wealth to those bold enough to steal it. One can imagine the constant plotting that went on, the many attempts to bribe guards and compliant priests. Frequently, small groups of men would assemble at a quiet nocturnal rendezvous. A few words of greeting and they would slip into the darkness. Perhaps a cooperative necropolis guard would stealthily shine a light to show the way to the entrance to an untouched tomb. Sometimes a swift dagger stroke would remove a vigilant sentry. Then the robbers would burrow into the tomb, hastily search the burial chamber for portable loot, and slip quietly away before the relief guard appeared for duty. Within a few days the booty would have been sold or melted down for its precious minerals or gems. It's easy to imagine such happenings. Grave robbing was almost inevitable, for, by taking all their wealth with them, the pharaohs seemed to issue an open invitation to grave robbers. Nearly all the royal tombs in the Valley of Kings were emptied of their treasures within a few genera-

The Valley of Kings.

tions. Not even the death penalty deterred the tomb robbers.
The rewards were too high.

By the time the Romans visited the Valley of Kings only a
number of empty tombs remained, so the disappointed travelers did nothing but inscribe their names by torchlight on the
tomb walls. During the Middle Ages, hermits settled in the
royal sepulchres. Arab treasure hunters followed them. They
ransacked every corner of the desolate valley in search of
unopened tombs. So did Napoleon's scientists during a
lengthy stay in 1799. They counted eleven royal tombs and
found a twelfth. It was empty.

Twenty years later the celebrated circus strongman turned
tomb robber, Giovanni Belzoni, descended on the Valley of

Kings. Belzoni was familiar with the ways of the pharaohs and possessed an incredible instinct for knowing where to dig. Armed with a battering ram and the services of twenty experienced laborers, he soon found the empty tomb of Ramesses I. Then, a few days later, he uncovered the tomb of Sethy I, a beautifully painted sepulchre, empty except for a wonderful, translucent sarcophagus that had once contained the royal mummy. We know now that royal priests had entered the tomb on at least two occasions to move the royal mummy to safety before grave robbers ransacked the sepulchre and carried off everything portable.

Not even Giovanni Belzoni was able to find an undisturbed royal tomb. Apparently all the royal sepulchres had been emptied in ancient times by tomb robbers working in league with guards and priests. The pharaohs were robbed as quickly as they were buried. Or had some been overlooked? Generations of archaeologists combed the Valley of Kings looking for the ultimate archaeological prize—an undisturbed pharaoh's tomb.

The nineteenth century saw a dramatic growth in the tourist trade through Thebes. The town's tomb robbers made so much money from a seemingly inexhaustible supply of mummies and fine antiquities that the authorities in Cairo became suspicious. Their attentions focused on one Ahmed Abd el-Rasul, whose stock of antiquities always seemed to include some unique pieces. In early 1881 Rasul and his brother were arrested and tortured to no avail. But soon afterward a violent family quarrel over the division of the spoils sent Rasul's brother to the police. He confessed everything, recounting how the Rasul family had come across an incredible cache of mummies in a rocky cleft behind Thebes. A few days later he led the police and archaeologist Emil Brugsch to the rocky defile.

Brugsch, after arming himself with a pistol for fear of reprisals from the villagers, had himself lowered into the narrow entrance. As he lit his candles he was confronted by an extraordinary sight: the entire cleft was full of mummies. "The Arabs had disinterred a whole vault of pharaohs," he wrote later. "And what pharaohs! Thutmose III and Seti I, Ahmose the Liberator and Ramses II the Conqueror." Here were the mummies of the greatest pharaohs of all, mingled with an incredible jumble of grave furniture and ornaments, as well as coffins belonging to queens and lesser officials. The Rasuls had stumbled over the secret hiding place of the royal mummies, adopted as a last resort when the Valley of the Kings was deemed unsafe for any pharaoh to lie in. Loyal priests had smuggled the bodies to the secret cache, where they had dumped them hurriedly, perhaps only one step ahead of the grave robbers.

The forty royal mummies and their priceless possessions were carefully transferred to the Cairo Museum. Mohammed Rasul was rewarded for his pains with an appointment as a tomb guard, surely the most incredible piece of official stupidity in Egyptian history.

With the discovery of this fabulous cache most people believed that the Valley of Kings contained no more royal burials. As more information emerged from the royal finds in Rasul's cache, it became clear that every pharaoh from Thutmose I (c. 1526–1512 B.C.) to Amun-hotpe III (c. 1417–1379 B.C.) had been buried there and could be accounted for. But one small gap remained, that of a little-known pharaoh named Tut-ankh-Amun who reigned from 1361 to 1352 B.C. His two successors were buried in the valley, but of his tomb there was no sign.

Tut-ankh-Amun was born at a time of great political upheaval in Egypt. During the Eighteenth Dynasty, which lasted from about 1567 to 1320 B.C., Egypt occupied a prominent position in the ancient world. It was a great center of international trade, especially famed for its precious raw materials and ever-fertile wheat fields. The green Nile floodplain generated enormous food surpluses that supported all the panoply and show of the Egyptian court and the religion of the great god Amun at Thebes. A huge bureacracy administered the day-to-day affairs of the state and Egypt's relations with dozens of other nations. Tut-ankh-Amun's predecessors had expanded the Egyptian empire far beyond the boundaries of the Nile. Egypt was a powerful military state, her prestige enormous.

The events that shaped Tut-ankh-Amun's reign began some seven years before he was born. By that time, the pharaoh Amun-hotpe III had reigned for at least twenty-nine years and was growing old. He appointed his son Akh-en-Aten, at that time known as Amun-hotpe IV, as his co-regent. Akh-en-Aten seems to have had a strong interest in religion, at that time a complex interest to pursue, for Egypt was a maze of local and national religions and cults. Akh-en-Aten, a strong believer in monotheism, felt the time had come for a single national religion. The god he chose to worship to the exclusion of all others was the sun god, Aten, personified by the solar disk itself.

Akh-en-Aten spent most of his time propagating the religion of Aten, declaring himself the son of the sun god and his co-regent. Accordingly, he changed his name from Amun-hotpe to Akh-en-Aten. A vast temple of Aten was planned at Thebes and the royal capital was moved to a new site between Memphis and Thebes, to a place he named Akhet-Aten, now known as Tell el-Amarneh. While the pharaoh was busy with religious matters, foreign affairs were neglected. Egypt's vassals took advantage of the chaos on the Nile and carried on more or less as they pleased. Tut-ankh-Amun was probably born to Sit-Amun, daughter and wife of Amun-hotpe III, after Akh-en-Aten had been co-regent for eight years.

By this time Akh-en-Aten had but one preoccupation: the obliteration of all religious cults that in any way threatened the preeminence of Aten. Sculptors hacked out all references to Amun and other gods from temples and statues. The temples of Amun at Thebes were ignored and desecrated. Akh-en-Aten himself seems to have become mentally unbalanced to the extent that the very stability of Egypt was threatened. Tut-ankh-Amun must have experienced the traumas and tantrums of Akh-en-Aten's court. Fortunately, however, the pharaoh was still surrounded by statesmanlike advisers, one of whom, Ay, had originally served as Master of the Horse and then been elevated to a state adviser to the pharaoh. It seems that Ay paid only lip service to the cult of Aten, being more concerned with the survival of the state than with Akh-en-Aten's peculiarities. Fortunately for Egypt, both Akh-en-Aten and his successor, Semenka-Re, died within a short time of each other in 1361 B.C. and Tut-ankh-Amun came to the throne. Whether the two were assisted to heaven by the industrious Ay will ever remain a secret.

Tut-ankh-Amun was only nine when he became the most powerful ruler on earth. Ay took up the reins of government and served as regent and vizier to the new pharaoh. He also had himself appointed crown prince designate, so that he could legitimately succeed Tut-ankh-Amun, a master stroke of intrigue if ever there was one. Acting on the pharaoh's behalf, Ay moved cautiously to restore order and the fortunes of the cult of Amun. Tut-ankh-Amun's official inscriptions state how he restored temples that had fallen into ruin, their buildings overgrown with vegetation and weeds. The young king and his equally young queen, Ankhes-en-Amun, were kept busy with the complex round of rituals and ceremonies that custom prescribed for the pharaoh. One of Ay's priorities must have been to restore public confidence in the monarchy after the chaos of Akh-en-Aten's reign.

Then, in 1352 B.C., just as he was of an age to assume the full reins of pharaonic power, the young king suddenly died. He died childless, but two stillborn children, both girls, were mummified and buried with him. The dead pharaoh, although accorded a magnificent funeral, was buried in a smaller tomb than were his predecessors, a tomb originally intended for Ay himself. His faithful vizier succeeded to the throne and ruled Egypt for four years after Tut-ankh-Amun's death. Whether he arranged for the young king to be poisoned just when he was becoming a possible political threat we do not know. The process of mummification removed all traces of any foreign substances in the king's body. We can only assume he died of natural causes.

Such, then, is the story of the obscure king whose grave was still undiscovered eighty years ago. Everyone suspected it lay somewhere within the Valley of Kings, even if it had been obliterated in antiquity, and the tantalizing possibility of its presence made the valley one of the Egyptologists' prime excavation targets. A concession to dig in the Valley of Kings was highly prized and was available only to the most wealthy of patrons. From 1899 to 1902 their excavations in the valley were carefully supervised by Howard Carter, a British archaeologist who was chief inspector of monuments for Upper Egypt.

Howard Carter was an artist and draughtsman who first came to Egypt in 1892 at the age of eighteen. His sketches of the inscriptions at Beni Hasan were so widely admired that he was invited to dig with several famous archaeologists, among them the immortal Sir Flinders Petrie, the greatest Egyptologist of all time. When he became chief inspector of monuments, Carter visited the Valley of Kings almost daily. There he met a wealthy American businessman named Theodore Davis, who had just won the concession to excavate in the valley. Davis had come to Egyptology late in life, but was soon pouring money into large-scale excavations. He spent nine years digging in the Valley of Kings, where he found six important tombs and several minor burials. Carter worked with the enthusiastic American on two tombs and had plenty of time to ponder what soon became an obsession—the whereabouts of Tut-ankh-Amun's tomb.

In 1905 Carter quarrelled with the government and resigned. For two years he eked out a living as an artist at Thebes. Then one day he was introduced to George Edward Stanhope Molyneaux, Fifth Earl of Carnarvon. The two men—Carter the craftsman and meticulous artist, Carnarvon a wealthy aristocrat of the old school and a man whose cultivated taste in rare books and works of art was well known—took to each other immediately. Lord Carnarvon had first visited Egypt in 1901 at the age of thirty, after a serious motor accident in Germany. Each winter the Carnarvon family took up residence in Egypt so that the earl could avoid the unhealthy damp of the English winter. He began to collect Egyptian antiquities and soon teamed up with Howard Carter. Year after year Carnarvon financed excavations at Thebes, digs Howard Carter supervised on his behalf. The pair made many important discoveries in the vicinity of the Valley of Kings, but the valley itself was closed to them. Each season the two men watched enviously as Theodore Davis uncovered the intact tomb of Queen Ty's parents, the only undisturbed tomb ever found in the valley. But in 1914 Theodore Davis relinquished his concession. In his final publication the wealthy American wrote, "I fear that the Valley of Kings is now exhausted." A year later he died.

In his final season Theodore Davis uncovered a small underground chamber that contained some objects which bore the name of Tut-ankh-Amun. He promptly claimed that he had located the remains of the lost pharaoh's tomb. In fact, these few finds were leftovers from an early and rapid theft from Tut-ankh-Amun's still-buried tomb nearby. Then Davis made another discovery that seemed of little importance at the time. A small pit containing about a dozen white clay jars came to light. The jars held bundles of linen, some animal bones, and various embalming substances. Davis thought the jars of no importance and turned them over to the Metropolitan Museum of Art in New York, where Hubert Winlock, the Met's Keeper of Egyptian Antiquities, soon realized that the cache consisted of materials used during the embalming of Tut-ankh-Amun's mummy. Also found were the remains of a banquet eaten by about eight people, a meal evidently consumed at the time of the funeral.

Winlock did not publish his remarkable findings, but did mention them to Howard Carter. The Winlock discovery set Carter thinking. While he was now certain Tut-ankh-Amun had been buried in the valley, he wondered whether it was worthwhile looking for a tomb that could have been obliterated centuries before. The obstacles to further excavation were formidable; huge piles of rubble and sand were scattered over the floor of the valley. Was it worth the effort to shift thousands of tons of soil to search for a mere possibility? These were the days before mechanical earth-moving equipment. The only available tools for the job were adzes and hoes, baskets, and a plentiful supply of very cheap labor. Some sixth sense, perhaps the well-tuned instinct of the experienced archaeologist, caused Carter to embark on what to many seemed a crazy enterprise—a search for a tomb that might not exist.

Although Lord Carnarvon took up Theodore Davis's concession in 1914, it was not until 1917 that work in the valley began in earnest. Howard Carter decided to concentrate on a triangle of ground between the empty tomb of Ramesses II, his son Mery-en-Ptah, and Ramesses VI. Section by carefully planned section, Carter cleared the valley floor, moving from one sector to another as each was cleared. Except for the foundations of some workmen's huts and a cache of alabaster jars, the excavations yielded only endless piles of dry rubble. After six seasons of hard labor, Carnarvon was ready to give up. The excavators had moved 200,000 tons of soil with almost nothing to show for it.

In the summer of 1922, Carnarvon sent for Carter and told him to pack it in. But Carter was not so easily dissuaded. He pulled out a map of the valley and showed his patron a spot they had left untouched in 1917, on the grounds that a dig would have inconvenienced visitors to the tomb of Ramesses VI nearby. The undisturbed area was a small one and would require only one more season to investigate. Carter begged for the chance to dig for one more year and even offered to bear all

Necklace of the Rising Sun.
From Tut-ankh-Amun's tomb.
Length: 16 inches.

the costs himself. Carnarvon was so touched by Carter's offer that he agreed to a final season of excavation on the same terms as before. It was a fateful decision for both men.

Carter started work on November 1, 1922, only a few feet away from the spot where he had begun digging six years before. The workmen were instructed to clear the soil away from an area around the entrance to the tomb of Ramesses VI. The very first day more ancient workmen's huts came to light, part of the very same group Carter had partially excavated in 1917. Three days later, as the workmen began to clear away the huts, they came across a hidden step cut in the rocky valley floor thirteen feet from Ramesses' tomb. Since the huts had belonged to the workmen who had labored on the tomb of Ramesses VI in 1148 B.C., the underlying step obviously dated to an earlier period. Twenty-four hours later Carter was gazing at a rocky staircase of twelve steps that converged on a partially exposed blocked and plastered doorway. Breathless with excitement, Carter cleared away some of the rubble and exposed the plaster work. It bore some unbroken seals, the official jackal seals of the royal necropolis. The tomb was apparently intact!

Since the workmen who toiled on Ramesses VI's tomb had built their huts over the hidden entrance, the burial had certainly remained undisturbed since the Twentieth Dynasty. Some of the plaster had fallen away from the doorway. Carter shone his torch into the small, dark hole by the lintel and glimpsed a passageway filled with rubble.

At this supreme moment in his archaeological career, Carter displayed incredible patience and restraint. He filled in his excavation, placed trustworthy guards on the tomb, and sent a historic cable to Lord Carnarvon who was still in England: "At last have made wonderful discovery in the Valley; a magnificent tomb with seals intact; recovered same for your arrival; congratulations." Carter had found the tomb only a few feet from the place where he had started digging six years before.

For three long weeks Carter waited for Lord Carnarvon and his sister to arrive from England by steamer. On November 23 Carnarvon arrived in Luxor. The very next day the entire sixteen steps of the stairway were cleared. As the base of the sealed doorway emerged from the rubble, the two men stopped to gaze at some intact seals on the plaster. They were those of Tut-ankh-Amun himself. Although some signs of damage could be detected, the tomb had clearly been resealed by officials of the necropolis. There was a good chance that Tut-ankh-Amun's mummy lay in the tomb.

The seals were carefully photographed and removed. Then the doorway was cleared to reveal a sloping tunnel completely filled with stones and rubble. This, again, showed signs of disturbance and later resealing. The rubble was shoveled out. Thirty feet further along the passage was another doorway, again impressed with Tut-ankh-Amun's seal. Again, there were signs of illegal entry, so Carter steeled himself for a ransacked and empty tomb. After three hectic days of work, everything was ready for the great moment. Lord Carnarvon and Howard Carter paused before the doorway—a doorway they knew might lead to the greatest archaeological discovery of their careers.

Howard Carter carefully pried away some stones at the top of the doorway. The others waited in restless silence as he passed a candle through the hole to check for dangerous gases. At first Carter could see nothing. His candle flickered as hot air escaped from the long-sealed tomb. But presently, as his eyes became accustomed to the faint light, he saw the glint of gold and a jumble of strange objects. The gold swam in front of his eyes as he gazed absolutely spellbound at the incredible scene before him.

Impatiently Lord Carnarvon waited behind the gazing Carter. The silence became unbearable. Carter was struck dumb with amazement. After holding back for what must have seemed an interminably long time, Carnarvon asked anxiously, "Can you see anything?"

There was a short pause, then came Carter's whispered reply: "Yes, wonderful things."

A few moments later, Carter stepped back from his peephole, sweating and speechless. Carnarvon grabbed a torch and peered through the hole at the incredible sight behind the stone wall. "It was," recalled Carter later, "the day of days, the most wonderful I have ever lived through, and certainly one whose like I can never hope to see again."

What the two men had seen was the antechamber, the storeroom that lay before the actual mummy chamber. All they had glimpsed in this first look was a tiny part of the entire tomb, but they had seen enough to know that the results of their long search surpassed their wildest dreams.

Half a century later, we can marvel at the extraordinary self-control the two men exercised at this supreme moment in their lives. For a moment Carter almost gave in to an over-whelming impulse to burst into the chamber, to open box after box and to handle the extraordinary treasure that lay before him. As he later wrote, he felt almost embarrassed, as if he had strayed into someone's private room. "The very air you breathe," he wrote, "unchanged throughout the centuries, you share with those who laid the mummy to rest." There was even a farewell garland lying on the threshhold.

As their eyes became accustomed to the darkness, the two archaeologists could pick out individual objects. Three large, gilt couches lay opposite the passageway, carved in the form of monstrous, stretched-out animals. Their gilded sides glittered in the torchlight. To the right stood two life-sized, gold-kilted figures facing each other like sentinels, armed with mace and staff. Between them was another sealed doorway. With a thrill of excitement, Carter realized there was no mummy in the treasure chamber. Perhaps the pharaoh himself lay behind the two sentinels.

Carter and Carnarvon spent hours simply gazing at the antechamber, at painted and inlaid caskets, alabaster vases, carved chairs, a confused pile of chariot wheels, and hundreds of exquisite smaller treasures. As evening approached, they emerged from the tomb, placed a wooden grille over the doorway, and set a strong guard on Tut-ankh-Amun's sepulchre.

As the party rode home through the darkness, everyone was strangely silent and preoccupied, overcome with the events of the day. Far into the night Carter, Carnarvon, and their companions sat and talked. They found that each person had gathered different impressions, had spotted items the others had not. Howard Carter posed question after question to his excited listeners. "Is there a mummy behind the sealed door?"

The antechamber before clearance.

Carter and Carnarvon wrapping up one of the two statues of Tut-ankh-Amun in the antechamber for removal from the tomb.

he asked. "Have tomb robbers done more than rifle through the antechamber?" "How many rooms lie beyond the antechamber?" No one seems to have slept well that night. Carter could not stop thinking of the arduous task ahead of him. Perhaps he alone realized that their work had hardly begun.

On November 27 the party returned to the tomb early in the morning. Carter's assistant, Arthur Callendar, laid electric cables from a neighboring tomb which enabled them to hang powerful lights in the antechamber. Carter immediately scrutinized the sealed doorway between the sentries and determined that a small hole had been made in the plaster and had then been repaired. Perhaps at one time a small boy had been sent into the chamber beyond to see what lay there. There were clear signs of a forced entry and a rapid ransacking of the treasure chests in the antechamber too. But the robbers never had a chance to reach the mummy itself. Apparently they were disturbed at their work, for they fled with their booty, leaving most of the tomb unrifled. Later the necropolis officials tidied up the damage and repaired the doorways into the tomb, restoration work that cannot have taken more than a day. There were signs of at least two robberies, the first concerned with small portable objects of gold and silver, the second with precious oils and unguents. One thief even left his finger prints on the inside of the vessel from which he emptied fine oil into a convenient water skin.

These seem to have been the only illegal assaults made on the tomb, for its location was forgotten soon afterward. Unlike other pharaohs, Tut-ankh-Amun apparently died unexpectedly, long before the elaborate tomb being prepared for him was ready for occupation. So the necropolis officials cast about for a suitable substitute. Maya, the superintendent of the royal necropolis at the time, ordered the workmen to prepare Tut-ankh-Amun for burial in Ay's tomb, a chamber already hewn from the rock. Two centuries later, Ramesses VI decided that his sepulchre would be built into the rock face directly above the forgotten entrance to Tut-ankh-Amun's tomb. Thus, quite by chance, the new royal tomb protected the sepulchre until modern times.

Carter's immediate reaction was to break down the sealed doorway at once to settle the question of the mummy, but his incredible self-control won the day. The archaeologists reluctantly turned their attention to the antechamber. Obviously, the first step would have to be a complete inventory and photographic record of the jumble of treasure around them.

The tomb soon after discovery.

But there was so much to puzzle over and to admire; everything was so fresh and complete. "Any one of the objects," wrote Carter, "would have filled us with excitement under ordinary circumstances, and been considered ample repayment for a full season's work." The artistry of the furniture and jewelry was extraordinary. Tut-ankh-Amun's seal lay on all the larger objects and many of the smaller ones. There could now be no doubt as to the identity of the mummy that perhaps lay behind the sealed door.

Carter and Carnarvon spent all day in the antechamber, exclaiming at new objects and contemplating the huge task that lay before them. Then, suddenly, they noticed a small, dark hole under one of the burial couches. It was another sealed doorway, again with a hole torn in it. But this time no one had bothered to repair the tomb robbers' damage. Carter cautiously crawled under the couch and shone a light through the hole. Gold glittered in the darkness as the flashlight revealed a jumble of small, exquisite objects haphazardly strewn on the chamber's floor.

This treasure store was much smaller than the antechamber and no one had tidied up after the tomb robbers. Probably a single plunderer had crept into the chamber and ransacked it from one end to the other. He had passed a few objects out through the opening and left the rest in chaos.

The new discovery had a surprisingly sobering effect on the party. Suddenly they faced the immensity of the job ahead. Tut-ankh-Amun's tomb was unique, quite outside any archaeologist's normal range of experience. Carter wondered if the job was beyond him.

The first priority was to secure the tomb against unauthorized entry. Carter ordered a gate of tough steel bars, then placed his most reliable guards on watch. Meanwhile, wild rumors were circulating in Thebes: a great treasure had been found in the valley and had been spirited out of Egypt by plane; the burials of several pharaohs had come to light; unbelievable wealth had been discovered for the first time. Dealers' shops and the bazaars buzzed with gossip, and Carter and Carnarvon were besieged with inquiries. To put an end to the uproar, they decided to stage an official opening of the tomb. On November 29, 1922, a large and varied party of distinguished guests assembled at the tomb for a formal inspection of the marvels that lay within. The local correspondent of the

London *Times* was present and filed a long dispatch that sent the public into a frenzy of excitement. Howard Carter's problems were only just beginning.

The tomb entrance was filled in as Carter went to Cairo to make thorough preparations for clearing the antechamber. Every object in the tomb had to be recorded and photographed in place. Many pieces were too fragile to be removed without some restoration first. Obviously Carter needed help. Fortunately, expert assistance was not far away. When the *Times* carried the news of Carter and Carnarvon's triumph, offers of help poured in from all over Europe and America. The Metropolitan Museum of Art lent photographers and artists, the Egyptian Antiquities Department offered facilities. Individual Egyptologists rushed to the scene as well, including Alan Gardiner, the world's leading authority on hieroglyphs.

Carter's immediate logistical problems were formidable. He purchased mountains of packing materials, a mile of bandages and a further mile of wadding, thirty-two bales of calico, all kinds of chemicals and photographic equipment, and even a motorcar. So much restoration and packing work had to be done on the site that Carter set up a conservation laboratory nearby in the empty tomb of Sethy II. There the contents of the tomb were prepared for shipping to Cairo. In those days there were no tarmac roads to the Valley of Kings, nor were there helicopters to transport delicate finds from door to door. Every statue, every item of furniture, and even the mummy itself had to be carried over dirt tracks by large gangs of men. All Carter had at his disposal were a few lengths of railroad track that had to be laid and relaid again as the precious loads made their slow way to the Nile at Luxor. The alternatives were camels or porters, so Carter used a gang of fifty men to move the precious trucks and the rails. Their progress was slow: they covered only a third of a mile each hour and it took fifteen hours to make the complete journey to the Nile. In addition, the move was made at the height of summer when, at times, the rails became almost too hot to touch. The steamship that carried the finds downriver to Cairo took another seven days.

By December 18, a steel door had been installed and a team of at least seven experts was on hand. During the following months, as Carter began to list the antechamber's contents, he was finally able to appreciate the full range of treasures crammed into this 300 square-foot space. Clearing this cramped area was, as Carter said, "like a giant game of spillikins." It was an exacting job, for many of the most delicate objects were intermeshed with one another and each presented special problems. There were, for example, delicate ornaments of patterned beadwork and funeral bouquets that fell apart at a touch unless first hardened with paraffin wax. Tut-ankh-Amun's chariots and funeral couches had been constructed in such a way that they could be brought into the tomb in pieces and then reassembled. Carter's problem was the reverse—he had to disassemble them and remove the separate parts. After three thousand years, the bronze hooks had set hard in their staples and would not budge. It took five people to dismantle the couches. The chariots were even worse, for they had been disturbed by the tomb robbers and been restacked by the priests. The leather trapppings were little more than a black, glutinous mass.

It took seven weeks to clear the antechamber. Harry Burton, a photographer from the Met in New York, photographed each object in place. Then two artists added the item to their detailed drawing of the antechamber before Carter and Callendar supervised its removal. Only archaeologists handled the precious finds, both for conservation and for security. Once a day a closely supervised company of laborers would carry a precious cargo of stretchers out of the tomb over to the laboratory in Sethy II's sepulchre. What an extraordinary sight each procession was! Painted wooden chests, stools, a golden shrine, even a mannequin to which the king's robes could be fitted, as well as a host of minor objects—fly whisks, bows,

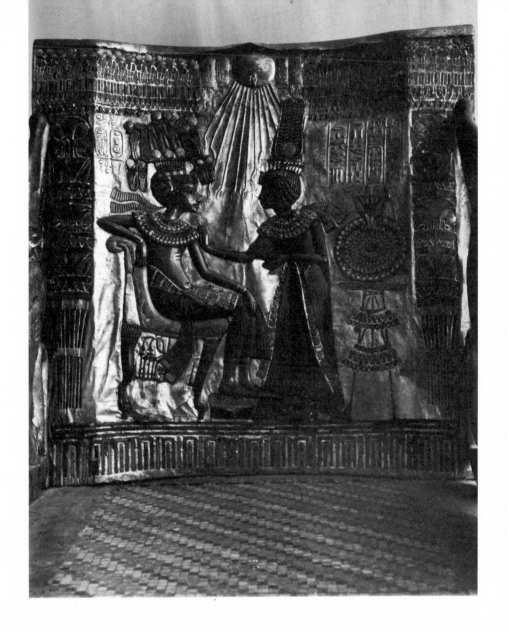

vases, a wine strainer—were brought into the bright sunshine
of the twentieth century.

Perhaps the finest object was a throne overlaid with gold
and richly decorated with glass, faience, and semiprecious
stones. The legs were surrounded with lions' heads, and magnificent serpents formed the arms. But the back of the throne
made Carter gasp. In a scene inlaid in glass, the pharaoh
relaxes on a cushioned throne while the queen, standing in

front of him, puts the final touches on the pharaoh's toilet. In one hand she holds a small jar of ointment; with the other, she gently anoints her husband's shoulder. The colors of this charming scene must have dazzled when new. Even centuries later, they glowed with a soft translucence that led Carter to exclaim that the throne was "the most beautiful thing that has yet been found in Egypt."

By this time, the clearance of the tomb was being closely followed by the press. Carter was deluged with congratulatory cables, then with thousands of letters. "They were a curious lot," Carter wrote of his correspondents. There were offers of assistance, as well as inquiries regarding moving-picture rights and fashion-design copyrights. Some told Carter how to appease evil spirits, others sent religious tracts and denounced the archaeologists for committing sacrilege. "An interesting psychological study they would make if one had the time," Carter remarked to a colleague.

Visitors to the site soon became a serious problem. Tourists in the thousands flocked to the entrance of the tomb. Every time a convoy of stretchers left the entrance, dozens of camera shutters clicked. The archaeologists were importuned by reporters in search of sensational stories and by the famous and wealthy seeking guided tours. By now a low wall had been built around the tomb. Each morning, visitors arrived "on donkeys, in sand-carts, and in two-horse cabs." They staked out a claim by the wall and stared. People read, talked, knitted, and photographed everything in sight. At the end of the first season, Carter estimated that a quarter of the archaeologists' time had been consumed with visitors. It was difficult to be gracious when there was real danger of irreparable damage to the contents of the tomb. Most annoying were the visitors who pulled every kind of string to get in to see the tomb and then left muttering, "Well, there wasn't much to see after all." The reporters were worse, until Lord Carnarvon gave exclusive rights to the London *Times.* Even so, Carter spent much of his time warding off the public and answering questions.

By the middle of February 1923, the antechamber was swept clean. As the work of clearance ended, Carter's eyes turned again and again to the sealed doorway. What would they find behind the damaged plaster, guarded for so many centuries by the two silent sentries?

On February 17, 1923, a party of twenty experts and distinguished people assembled in the antechamber to witness the opening of the sealed doorway. A low working platform was erected, high enough for Carter to reach the top of the doorway. The guests were invited to sit down as Carter advanced to the doorway with a small hammer and trembling hands.

With infinite care, Carter chipped away the plaster from the wooden lintel. After ten minutes of careful work, he was able to insert a flashlight into a small hole. To his astonishment, a solid wall of gold blocked the entrance of the chamber. Carter and two colleagues carefully removed the coarse stone slabs that blocked the doorway. As the golden wall came into view, a thrill of excitement passed through the spectators. Two hours later, most of the entrance was cleared. Some agonizing moments of delay ensued as Carter gathered up the scattered beads of a necklace dropped on the threshhold by a tomb robber three thousand years before.

The floor of the chamber that lay beyond the threshhold was four feet lower than that of the antechamber. There was only a narrow space between the doorway and the huge gilt shrine that protected the royal mummy. Carter lowered himself into the chamber and shone an electric light into the tiny passageway. After removing two alabaster vases that blocked the way, Carter signaled to Carnarvon to join him. Together they squeezed along the passage. Openmouthed, they stared at the great gilt shrine, glittering with gold inlay and panels of brilliant blue faience. Its massive bulk—17 by 11 by 9 feet—filled almost the entire burial chamber. The walls of the

Howard Carter opens the second shrine.

chamber itself had been hastily painted with scenes and inscriptions. Nearby lay the oars the pharaoh needed to ferry himself across the waters of the underworld.

The closed doors of the shrine lay at the east end of the chamber. They were bolted but not sealed. Had tomb robbers wreaked destruction on the sarcophagus that lay within? Eagerly Carter slid back the bolts and swung open the doors. Before him was a second shrine with bolted doors and an intact seal. A linen pall decorated with golden rosettes hung above the inner shrine.

At this point, Carter and Carnarvon paused again, simultaneously experiencing a sharp sense of intrusion. They were, they felt, in the presence of a king to whom they should make reverence. So they closed the doors silently and continued their preliminary examination of the burial chamber. Another surprise awaited them, an open doorway that led to a small chamber containing a marvelous golden shrine guarded by four goddesses of the dead. This shrine obviously contained the canopic jars so important in Egyptian funerary rites. Nearby the jackal god Anubis, wrapped in a linen cloth, sat on his shrine. There were further shrines and chests, too, model boats, another chariot. Carter opened a magnificent casket containing a beautiful ostrich feather fan as fresh as the day it was made.

The first survey of the burial chamber was but a hasty one, for Carter realized the others were waiting their turn. In pairs, the visitors stepped down into the chamber. As they emerged, Carter watched their faces. Everyone, dazzled and bewildered, threw their hands up in front of them as if unable to describe the wonders that lay within. "It was," Carter wrote soon afterward, "an experience which, I am sure, none of us who were present is ever likely to forget." The emotions aroused by the spectacle of the burial chamber made the archaeologists feel they had actually been present at the burial ceremonies of the pharaoh himself.

A week later Carter closed down the tomb for the season and placed it under heavy guard. Two months afterward, Lord Carnarvon was bitten by a mosquito. The bite became infected. Three weeks later, on April 6, 1923, he died in a Cairo hotel. His death created a public sensation, for people thought he was the first victim of the legendary curse of Tut-ankh-Amun, a terrible penalty for disturbing the long sleep of the pharaoh. Speculation ran wild, for two other archaeologists associated with the investigation died suddenly soon afterward. Over the years no fewer than twenty-one individuals were claimed by the press to be victims of the curse. But perhaps the more impressive statistic is the number of people who did *not* die. Carter lived to be sixty-six, while the anatomist who performed the postmortem on Tut-ankh-Amun lived to be over eighty. All the same, the myth lived on, perpetuated by a rash of Hollywood movies about the curse of the pharaohs. One starred Boris Karloff as a hyperactive mummy. Romantic novelists have made hay with the myth, too. But, whatever one's views on the curse, no one can explain the curious fact that all the lights in Cairo failed at the precise moment that Carnarvon died. And, at that very same moment, his dog in faraway England suddenly howled and dropped dead.

Despite Carnarvon's death, Howard Carter was determined to continue. After prolonged negotiations, the Carnarvon concession was renewed, on terms more favorable to the Egyptian government. In 1924–1925 the objects stacked between the shrine and the walls of the burial chamber were removed. Then the wall between the antechamber and the burial chamber was taken down, so that the delicate work of taking apart the outer gilt shrine could begin. Carter expected to find at least five shrines, one inside the other, but in the end, found only four. Each was removed piece by piece by dismantling the gold-covered planking at the very tongues and grooves where they had originally been joined. It took eighty-four days of intense labor to unveil the magnificent yellow quartzite of the king's sarcophagus. There was so little space in the chamber that the walls of the outer shrine had to rest against the side of the chamber until there was space to move them out.

When a third shrine with sealed doors was revealed within the second, Carter decided to go ahead and open its doors at once. The cords and seals were removed, the bolts slid back. A fourth and even more gorgeous shrine lay within, this time with unsealed doors. With bated breath, Carter drew back the bolts. As the doors swung open, a goddess sculpted on the end of the huge yellow sarcophagus within seemed to raise her hand and wings to ward off the intruders.

Some weeks later, the yellow quartzite sarcophagus stood in the middle of the burial chamber, clear of its four shrines. At this point, diplomacy intervened. A large group of archaeologists and officials gathered to witness the opening of the casket. Blocks and tackles were attached to angle irons along the huge granite sarcophagus lid, which weighed over a ton. As bright lights revealed the inside of the sarcophagus, first impressions were disappointing. The inner coffins were covered with fine linen shrouds. Silently, Carter rolled the shrouds back. As the last was removed, everyone gasped. A fabulous golden effigy of the young king lying on a lion-shaped dais filled the sarcophagus. The metalsmiths had even used two different alloys of gold to render a different flesh texture akin to the grey of death. And, most touching of all, a withered bouquet of flowers lay next to the royal symbols of the cobra and the vulture (Upper and Lower Egypt) on the king's forehead. Perhaps, thought Carter, this was the final tribute of the young, mourning queen. In the silence, he could almost hear the ghostly footsteps of the departing mourners.

In the 1925–1926 season, fully three years after the discovery of the tomb, Carter removed the royal coffins from the burial chamber. The huge, gilt-covered effigy coffin was first. The silver pins that held the lid to the body of the casket were

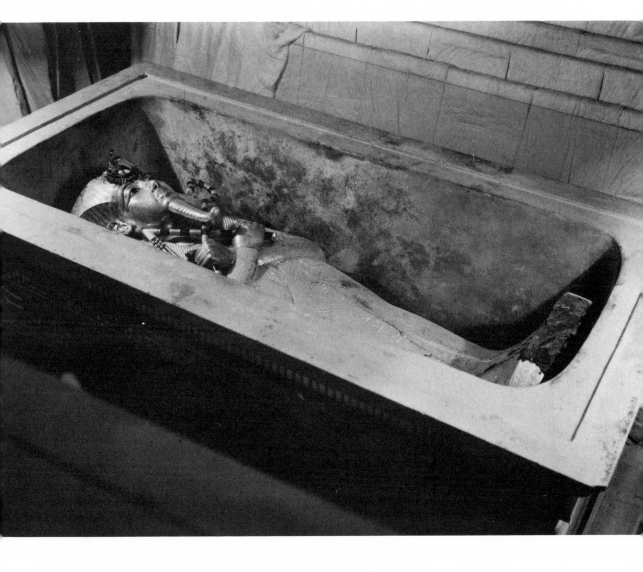

carefully drawn out and a lifting tackle was attached to the
silver handles to raise the lid. A second, magnificent, gold-
covered coffin lay within, again covered with a linen shroud
and withered garlands. There was so little space inside the
sarcophagus that Carter lifted the first and second coffins out
of their stone cocoon and laid them on planks. Then, daringly,
the first coffin was lowered back into the sarcophagus while
the second was suspended in midair by fine copper wires for a
few breathless minutes.

By this time they were close to the pharaoh's mummy
itself. The lid of the second coffin was carefully lifted off,
revealing more linen coverings and a third coffin. Another

Tut-ankh-Amun inside his
sarcophagus.

surprise awaited the onlookers. The inner coffin, a little over six feet long, was of solid gold, later found to be about one-tenth of an inch thick. Carter was overwhelmed by the incredible wealth of the Golden Monarch, at the extraordinary display before him. Small wonder the pharaohs had been robbed in their graves!

At this point, the inner coffins were moved to the antechamber, where Carter proceeded to the ultimate task, that of exposing the royal mummy within the golden coffin. With great difficulty the lid was raised, revealing the mummy of Tut-ankh-Amun wearing a golden mask and darkened by the many unguents poured on its bandages. The mummy was covered with necklaces, pendants, and beads, but was obviously in a perilous state because of an overdose of unguents.

On November 11, 1925, at 9:45 A.M., Dr. Douglas Deny, an anatomist from Cairo, began the formal examination of Tut-ankh-Amun's mummy in front of a select audience. He started by cutting away the outer wrappings—bandages, sheets, and linen pads. With every incision, he exposed more ornaments. Excitement mounted as Deny started on the bandaged head. The pharaoh was wearing a gold diadem, a broad headband, and a beautifully decorated skullcap that fitted tightly over his shaven head. Then, with a few deft strokes, Deny exposed the features of the long-dead pharaoh.

Tut-ankh-Amun gazed serenely at his audience. His "refined and cultured countenance" smiled slightly, the masked lips slightly parted. Everyone was astonished to find just how accurately the contemporary artists had portrayed the king's features. They depicted Tut-ankh-Amun as a handsome and finely featured youth, which, his mummy showed, he actually was. The ears were pierced, the skull curiously elongated. The pharaoh's forearms were smothered in bracelets, his fingers and thumbs encased in gold sheaths and rings. A magnificent, gold-decorated dagger lay inside the king's waist girdle. Another, with a virtually unrusted iron blade, lay in a golden scabbard by the ceremonial apron around the pharaoh's waist.

Tut-ankh-Amun fishing with a
spear from a reed canoe.

Tut-ankh-Amun wore gold sandals, with separate gold sheaths for each toe. No less than 143 different objects were placed over, or on, the king's body.

Once most of the wrappings had been removed from the body, the king's corpse was lifted from its coffin. The bitumen that anchored the wrappings to the gold coffin had to be chiseled away. It was then possible for Dr. Deny to examine the pharaoh's body. After a meticulous autopsy, Deny confirmed that Tut-ankh-Amun had died when about eighteen to twenty years of age. He was of slight build, perhaps no more than 5' 6" tall. There were no injuries, signs of poisoning, or indications of a violent death.

Many years later a team of anatomists from Cairo and Liverpool universities X-rayed Tut-ankh-Amun's mummy. They confirmed Deny's and Carter's conclusions as to the age and stature of the king. Then they analyzed the pharaoh's tissues using a new technique that showed his blood groups were $A_2$ and MN, identical to those of Semenka-Re, whose mummy had been identified some years before. The skull measurements of the two young men, and indeed their facial features, seemed almost identical. The anatomists suggested that the two men were brothers who died within a few years of one another. Perhaps both of them were the children of pharaoh Amun-hotpe III and his daughter Sit-Amun. We do not know. This remains one of the many mysteries that still surround the tomb of Tut-ankh-Amun.

Howard Carter continued to work on the tomb of Tut-ankh-Amun until 1928. He cleared the treasure chamber connected to the burial chamber and the small annex to the antechamber. After ten years of strenuous work, he left the valley forever, exhausted and in ill health. Carter died at the age of sixty-six. Although he never completed the herculean task of studying the contents of the tomb, he did complete a three-volume popular account of his discoveries. Meanwhile, Lord Carnarvon's widow had been persuaded to donate all the finds to the Cairo Museum, where they remain on permanent display. She, in turn, was indemnified by the Egyptian government for all the expenses incurred by the family.

Although more than half a century has passed since Howard Carter first gazed on the tomb of Tut-ankh-Amun, the burial of this obscure pharaoh still seems to evoke remarkable public interest. Thanks to the generosity of the Egyptian government and the Cairo Museum, Americans, beginning in 1977, had the opportunity to view the treasures of Tut-ankh-Amun as the collection toured selected museums across the United States.

Perhaps it is the legendary mystery that surrounds the ancient Egyptian kings, perhaps Tut-ankh-Amun's mind-boggling wealth, possibly the stirring drama of the discovery itself that generates such rapt interest whenever the young king is mentioned. Wandering through the Tut-ankh-Amun galleries in the Cairo Museum, one is conscious of the boy pharaoh's spell. And, as one gazes on the serene, golden countenance of the pharaoh, it's possible for just a moment to imagine oneself—as Howard Carter did—in the presence of a king who lived three thousand years ago.

# CHAPTER

# 10

# CHAIRMAN MAO'S ARCHAEOLOGY

"OUR NATION HAS THOUSANDS OF YEARS OF HISTORY: IT has good points and it has numerous valuable and rare and unusual objects. Make use of the old ways for present purposes, and adapt Western ways for present use." Thus did Chairman Mao define the role of archaeology in the building of modern China.

Unique among nations, the Chinese use archaeology as a means of forging a national identity and of generating pride in the technological skills passed down from the ancients. It is not only archaeologists that are involved in this effort but the wider community as well—government bureaucrats, soldiers, workers, students, and entire local communities.

Today in China there is tremendous popular concern for preserving ancient cultural objects. People are identifying with the past as never before, largely because archaeology has been recognized as a useful instrument in realizing Mao's new plan for Chinese society. By pointing up parallels between China's past and present, archaeology promotes an understanding of contemporary society in terms that are readily intelligible to all members of society.

Most western archaeologists, remembering the archaeological myths spun by Nazi archaeologists before World War II and recent, more subtle attempts to use archaeology for political purposes in Rhodesia and elsewhere, would strongly disagree with the Chinese use of archaeology as an instrument for reinforcing the party line. Again and again in Chinese political tracts we read statements like: "The people, and only the people, are the dynamic in creating world history. In feudal society, only the farmers and artisan workers were the basic class who created wealth and culture." Archaeology in China is used to underscore the suffering of the workers in prerevolutionary society, to emphasize that the credit for technological achievement goes to the masses rather than to the corrupt aristocracy. Many of the artifacts found in Chinese archaeological sites bear a remarkable resemblance to the tools used by well diggers and bridge builders in modern China. The point is simple: the workers, by their ingenuity, have solved complex technological problems for thousands of years, without the aid of complex machines such as are used by other nations. Archaeology is even used to emphasize China's friendship with its present neighbors. The textile imports found in ancient cemeteries are pointed to as evidence that China has always been interested in friendly relations with other Asian nations.

The new nation has embraced archaeology enthusiastically. The Chinese people themselves are totally involved in a pastime that in many other societies is considered an expensive luxury. The other side of the coin, of course, is that the government totally controls archaeological research and conservation. But, given the finite nature of archaeological sites, which, once dug, are destroyed, there is something to be said for the Chinese approach to conservation of the past.

Chinese civilization has always seemed exotic to outsiders. Ever since the Venetian merchant Marco Polo visited Asia in the thirteenth century A.D., westerners have thought of the Chinese as a very ancient and mysterious people. Marco Polo

GREAT WALL

▲ PEKING
*CHOUKOUTIEN*
*MAN-CHENG*
*YI-TU*
HOPEI
SHANTUNG
▲

KANSU

SHENSI
SHANSI

*ANYANG*
HUANGHO R.
● *CHENG-CHOU*
HONAN

CHINA SEA

CHINA

YANGTZE R.

*CH'ANG-SHA*
HUNAN

N

0 ——— 300
MILES

Locations and sites mentioned
in Chapter 10.

loved to spin elaborate tales of his travels in far-off lands. Chinese civilization, he wrote, was so prosperous that the great khan received a hundred thousand white horses with rich trappings from his subjects every New Year.

But western disillusionment with the East set in in the eighteenth century, when Protestant missionaries returned from China utterly disenchanted with the people and their suspicious rulers. China was, one disgusted cleric wrote, "a second-class country, peopled by those who, lacking the light of God, must inevitably be regarded as inferior beings." Needless to say, the clerical view must be regarded as less than objective.

Whatever the prevailing feeling toward China, westerners have always agreed on one point: the Chinese have enjoyed a sophisticated civilization for many thousands of years. What was this civilization like in ancient times? Until quite recently, nobody knew.

The Chinese themselves are very conscious of their history; they revere the past. Their tradition of historical scholarship goes back several centuries before Christ, a tradition based on the notion that accumulated human experience is a useful guide for the future. As a result of this view, their culture developed an extraordinary continuity, even though the actual events of history include just as many political upheavals as experienced by other countries.

The Chinese have long possessed a legendary history. According to this ancient lore, the universe was created by a personality named P'an-ku. He was followed by a whole series of legendary monarchs and heroes who invented houses, fire, agriculture, writing, and all the social and political complexities of Chinese society. Then came the three great dynasties—Hsia, Shang, and Chou—dynasties that mark the beginning of recorded Chinese history.

The details of this long recorded history are very vague, a curious melange of historical fact, legend, and sheer fantasy. Confucius, who died in 479 B.C., insisted that a single emperor had always ruled China. His assumption passed into Chinese history. So did the arguments of an ancient Chou philosopher who thought that early Chinese society had advanced through various stages of technological development. The earliest Chinese had used no metals, he said, only stone and wood. They were followed by bronze-working peoples, while iron came into use much later.

Although no one used archaeology to write early Chinese history, plenty of scholars avidly studied the inscriptions on stone and bronze vessels, a tradition of antiquarianism that extended back over a thousand years. Still, even given this reverence for the ancient civilization, no one seemed particularly interested in sorting out historical fact from fiction.

Archaeology has changed all that. During the 1920s and 1930s, Chinese intellectuals began to challenge the official version of their history. They began to look at the ancient sources with a critical mind and to search for traces of ancient civilizations in the ground. Numerous traces of long-abandoned villages and towns could be seen in cultivated fields and near great rivers like the Huangho and Yangtze. The world was electrified when European and Chinese archaeologists found the remains of very ancient prehistoric hunter-gatherers and their quarry in the Choukoutien caves near Peking in the 1930s. The beetle-browed skulls of "Peking Man" were dated to about 400,000 years ago, a time when long-extinct animals roamed the Chinese countryside. Incredibly, these remarkable finds seemed irrelevant to traditional Chinese historians. But other, more forward-looking scholars realized their wider significance: they recognized that archaeology could add a whole new dimension to Chinese civilization.

In 1928, a group of Chinese archaeologists attached to the newly founded Academia Sinica, the institute of sciences in Peking, decided to launch a bold search for ancient civilization in Northern China. They pored over the few available historical documents pertaining to this region and decided to concentrate their efforts on an area near the town of Anyang near the Huangho River. All evidence indicated that this area had been the seat of powerful Shang rulers who had presided over a distinctive, early civilization centered in the Huangho Valley at least two thousand years before Christ.

To determine where to excavate, the archaeologists followed up on some intriguing local legends. For many years, the farmers tilling the soil near the village of Hsiao T'un by Anyang had been digging up curious bone fragments, many of them decorated with strange symbols. Regrettably, some of these found their way into the hands of local apothecaries, who ground them up for medicine. The few that reached scientific hands were immediately recognized as Shang oracle bones. Furthermore, the place they came from had strong Shang associations in local lore.

For nearly ten years, from 1928 to 1937, the archaeologists of Academia Sinica carried out lengthy excavations at Hsiao T'un under the direction of Tung Tso-pin and Li Chi. At last the Shang civilization emerged from the shadows of history. The Shang were revealed as farmers and skilled metalworkers whose rulers lived in secluded compounds and were buried in elaborate tombs, complete with their chariots and trusted retainers. Many of the finest of the Shang craftsmen's products were found in the tombs of rulers and nobles. The common people lived in small villages scattered over the Shang domain. They cultivated barley, wheat, millet, and other crops and kept sheep, pigs, oxen, and dogs. Skilled artisans often lived in special enclaves near the royal residences, working with bronze, jade, clay, and inlaid wood to produce magnificent objects that graced the royal palaces and burials.

Shang society was rigidly stratified into a hierarchy of classes governed by elaborate social rules. From the start, this civilization and its successors were distinctively Chinese. The Shang script foreshadows the established Chinese writing system of later times, and Shang cooking vessels indicate that Chinese cuisine was already evolving in sophisticated directions radically different from those of western kitchens. The archaeologists who worked at Anyang soon realized that the roots of Chinese civilization extended at least three thousand years into the past. And the expertise of early craftsmen fully matched that of later dynasties.

Startling evidence both of technological skill and of the harsh conditions of Shang society came from royal burials and chariot tombs. Although some royal burials were excavated in the 1930s, new revelations have come from official government excavations in recent years. A royal grave dug at Yi-tu in 1965 in Shantung province unearthed a grisly human sacrifice. The archaeologists uncovered a rectangular shaft twenty-five feet deep, its walls sloping gently inward to a step near the base. A wooden funeral chamber lay below the step, protected by a layer of charcoal. Beneath this timber-framed chamber, the excavators found three sacrificial pits. The lowest contained the seated body of a human victim with a bone pin in his hair; the other two entombed a dog and another human sacrifice, this time a man who may have been buried alive with a wooden post to hold him down.

The burial chamber had been robbed at least three times, so no traces of the royal personage remained for the archaeologists to examine. But their careful sifting through the soil yielded fragments of ritual bronze vessels, spears and arrowheads, symbolic jade objects, and two massive, bronze axe heads that may have been the symbols of office granted to the long-dead ruler. The step above the burial chamber contained further human sacrificial victims buried in wooden coffins. Four ramps led from this step to the surface. The southern approach, considered the main entrance, extended to the bottom of the grave. Where it joined the burial chamber the archaeologists found twenty-four human skulls and thirteen skeletons of young men stacked in three layers where they had been slaughtered in sacrificial tribute. The shaft was filled with tightly packed earth that effectively sealed its macabre contents. The design of the Yi-tu royal tomb closely resembled those of the Shang kings at Anyang excavated before World War II.

Between 1600 and 1027 B.C. the Shang kings went to war in fine chariots, at that time strategic weapons of the utmost importance that gave a critical tactical edge to their owners. Only the wealthy could afford chariots, for they were intricate, carefully crafted machines fashioned from precious materials. Many people chose to be buried with their valuable chariots, so that they could ride them in the afterlife. In 1972 a Shang chariot, buried deep in fine soil that had eaten away the chariot's wood, came to light near Anyang. The decomposed timber had been replaced by harder particles of the soil that subsequently hardened even more than the surrounding earth. When the archaeologists opened the grave they identified the harder, discolored soil, brushed away the less-hard grave filling, and unearthed the ghostly shape of a long-decayed chariot. Such excavation requires extraordinarily precise technique.

The chariot had a stout shaft that supported a driver's platform with sturdy timber sides. The axle shaft was joined to this same shaft. The finely spoked, intricate wheels with bronze hubcaps were carefully unearthed from the grave fill. Since no bronze nails were found in the immediate area, the Chinese assumed the various parts of the vehicle were lashed together with thongs. The yokes, bronze harness parts, and ornaments still rested in place on the skeletons of two horses. The driver of the chariot had been killed, too. He lay stretched out behind his perch. Both driver and horses had been covered with mats after the burial was laid out.

In the case of the Shang, recent Chinese archaeology has added many details to the previously sketchy story of the earliest of far eastern civilizations. Although a great deal of work had been carried out on Shang sites by 1937, political conditions became so unsettled after that time that archaeological excavations came to a virtual standstill for over twenty years. Several archaeologists were killed by insurgents. In addition, the supervision of key sites and known royal burials during the period of unrest was so lax that hundreds of tombs and settlements were looted for their valuable bronzes, beautiful vases, and jade objects. Tomb frescoes were ripped from the walls of long-buried sepulchres and statuary was taken apart and reassembled after export for sale to dealers and collectors all over the world.

Regrettably, many of the people who collected Shang bronzes and fine statuary, whether these objects were from legal or illegal excavations, considered their pursuit harmless, if extravagant. Some simply found pleasure in owning valuable and unique objects; the historical context of the objects was unimportant to them. All that mattered was the price and quality of the artifact. Thus Chinese archaeology, like that of the ancient Egyptians and the Maya of Mexico, was in imminent danger of vanishing into thousands of private collections long before any serious, large-scale excavations could be planned.

As long ago as 1925 the great writer Lu Hsun commented on the artifact scavengers: "Some foreigners are very eager that China should remain one great antique for them to enjoy forever. But," he went on, "our chief aims at present are: first, to exist; secondly, to find food and clothing; and thirdly, to advance."

Fortunately for science, the communist rulers who took over the government in 1949 looked at archaeology in a different way. Mao Tse-tung himself said, "Let the past serve the present." So a new generation of archaeologists set about creating order out of historical and archaeological chaos. The government established provincial and district museums and organized regional institutes of archaeology. The staff of these institutions began training field-workers, administering new antiquities laws that protected dozens of important sites, and educating local people in the value and importance of archaeological sites and ancient crafts as part of Chinese history.

The result of these efforts has been much greater control of illegal looting and many new and astonishing discoveries. A large number of these discoveries came about because of finds reported by farmers or laborers, the very people who earlier would have sold their finds to an apothecary or a dealer. In addition, the huge public works undertaken by the new government meant that thousands of observant peasants were put to work on immense earth-moving projects, such as the construction of dams. While engaged in this work, they also, in effect, served as archaeological scouting parties, and their alertness resulted in many dramatic finds.

"A splendid old culture was created during the long period of Chinese feudal society," said Chairman Mao. And the Chinese believed him. "During the Great Proletarian Cultural Revolution, China's archaeological workers took an active part in the revolutionary struggle, and at the same time did much work in their field. They did not work in isolation but among the people following the mass line. . . . This has made archaeological work develop smoothly and yield richer results than ever before."

Archaeological research has received strong encouragement partly because its spectacular discoveries can be used to foster a sense of national unity and pride. But there are other motives as well, as evidenced by this party pronouncement: "Tempered in the Cultural Revolution and advancing along the revolutionary path pointed out by Chairman Mao, Chinese archaeologists are contributing much evidence for the scientific materialist view of history." The current official view of Chinese history is to regard it, along Marxist lines, as a series of theoretical stages, beginning with primitive society and advancing through slavery and feudalism to the present revolutionary society. The archaeological finds of recent years provide, in the eyes of Chinese scholars, ample support for this scheme.

It was with considerable eagerness, for example, that Chinese archaeologists reported the finding of a Chou nobleman's tomb dating to between 110 and 221 B.C. The sepulchre contained not only the body of the nobleman but also the skeletons of eighteen slaves with iron collars around their necks. Thus, the archaeologists said, there was obviously a slave class in early Chinese society.

The most glorious and long-lived of the early Chinese states was that of the Han emperors. To this day, the Chinese people call themselves "the people of Han." The first Han leaders emerged in 206 B.C. Their dynasty was to rule China almost without interruption for four hundred years. The Han quickly established a power base and extended their territory deep into central Asia. They developed the Great Silk Road, the route that carried China's most famous product to the markets of the Roman Empire. All in all, they established remarkable communication systems, expanded trade, organized national iron and salt industries, and encouraged philosophy and the arts.

The emperor, known as the "Son of Heaven," became an institution in himself and was the core of the Han state. He ruled over a despotic government administered by a vast bureaucracy of nobles and officials. The emperor appointed his own relatives to maintain the imperial presence in ten principalities throughout his domains. His relatives, in turn, ruled like emperors, accountable only to the Son of Heaven.

The nobles and lesser officials of the Han dynasty were preoccupied with the belief that they could take all their earthly possessions with them to the next world. Their elaborate tombs were crammed with magnificent objects as well as the prosaic artifacts of day-to-day life. The goal was to transfer one's pleasant earthly life to the next world—with no amenities left behind.

The archaeologists who dug Han tombs were accorded fascinating insights into Chinese life of two thousand years ago. They found acrobats, modeled in clay, performing before a noble family; miniatures of people, animals, and farmhouses; even models of carts and boats. The tombs provided an extraordinarily detailed record of how the ancient Chinese had gone about their daily business.

But what of the emperor and his closest relatives? How did they live and die? No one has yet tried to excavate a Han royal burial, entombed as they are under vast artificial hills erected by forced labor. But some rather grim indications have come down to us. The Emperor Ching-ti, who died in 141 B.C., employed thousands of convicts to erect his tomb. The resting places of many of these unfortunate souls have been found near the royal enclosure. Some skeletons still bear the neck and leg irons that imprisoned the convicts in life. Several had been decapitated.

The Han principality nearest Peking had a population of 600,000. Emperor Wu-ti appointed his elder brother Liu Sheng to be prince of this Chung-shan principality. Liu Sheng ruled for nearly forty years until his death in 113 B.C. His wife Tou Wan survived him for about ten years. Both were buried with elaborate imperial ceremony in royal graves dug deep into the barren Lingshang hillsides near the town of Man-Ch'eng. There they rested until June 1968, when a detachment of the People's Liberation Army made one of the most dramatic archaeological discoveries of all time.

"One evening," wrote one of the soldiers involved, "comrades of the 12th Troop on night patrol discovered a subterranean structure." The excited soldiers immediately reported the find to their company headquarters. "When the company commander, Comrade Kou Chou-lin, heard the news, he leaped from his bed and drove many miles to the scene of the report," continued the soldier. Kou Chou-lin and his men made their way cautiously into the newly discovered cavern. They found themselves inside a vast chamber, "big enough to hold a thousand men, a feat of careful engineering, a veritable underground palace." The feeble light of their flashlights could not even reach the end of the tomb.

Kou Chou-lin stared in amazement. Everywhere he turned, his flashlight caught the glint of gold, silver, and jade. Bronze and clay pots stood in long, orderly rows. Kou Chou-lin trod delicately between the pots and peered at the inscriptions on the vessels. "Palace treasure of Chung-shan," he spelled out aloud. "This must be a very ancient tomb. We must report it at once." The soldiers retreated in awe, mounted an armed guard over their remarkable find, and reported the discovery to higher authority.

Within hours, the Academy of Sciences in Peking had archaeologists on the scene. They entered the tomb with bright lights and emerged in a state of great excitement. "This is the tomb of Liu Sheng, Prince of Chung-shan of the former Han," one archaeologist exclaimed. "It dates to about two thousand years ago."

Meanwhile, soldiers eagerly exploring further in the area noticed huge piles of rocky chips on a neighboring hillside. They poked around the piles and came across a sealed entrance to another cavern, a massive fortification of stone blocks sealed with molten iron. Was this another tomb? Under careful supervision, army demolition experts blasted open the entrance. It proved to be the sepulchre of Liu Sheng's wife Tou Wan.

The government now moved swiftly. An impressive archaeological team of national and local experts arrived on the scene. Army officers organized digging teams composed of the "local revolutionary masses." The archaeologists soon realized they had a formidable task ahead, one fully as complex and demanding as that facing Howard Carter when he cleared the tomb of Tut-ankh-Amun half a century before. Fortunately, by government fiat, they were able to rely on assistance from the military as well from experts on preservative methods. The best archaeological technicians in China were soon on the scene. Years of carefully educating local communities in the importance of China's archaeological treasures had paid off in a unique discovery.

In the midst of these frantic preparations, Kuo Mo-jo, a member of the Central Committee of the Chinese Communist Party, arrived for an official inspection. "He presented us with a portrait of Chairman Mao," wrote a soldier, "and then took up his brush to write a poem, hymning the praises of the creative wisdom of our country's workers and the treasure of her ancient art." It was rumored that Chairman Mao himself was taking a personal interest in the excavations.

Liu Sheng's tomb was sealed by two brick walls. The cavity between them had been filled with molten iron that must have been smelted on the site. This task alone would have been a formidable undertaking. An entrance passageway blocked with earth and rocks led into the tomb itself. The excited archaeologists organized the clearance of the passage, then measured the dimensions of the huge rock cavern before them. Liu Sheng's sepulchre was 171 feet long, Tou Wan's somewhat larger. More than 64,000 cubic feet of rock had been laboriously dug from the solid hillsides to form the sepulchres. Even with modern equipment, it would require several hundred men at least a year to excavate the chambers. Liu Sheng and his wife employed thousands of laborers at enormous cost. The austere archaeologists were shocked. As they later wrote, "The archaeological work has mercilessly exposed their evils and extravagance, as well as their brutal exploitation and oppression of the working people."

Once through the passage, the archaeologists found themselves in an antechamber, off of which led two side passages. Liu Sheng's six carriages, sixteen horses, and eleven dogs lay in these defiles. He also took with him a horse-driven grindstone, complete with horses, and ample food and wine for a long journey. The antechamber itself led into a central chamber, originally hung with finely embroidered curtains that had decayed over the centuries. Both chambers had wooden walls and tiled roofs.

The central chamber held hundreds of fine vessels and figurines, laid out in rows. This chamber in turn led to a stone doorway and the burial chamber itself. Liu Sheng's coffin lay on a platform on the north side of the chamber; a bathroom was situated on the south side. A walkway extended around the stone-lined burial chamber. Tou Wan's sepulchre was of similar design.

For several incredible months, the archaeologists and their military assistants worked on clearing the two tombs. They removed more than 2,800 funerary objects from the sepulchres, an unbelievable treasure. There were magnificent bronze and gold vessels, gold, silver, and jade ornaments, fine clay vessels, lacquered vases, even fine silks. Everything was of the finest quality, of a magnificence that could only be associated with royalty. The soldiers looked on incredulously as the contents of the tombs were carefully cataloged and moved into the open air. Every piece bore signs of many hours of painstaking craftsmanship. Some were inscribed with details regarding their place of origin and cost.

Two bronze jugs from Tou Wan's tomb had come all the way from Shansi province. One of them was inscribed with a price: 840 cash. This, Chinese sources tell us, was twice the annual poll tax on a family of two adults and three children. With glee, the soldiers recalled the words of Chairman Mao: "In China, education has always been the exclusive preserve of the landlords, and the peasants have had no access to it. But the landlords' culture is created by the peasants, for its sole source is the peasants' sweat and blood." Every find from these two rich burials seemed to confirm Mao's teachings.

Perhaps the most beautiful pieces from the two-thousand-year-old tombs are a lamp and an incense burner. Tou Wan's body was watched over by a gilt-bronze lamp modeled in the form of a young serving girl. The servant is kneeling, a lamp in her hands. Both the lamp and its shade are adjustable, so that the direction and intensity of its rays can be changed at will. The girl's head can be removed to fill the lamp. Smoke from the lamp was diverted into the body through the hollow right arm, so that the room remained clear of fumes. The lamp bears the words "Lamp of the Palace of Eternal Trust." We know that Tou Wan's grandmother lived in a palace of that name;

the lamp may have been a wedding present to her granddaughter.

Liu Sheng took a magnificent incense burner with him to the next world. The bronze burner was shaped in the form of a precipitous mountain peak. Hunters cavort on its slopes as they pursue wild animals. The peak appears to float in clouds of inlaid silver and gold. When the incense was lit, the pungent smoke would swirl out through numerous holes in the burner to wreathe the mountain scene. It is an exquisite piece, far more refined than any burners found in earlier excavations.

Some of the other bronze vessels were equally magnificent. Two gilded wine containers modeled with intricate dragon and knob designs still glowed with lustrous color after two thousand years. A flying bird holding a round dish with three candlesticks formed an elegant lamp. The bronzes bore intricate patterns and the glitter of gold and silver inlay was to be seen everywhere. The archaeologists were astonished. They had no idea such sophisticated craftsmen lived in Han times.

The corpses of Liu Sheng and Tou Wan were the most remarkable discoveries of all. Both wore magnificent jade suits sewn together with gold thread. Although the Han emperors and their nobles were known to have been buried in such suits, this was the first time complete jade burial clothes had been found. Funeral superstitions about jade dated far back in China. Even simple farmers placed jade rings with the dead over four thousand years ago. The Han emperors and their nobles believed in Taoist magical traditions, traditions that called for the use of jade to stop up the nine orifices of the human body. Taoists believed that jade prevented the body from decaying. Many people apparently were content to place one jade object in each of the nine openings, but Liu Sheng and his wife went to the limit. They were buried in complete jade suits, evidently a privilege of only the most important and noble aristocrats. The rank of the corpse was also indicated by the material used to wire together the thousands of thin jade plaques that made up the suit. The emperor and his chosen favorites were allowed gold-threaded suits; slightly less prestigious people were accorded silver or bronze, according to their rank.

The experts who examined the intricate suits were amazed at the painstaking craftsmanship. Liu Sheng's suit consisted of 2,690 pieces of jade sewn together with 39,025 lengths of gold thread. Each piece of jade was cut into a small rectangular or square wafer one-eighth inch thick and perforated at each corner. Many were shaped to different angles of the body. The workmen used tiny saws with delicate teeth to saw the jade into pieces. The 0.03-inch corner holes were drilled with tubelike drills filled with abrasive sand. The gold thread was intricately woven into twelve-stranded wire, tied together with nine different knots. Each suit, carefully made to measure, was assembled in twelve separate sections, such as the head, gloves, or legs. Each section was then edged with red cloth and set aside until the death of its intended wearer. Before burial, the suits were tightly sewn together around the corpse, so that no part of the body was left exposed. The suited prince and princess were laid to rest in their coffins, their heads reposing on bronze pillows inlaid with gold. Liu Sheng was accompanied by an iron knife and two swords. Each corpse grasped two ceremonial jade crescents.

When first discovered, the jade-suited corpses were in a state of total disarray. As the bodies decomposed and the wooden coffins rotted to dust, the jade suits collapsed and the gold threads broke. All that remained was a tightly compacted jumble of dusty jade and gold. With infinite care, the excavators sorted the piles of priceless jade and removed the fragments to a laboratory in Peking for restoration. Laboratory experts tried to record the original position of each jade square. They fitted many of them in groups, using networks of wire, paper, and plaster of paris to solidify the fragile assemblages. Once in the laboratory, every piece was photographed and cleaned and the gold wire restored to its original state. Then Liu Sheng and Tou Wan's suits were reassembled piece by piece on aluminum frames from the reconstructed fragments. The experts estimated that each jade suit took a single craftsman more than ten years to complete. The price of eternity came high for royalty in Han China. But it was all in vain: all that remained of Liu Sheng, a man who ruled over and taxed 600,000 people, was a handful of teeth. Happily, the products of his skilled artisans endured for the world to admire.

The archaeologists recalled that Liu Sheng was a corrupt and depraved man. Historians wrote that he was "fond of wine and women." One of the bronze wine jars found among the many in his tomb bore a revealing inscription, a prayer for prosperity: "May good food fill your gate, expand your girth, extend your life, keep illness at bay." Both Liu Sheng and his wife enjoyed lavish funerals at a time when thousands of their people were starving as a result of terrible floods. But by destroying their bodies, history has exacted a just retribution.

History was kinder to another Han lady, discovered in 1971 at Ma-wang-tiu near Ch'ang-sha in Hunan. Her grave mound lay on the summit of a low hill, the tomb a vertical, rectangular earthen pit approached by a sloping passageway. Thick jackets of dense white clay and over 5,000 kilograms of charcoal lined the deep burial pit, dug over fifty feet into the hill. A six-walled wooden coffin lay in the center of the pit, with moisture-absorbent charcoal packed tightly against the perishable wood. The charcoal kept out all oxygen as well as all moisture and, as a result, led to quite incredible discoveries, for even the most fragile of materials had survived.

The cypress chambers that housed the coffins lay at the bottom of the tomb. An outer chamber held an inner casket, which in turn enclosed three coffins that fitted inside one another with extraordinary precision. The outer and middle coffins were lacquered and decorated with beautifully colored designs: multicolored clouds chased across fair and stormy skies; humanlike monsters fought one another, played musical instruments, or hunted. Fine satin-stitch embroidery and hundreds of feathers glued to background fabric covered the wooden inner coffin.

The innermost coffin contained the perfectly preserved body of a woman about fifty years old. Her corpse had been wrapped in over twenty layers of cloth bound with silk ribbons. Two beautifully decorated quilts covered the lady. The woman lay on her back, her hands on her ample stomach, head turned to the north. A ceremonial jade filled her open mouth. There were almost no signs of deterioration. Her skin was still soft and an injection of preservative fluid into her arm even raised a small swelling that soon subsided. Inscriptions buried with the coffin identified the body as that of Lady Tai, the wife of a marquis of Tai, who lived between 193 and 141 B.C.

Lady Tai was carefully removed from her elaborate coffin and taken to Hunan Medical College for an autopsy. The corpse measured 1.54 meters long and weighed 39.3 kilograms. As a young woman, Lady Tai had borne children. At the time of her death, she walked with a bent posture and suffered from gallstones. She had a serious heart condition and had indeed died of heart failure soon after eating a melon. Lady Tai was described as "well nourished, with plenty of subcutaneous fat." She had led, said the doctors, "the idle, dissipated life of the exploiting classes."

Lady Tai's husband was prime minister to the prince of Ch'ang-sha. His wealth paid for a magnificent funeral and tomb for his wife. Three hundred twelve bamboo slips inventoried the contents of her tomb. Her food supplies—chicken, fish, even spareribs and eggs—were packed in boxes. Lacquer jars, boxes, and chopsticks were as fresh as the day they were buried. One hundred sixty-two wooden figurines of her servants, musicians, and household items were packed in the tomb to ensure that Lady Tai would be adequately cared for in the next world.

Lady Tai's elaborate wardrobe astounded the experts most of all. Coats, stockings, gloves, shoes, and over forty boxes

Drawing of Lady Tai's funeral banner.

packed with rolls of silk accompanied the noble lady to heaven. Both plain and brightly decorated silks were found, some adorned with animals, flowers, or delicate clouds. Some of the gauze silk was as light as the most fragile nylon fabrics of today. Silks such as these brought the Han emperors in contact with the Roman Empire via the Great Silk Road, a trade route from western China to the outermost Asian frontiers of imperial Rome. Chinese silk was literally worth its weight in gold in Roman markets.

The most remarkable silk object of all, Lady Tai's funeral banner, was draped over the inner coffin. The T-shaped banner, mounted on a bamboo frame, had been carried to the tomb in front of the carriage that bore Lady Tai's corpse. It is thought to depict the fate of Lady Tai's soul after death. The silk was painted a deep red and then covered with elaborate painted designs. Tassels hang from the banner's four lower corners. The banner measures over six feet long and over a foot and a half wide.

The bottom section of the banner depicts an underworld inhabited by snakes, snouted fish, and antlered creatures that may represent demons. A human-faced monster supports a platform on which members of Lady Tai's household are performing burial offerings.

Two large intertwined dragons support a second platform above the underworld. Lady Tai, accompanied by five female attendants, stands with bent back and walking stick on this platform. A human-faced bird hovers over the scene. Perhaps the soul of Lady Tai is being welcomed back to her household for a short visit before it finally departs forever.

The heavenly paradise at the top of the banner is guarded by the sun and the moon. The crescent moon is associated with Chang-ngo, a goddess who fled long ago to the moon and was said to live there in the form of a toad. A raven has alighted in the red sun, while two guardians wait at the gates of heaven above the Lady Tai. At the very top of the banner sits the primordial ancestor Fu-hsi or Tai-i, with his long serpent tail and five bird companions. He waits to receive the two elements of Lady Tai's soul that will be carried to heaven by the intertwined dragons. Fu-shi will then prepare the soul for rebirth as an ancestor spirit, free to come to the aid of the deceased lady's descendants.

For centuries, Lady Tai lay in solitary state, surrounded by her clothes, her favorite lacquered vessels, even her zither and pipes. A silent army of attendants lay with her. Now she adorns a museum, while her possessions have traveled all over the world to be admired by people who have never met the wonders of ancient Chinese civilization.

Lady Tai's husband was a relatively minor official who held sway over a mere 700 families. But the income from his holdings was sufficient to ensure a rich burial, as prescribed by regulations, for both his wife and himself. To Chinese archaeologists, Lady Tai's elaborate and perfectly preserved funeral furniture is confirmation that Han nobles "ruthlessly oppressed the working people." Such finds, say the Chinese, "will enable us to learn more about the class struggle in ancient China."

To the world at large, of course, the tombs of Liu-Sheng, Tou Wan, and the Lady Tai provide an extraordinary revelation of some of the mysteries that have surrounded ancient China for centuries. If these discoveries have brought China and the West closer together through archaeology, then the past has truly served the present.

# SOURCES

While writing this book over a period of three years, I consulted hundreds of articles and books, many of them very specialized. Here, however, I've compiled a selection of basic sources for those interested in reading further about the various personalities, sites, and archaeological topics discussed in this book.

## Chapter 1

The general reader will have to go far to discover a better introduction to archaeology than C. W. Ceram's *Gods, Graves, and Scholars* (New York: Knopf, 1953), which has become a modern classic. It is particularly good on the discovery of the early civilizations. David Wilson's *The New Archaeology* (New York: Knopf, 1974) discusses some of the latest advances in modern archaeology. Anyone seriously interested in the method and theory of archaeology should consult either Frank Hole and Robert Heizer, *Prehistoric Archaeology: A Brief Introduction* (New York: Holt, Rinehart and Winston, 1977) or my own *In the Beginning* (Boston: Little, Brown, 3d ed., 1978). Both are college texts. World prehistory as a whole is the subject of Grahame Clark's *World Prehistory* (New York: Cambridge University Press, 3d ed., 1977) and of my *People of the Earth* (Boston: Little, Brown, 2d ed., 1977). John Pfeiffer, *The Emergence of Man* (New York: Harper & Row, 2d ed., 1972) and *The Emergence of Society* (New York: McGraw-Hill, 1977) are perhaps the best general surveys for the lay reader, however. Glyn Daniel, *The Origins and Growth of Archaeology* (Baltimore: Pelican Books, 1967) contains many excerpts from the writings of early excavators, while J. P. Droop, *Archaeological Excavation* (Cambridge: Cambridge University Press, 1915) is deliciously amusing reading. Sir Mortimer Wheeler, *Archaeology from the Earth* (Oxford: Clarendon Press, 1955) is a vigorous account of good excavation technique, while Robert F. Heizer and J. Graham, *A Guide to Archaeological Field Methods* (Palo Alto: National Press, 3d ed., 1966) is a widely used guide to digging in North America. Louis A. Brennan, *Beginner's Guide to Archaeology* (Stackpole Press, Harrisburg, Pa., 1973) is another widely read introduction to the field.

## Chapter 2

Louis Leakey already has a wide following—indeed, almost a fan club. The definitive Leakey biography is Sonia Cole's *Leakey's Luck* (London: Collins, 1975). Leakey's own autobiographical books, *White African* (Cambridge: Schenkman, 1966) and *By the Evidence* (New York: Harcourt, Brace, Jovanovich, 1974) are useful sources, but are very much Leakey's own viewpoint. Both John Pfeiffer's *Emergence of Man*, referred to above, and the Time-Life book *Early Man* (New York, 1965) provide a wealth of background information on early human evolution. Time-Life's new book series, *The Emergence of Man*, is also very informative, especially the volumes on the first humans and the missing link. *Olduvai Gorge 1931–1951* (Cambridge: Cambridge University Press, 1953) is Leakey's original description of the site. A new series of reports under the same title have appeared since 1969: volume I is a general update by Louis Leakey; volume II is the complete description of *Australopithecus boisei;* volume III is Mary Leakey's account of the early living floors. Although all are quite technical, the general reader may find some of the details fascinating. *National Geographic* magazine carries regular reports on the Leakey family's latest discoveries. Jane von Lawick-Goodall's *In The Shadow of Man* (Boston: Houghton Mifflin, 1974) describes her work among the chimpanzees.

### Chapter 3

Ozette is such a recently excavated site that there are few descriptions of the finds made there. Ruth Moore's *Hunters of the Whale* (New York: Morrow, 1975) is a popular account written in collaboration with Richard Daugherty. I have drawn on it extensively in Chapter 3 and would refer the interested reader to its fine photographs. The Northwest Coast Indians themselves have been much described. Perhaps the most famous survey is Philip Drucker's *Indians of the Northwest Coast* (Garden City, N.Y.: Natural History Press, 1963). Elizabeth Colson, before becoming a world-famous African anthropologist, wrote a definitive study of the Makah in 1955: *The Makah Indians: A Study of an Indian Tribe in Modern America* (Minneapolis: University of Minnesota Press, 1953). A good introduction to American archaeology as a whole is *The First Americans* (New York: Time-Life Books, 1973). A more detailed treatment: Jesse D. Jennings, *The Prehistory of North America* (New York: McGraw-Hill, 2d ed., 1974) is a college text. Peter Farb's *Man's Rise to Civilization as Shown by the Indians of North America from Primeval Times to the Coming of the Industrial State* (New York: Dutton, 1968) is also a widely read introductory text.

### Chapter 4

Rene Millon's magnificent study of Teotihuacán is still in progress, but the first volume of *Urbanization at Teotihuacán, Mexico* (Austin: University of Texas Press, 1974) has already appeared. It contains the maps on which the entire study is based and is well worth perusal. Peter Tompkins, *Mysteries of the Mexican Pyramids* (New York: Harper & Row, 1976) is an entertaining account of the discovery and early excavations at the great city. These are but two of many books on the subject; the interested reader is referred to Tompkins's book for a more extensive bibliography. For an examination of early relations between Indians and Spaniards, see my *Elusive Treasure* (New York: Scribners, 1977). The prehistory of Mesoamerica as a whole has not been summarized for the lay reader in any detail, although Michael Coe's *Mexico* and *The Maya* (New York: Praeger, 1962 and 1966) are well-written short syntheses suitable for the general reader. For a more specialized treatment, try Muriel Porter Weaver, *The Aztec, Maya and their Predecessors* (New York: Seminar Press, 1973). Gordon R. Willey's *North and Middle America, An Introduction to American Archaeology*, vol. I (Englewood Cliffs, N.J.: Prentice-Hall, 1967), although now a bit dated, was once considered the definitive text.

## Chapter 5

Austen Henry Layard, although one of the most colorful archaeologists of all, has been sadly neglected by biographers. Gordon Waterfield, *Layard of Nineveh* (London: John Murray, 1963) presents the great man's fascinating life in detail, especially his later diplomatic career. Nora Bejamin Kubie, *Road to Nineveh* (New York: Doubleday, 1964) is a more superficial account of Layard's archaeological work. Perhaps the best source of all on Layard is Layard himself. Both his popular accounts, *Nineveh and Its Remains* and *Nineveh and Babylon*, are readily available in many libraries, either in the original editions or in a reprinted form. I urge you to read Layard, for he possessed a unique gift for communicating his exciting finds to a lay audience. He was a member of a heroic archaeological generation and his writings reflect the excitement of the age. Seton Lloyd, *Foundations in the Dust* (Baltimore: Pelican Books, 1954) is a comprehensive survey of the history of Mesopotamian archaeology. Jacquetta Hawkes, *The First Great Civilizations* (New York: Knopf, 1973) provides a readable account of the Sumerians and Assyrians, while Samuel Kramer's *The Sumerians* (Chicago: University of Chicago Press, 1963) beautifully summarizes the world's earliest urban society.

## Chapter 6

Heinrich Schliemann, like Layard, has for the most part been overlooked by biographers. However, no one should miss Irving Stone's brilliant fictionalized biography, *The Greek Treasure* (New York: Doubleday, 1975). The research behind this book is extremely authoritative and the story line is both vivid and compelling. Archaeology has rarely been so competently popularized. Carl Blegen, *Troy* (New York: Praeger, 1961) is a straightforward, spare summary of this complex site. C. W. Ceram, *Gods, Graves, and Scholars* (New York: Knopf, 1953) also includes a good account of the discovery of Troy. The Mycenaeans and Mycenae itself are well covered by Lord William Taylor in *The Mycenaeans* (New York: Praeger, 1963). For those interested in consulting the original sources, E. V. Rieu's brilliant translations of Homer's *Iliad* and *Odyssey* were published by Pelican Books just after the Second World War. Other more recent translations are also available. Another very new source is Leo Deuel's *Memoirs of Heinrich Schliemann* (New York: Harper & Row, 1977).

### Chapter 7

The Evans family constituted an archaeological dynasty of extraordinary distinction. Joan Evans, the last of the dynasty, wrote an account of the family in *Time and Chance* (London: Longmans, 1943). Her book, based on family papers, is very authoritative as well as readable. Knossos is competently surveyed by Sinclair Hood, *The Minoans* (New York: Praeger, 1971) and by L. R. Palmer, *A New Guide to the Palace of Knossos* (London: Faber, 1969). The origins of Aegean civilization are much debated. Colin Renfrew, *The Emergence of Civilization* (London: Methuen, 1972) is a fundamental but rather technical source for readers interested in this topic. Arthur Evans's *Palace of Minos* (Oxford: Oxford University Press, 1921-1936) requires the reader to wade through a mass of detail, but it is a remarkable work. Mary Renault's fictional recreation of Knossos and the Minoans: *The King Must Die* (New York: Random House, 1963) is a good starting point for anyone interested in prehistoric Crete.

### Chapter 8

The Pyramids have inspired an enormous outpouring of popular and technical literature, much of it frankly crazy. Peter Tompkins, *Secrets of the Great Pyramid* (New York: Harper & Row, 1971) wades through the technical literature as well as the fascinating history of research at Gizeh with entertaining authority. I. E. S. Edwards, *The Pyramids of Egypt* (New York: Viking Press, 1972) and Ahmed Fakhry, *The Pyramids* (Chicago: University of Chicago Press, 1961) are the standard works on the structures themselves. Kurt Mendelssohn, *The Riddle of the Pyramids* (New York: Praeger, 1974) offers an ingenious explanation for why the Pyramids were built. No one should miss David Macaulay's enchanting *Pyramid* (Boston: Houghton Mifflin, 1975), an artist's account of how the Egyptians built the Great Pyramid. My own *The Rape of the Nile* (New York: Scribners, 1975) covers the history of tomb robbing on the Nile. For a discussion of ancient Egyptian civilization, see Cyril Aldred, *The Egyptians* (New York: Praeger, 1963).

## Chapter 9

The recent United States tour of objects from Tut-ankh-Amun's tomb has generated a flood of superficial accounts of this great discovery. The discerning reader will go straight to Howard Carter's own, very personal account of the discovery: Howard Carter and A. C. Mace, *The Tomb of Tut-Ankh-Amen* (London: Macmillan, 1923–1933). I. E. S. Edwards, *Treasures of Tutankhamun* (London: British Museum, 1972) is a useful short summary of the discovery and tomb prepared for the fifty-year exhibition in London. It is widely available, as is the most thorough popular account: C. Desroches-Noblecourt, *Tutankhamen, Life and Death of a Pharaoh* (London: Thames and Hudson, 1963). The Desroches-Noblecourt book is illustrated with exquisite photographs. All of these works contain bibliographies of more technical books and articles on the tomb.

## Chapter 10

The Chinese have produced a number of popular publications to accompany a widely traveled exhibition of ancient Chinese artifacts. *New Archaeological Finds in China* (Peking: Foreign Languages Press, 1974) is a concise description, interlarded with the Maoist line. William Watson, *Ancient China: The Discoveries of Post Liberation Archaeology* (New York: New York Graphic Society, 1974) and John Hay, *Ancient China* (London: The Bodley Head, 1975) are more complete summaries of the latest exciting finds. The best technical source on the archaeology of China is Kwang Chih Chang, *The Archaeology of Ancient China* (New Haven: Yale University Press, 3d ed., 1977). Paul Wheatley's *Pivot of the Four Quarters* (Chicago: Aldine, 1971) is a very learned and thought-provoking account of the origins of Chinese civilization.

# PHOTO CREDITS

148, 154, and 157, from Heinrich Schliemann, *Trojan Antiquities*. Pages 162 and 167, Hirmer Fotoarchiv, München. Pages 164–165, drawing by James D. Cooper in Heinrich Schliemann, *Mycenae* (Leipzig: n.p., 1878). Page 168, drawing by J. W. Whymper in Heinrich Schliemann, *Mycenae* (Leipzig: n.p., 1878).

### Chapter 7
Pages 174 and 180, painting by Sir William Richmond, © Society of Antiquaries of London. Pages 182 and 190, photo © Ashmolean Museum, Oxford. Pages 186–187, 193, 197, and 198–199, Hirmer Fotoarchiv, München.

### Chapter 8
Pages 202 and 212, Hirmer Fotoarchiv, München. Pages 207 and 222–223, Ken Lambert/FPG. Pages 208–209, from Edmé Jomard, *Description de L'Egypte* (Paris: n.p., 1821). Pages 215 and 217, from Samuel Manning, *A Visit to Egypt and the Holy Land* (London: Bible Tract Society, 1875). Page 224, Bernice Q. Johnson/FPG.

### Chapter 9
Pages 226, 241, 242, 244–245, 249, 252, 255, and 257, The Metropolitan Museum of Art, photographs by Harry Burton. Page 229, Hirmer Fotoarchiv, München. Page 237, © Griffith Institute, Ashmolean Museum, Oxford.

### Chapter 10
Pages 260 and 280, drawing by David Buck, copied from *Ch'ang-sha Ma-wang-tui i-hao Han-mu* (1973), I:40.

# INDEX